BIRDS IN JEOPARDY

Imperiled and Extinct Birds of the United States and Canada,

Including Hawaii and Puerto Rico

AVID S. DOBKIN, AND DARRYL WHEYE

Illustrations by Darryl Wheye

STANFORD UNIVERSITY PRESS

STANFORD, CALIFORNIA

1992

Stanford University Press
Stanford, California

© 1992 by the Board of Trustees of the
Leland Stanford Junior University

Printed in Hong Kong

Designed by Copenhaver Cumpston

Typeset in 9/11½ Sabon and Eras by
Keystone Typesetting, Inc., Orwigsburg,
Pennsylvania

Printed by Dai Nippon, Inc.

Library of Congress Cataloging-in-
Publication Data

Ehrlich, Paul R.
  Birds in jeopardy : the imperiled and
extinct birds of the United States and
Canada, including Hawaii and Puerto
Rico / Paul R. Ehrlich, David S. Dobkin,
and Darryl Wheye ; illustrations by
Darryl Wheye.
       p.   cm.
Includes bibliographical references and
index.
ISBN 0-8047-1967-5. —
ISBN 0-8047-1981-0 (pbk.)
  1. Rare birds—United States. 2. Rare
birds—Canada. 3. Rare birds—Puerto
Rico. 4. Extinct birds—United States.
5. Extinct birds—Canada. 6. Extinct
birds—Puerto Rico. 7. Birds, Protection
of—United States. 8. Birds, Protection of—
Canada. 9. Birds, Protection of—Puerto
Rico. I. Dobkin, David S. II. Wheye,
Darryl. III. Title.
QL676.55.E38   1992
333.95'8137'097—dc20
91-29555
CIP

To John and Susan Boething,

with deep appreciation for their support
of the Center for Conservation Biology

And to

those whose efforts to conserve birds
are reflected in what follows

A sample of the species that appear to have suffered most from the continuing fragmentation of the great Eastern forests of the United States and Canada. (For more on these birds, see p. 3.)

Clockwise from top left:

Swainson's Warbler, Ovenbird, American Redstart, Hooded Warbler, Acadian Flycatcher, Wood Thrush, and Yellow-throated Vireo.

PREFACE

Two hundred years ago, when the North American continent (for present purposes including Hawaii and Puerto Rico but not Mexico or the other islands of the West Indies) was home to fewer than 5 million people, about 700 species of birds were breeding here. Today, more than 280 million people live here, 33 species and subspecies of birds have become extinct, and well over 150 more are in trouble in all or parts of their range. Of those in trouble, more than half are recognized by the U.S. Fish and Wildlife Service (USFWS) either as Endangered (in imminent danger of extinction), or as Threatened (likely soon to be in such danger), or as "candidates" for listing (known to have suffered losses but still awaiting formal recognition of the severity of their declines). The remainder of those commonly thought to be in peril—those *not* under consideration by the USFWS—are recognized by the National Audubon Society, from substantial evidence, as in apparent decline. (We have used the USFWS and Audubon lists as the basis for the book's structure, but of course there are other birds thought to be in peril that are not on those lists, and we treat some of those and discuss as many more as have been identified.)

When we began writing *The Birder's Handbook* six years ago, reports of habitat degradation and loss, and of the associated losses in avian populations, were common in the conservation and ornithological literature, but then, and until now, no single volume or checklist identified all imperiled U.S. and Canadian birds or summarized their needs or the particulars of their declines. Here we offer a concise review of those birds recognized widely as imperiled, briefly describing their basic ecological requirements, the aspects of their biology that are pertinent to conservation, their historical and contemporary ranges, and the nature of the threats to their persistence. For those birds recognized by the USFWS as severely imperiled, we give current population estimates and some of the plans for their recovery. Birds pushed to extinction since 1776 are also treated, since the stories of their fates can help instruct us on how to save birds now in jeopardy. (We have chosen 1776 as our cutoff point somewhat arbitrarily, but reliable reports from before that point are few, museum specimens are rare, and documented extinctions are rarer still.)

We wish to emphasize that the conservation status of many birds is quite fluid, and changes (usually for the worse) can occur surprisingly rapidly. Many species not covered in this book may nonetheless be in peril by now, or at risk locally or even regionally. Although the data that form the basis for the National Audubon Society's Blue List (and its auxiliary lists) are extensive, they are still quite limited and provide a broad but far from comprehensive picture of the status of North America's avifauna.

Without the exhaustive efforts of generations of birders and ornithologists in the field, and the compilers who published the survey data that those field workers provided, this book would not have been possible, and probably would not have been thought necessary.

Tony Angell (Department of Environmental Education, State of Washington), Pete Myers (W. Alton Jones Foundation), Alan Launer, Dennis Murphy, and Kathy Switky (Center for Conservation Biology, Stanford University), and James Tate, Jr. (U.S. Fish and Wildlife Service) kindly reviewed all or parts of the text, and Tony Angell, Peter Pyle (Pt. Reyes Bird Observatory), and Tom Sisk (Stanford University) took time from their busy schedules to review the illustrations. We are especially indebted to Stuart Pimm (University of Tennessee) for urging us to expand the Hawaiian coverage, for many invaluable comments, and for reviewing the Hawaiian portions of the book once more.

For valuable consultation, we wish to thank also David Ainley (Pt. Reyes Bird Observatory), Daniel Anderson (University of California, Davis), Sheila Conant (University of Hawaii), David De Sante (Institute for Bird Populations), Ross D. James (Royal Ontario Museum and COSEWIC), Kenn Kaufmann (National Audubon Society), Lee Jones (Michael Brandman Associates), Stephen A. Laymon (Kern River Research Center), H. Ronald Pulliam (University of Georgia), Thomas Scott (University of California, Riverside), William D.

Toone (San Diego Wild Animal Park), and Joseph Wunderle, Jr. (Institute of Tropical Forestry, Puerto Rico). At the U.S. Fish and Wildlife Service, we must thank Loren Hays, Jim Jacobi, Larry Salata, Linda Schmale, and Richard Zembal. And at the Canadian Wildlife Service, Chuck Dauphiné and Bob Campbell gave us current information on COSEWIC and its listings of imperiled Canadian birds.

We also thank Zoe Chandik, Joan Dietrich, Gill Senn, and Joe Wible of Stanford's Falconer Biology Library for patiently tracking down source material, and Steve Masley and Pat Browne for their quick and competent handling of copying chores. Peggy Vas Dias of Stanford's Department of Biological Sciences provided a vital link among the authors. Our editor at Stanford University Press, Bill Carver, and Phillip Unitt (San Diego Natural History Museum), who edited the manuscript under the Press's direction, gave us much good advice and caught many errors and infelicities, for which we are grateful. Carver's and Unitt's contributions went far beyond those ordinarily made by editors. Unitt, in particular, made available to us, in the process, his vast knowledge of North American birds. Cope Cumpston, design and production manager at Stanford Press, conceived the book's design and laid out the pages, to handsome effect. Robert Ehle oversaw the book's delicate printing and binding operations. Nancy Watt and Bob Lloyd had many good marketing ideas, in-

cluding a magnificent poster, designed by Maura McAndrew. Dick Angstadt of Keystone Typesetting, Inc. in Orwigsburg, PA, managed an extraordinary typesetting effort: accurate, intelligent work from a truly filthy manuscript in amazingly little time.

This book, more than most, was in fact a group effort, and in retrospect we are astonished at how much was done in so little time. Its roots lie in the collaboration of the three of us in producing *The Birder's Handbook*, which was in part motivated by our concern for the conservation of biotic diversity in general and birds in particular. Wheye began the current effort by preparing the portraits of birds in peril. The portraits and a preliminary text were then taken to Stanford University Press, where Bill Carver encouraged us to extend the original goal and to produce a much more comprehensive volume that would reflect the academic roots of the project and the concerns of the Center for Conservation Biology, with the text to be authored by the *Birder's Handbook* team. It turned out to be a much more ambitious project than any of us had anticipated, but a more rewarding project, as well. We hope, too, that this book will prove timely and useful for those concerned with the fate of our North American birds and with the preservation of biological resources in general.

CONTENTS

BIRDS IN JEOPARDY

INTRODUCTION

If you enjoy watching birds, you doubtless are often reminded that you are a member of a species that poses a colossal threat to the global avifauna. As the human population has skyrocketed, bird populations have plummeted, and, as this book shows, the two trends are continuing today, throughout the United States and Canada. Many species and subspecies of North American birds—well over 150 of them—are in jeopardy, and unless current patterns of environmental degradation and habitat conversion can be reversed, many more are likely to become imperiled in the near future.

Humanity's impact on the avian world began long ago. Polynesians colonizing New Zealand a thousand years ago quickly put an end to the giant moas. These huge, slow-breeding birds had never known human hunters or other large predators, and were apparently very tame. As a result, they were soon hunted to extinction: the remains of over 100,000 moas have been found in the ruins of ancient Maori ovens.

The site of one of the worst known bird slaughters anywhere is now part of the United States. The Hawaiian Islands are home to the fossil remains of many bird species exterminated by the Polynesians who colonized the archipelago roughly 1,600 years ago. They killed birds for food, harvested them for feathers to make cere-

monial cloaks, capes, and helmets, and chopped down the forests that many of the birds inhabited. But we should not too righteously denounce those early settlers: as you will see, in the sections on Hawaiian birds, the process of extinction accelerated after the arrival of the Europeans and North Americans, and continues today.

On the North American mainland, the Carolina Parakeet and the Passenger Pigeon, once present in truly gigantic numbers, were wiped out by gunfire, the Great Auk and Labrador Duck by hungry sailors and colonists, and the Ivory-billed Woodpecker (if it is truly gone) by destruction of the extensive riverine forests that it required as habitat. Europe has had a similarly grim history. Much of Europe's woodland avifauna doubtless declined dramatically hundreds of years ago, as forests were cleared for farming, firewood, and lumber for the construction of buildings and ships. The Little Bustard and the Andalusian Hemipode disappeared from Sicily in the first half of the twentieth century as their steppe habitat was plowed to make way for cereal crops, and the Corn Crake has been declining all over Europe since the introduction of farm machinery and the practice of early mowing. In northern Finland, mechanized forestry has been destroying old growth and generally fragmenting the region's vast forests since World War II. These ravages have led to drops in the populations of many forest-dwelling species, including the Three-toed

This Introduction is based in part on P. R. Ehrlich. 1990. Birding for fun: People vs. birds. *American Birds* 44: 193–96. (With permission.)

Woodpecker, Siberian Tit, Song Thrush, Redstart, Pied Flycatcher, Brambling, and the crossbills. But these are simply the parts of the world we are familiar with: stories can be told of birds suffering from human activities over much of the rest of the planet, critically or terminally.

Today, the human assault on the natural world is accelerating, because of sheer numbers. At the end of World War II there were almost 2.5 billion people on the planet, some 150 million of them in Canada and the United States. Now—just 37 years later—there are 5.4 billion people in the world, and each year 95 million more—more than now live in Great Britain, Iceland, Belgium, Denmark, Norway, Sweden, and Finland combined—are added. Canada and the United States combined have almost doubled, to 280 million people. In fact, in the three and a half years since the three of us completed *The Birder's Handbook,* the Canadian and U.S. populations have increased by well over 7 million—roughly the number of people living in Los Angeles County.

As the human population grows, natural habitat disappears, and the toxic influence of human society spreads over the entire planet, even to Antarctica. Not only is Earth's population already too large, but bad (or nonexistent) planning, overconsumption by the rich, and the use of inefficient and dangerous technologies have needlessly multiplied the average individual's impact on the environment.

As more and more people have crowded into the eastern United States (and much the same can be said for California and the other sunbelt states), continuous tracts of forests and wetlands have been broken up by clearing and draining for housing developments, shopping centers, freeways, golf courses, and all the other features of "development." This fragmentation of eastern forests has led to sharp declines in the populations of many species of songbirds—including many that winter in tropical America—that depend on unbroken tracts of woodland. A sample of the species that appear to have suffered most is illustrated on p. vi: the Yellow-throated Vireo, Ovenbird, Hooded Warbler, American Redstart, Acadian Flycatcher, and Wood Thrush, all of them long-distance migrants. None of these is yet generally recognized as imperiled (and they are not treated in this book), but concern about them is growing, as it is about many other "neotropical migrant" species. Swainson's Warbler, for example, is in sharp decline, and ominously shares many of the ecological requirements of Bachman's Warbler, which is now probably extinct. Both birds winter in Cuba and nest in canebrakes (bamboo thickets) in the seasonally flooded swamps of the Southeast. Canebrakes are an increasingly scarce habitat, thanks to agricultural clearing and other land-use changes. Swainson's Warbler is not confined to breeding in such habitats, however, and its more diverse habits—it also uses woodland ravines filled with rhododendron and laurel—may have been the reason it has outlived its relative.

Culprits contributing to the decline of these forest species are easily observed if you go looking for birds in the East. Unless a major expedition is undertaken, most birding is necessarily suburban. And among the easiest-to-see birds in the Eastern suburbs are Blue Jays and Brown-headed Cowbirds, both of them deadly predators on the nests of warblers, vireos, flycatchers, and other small passerines. Other enemies in the easy-to-see category are cats and raccoons; like the jays and cowbirds, they are comfortable as "edge animals," thriving in the suburbs but adapted to living along woodland margins. And in the forest fragments now typical in the East, far too many nesting sites in the woods are close to "edges" and therefore exposed to higher levels of predation. None of these predators would have a significant impact on the populations of songbirds if other, less obvious forces brought into play by humanity were not magnifying their vulnerability.

But not only does the destruction of forests in the United States and Canada threaten these birds, so also does the disappearance of habitat in Central America, the Caribbean, and northern South America, where the migratory birds spend the winter. Many of our most beautiful passerines are not "ours," but rather denizens of the tropics that move north for a few months each year to breed. These migrants take advantage of the flush of insects in our spring and summer, and then return home for the remainder of the year. Evidence from local censuses in North America and from radar records of trans-Caribbean migrations suggests that populations of most forest-dwelling migrants have been reduced by roughly half in just the past few decades.

"Home" for these birds is an area where human populations are booming. The number of people living in Central America is projected to increase from about 120 million today to almost 200 million by 2020. That of tropical South America may well shoot from 245 million to 400 million in the same period. In his fine book *Where Have All the Birds Gone?*, John Terborgh points out the close correlation between the density of human populations in Latin America and the destruction of forest habitat critical to wintering migratory birds. The natural vegetation of Haiti, with the second highest human population density in the Americas (600 per square mile), is essentially gone. El Salvador, the most densely populated nation (650 per square mile), "has no natural vegetation left either, though the hilly interior . . . has regrown to scrub."

To judge from the impacts of human population growth already observed in Latin America, natural habitats of any significant extent are unlikely to persist there after local population densities exceed about 250 per square mile. On that basis, Terborgh considers the Dominican Republic, Jamaica, and Trinidad already over the edge, and notes that Cuba, Guatemala, Honduras, and Costa Rica are moving rapidly toward ecological breakdown. With the exception of Trinidad, all these countries are crucial for maintaining the populations of the birds that enliven North America during the breeding season. Where

the needs of people for food, fuel, shelter, and cash come into conflict with the needs of birds for a place to live, the birds inevitably lose out. Even in comparatively enlightened Costa Rica, whose government has been much more concerned with the preservation of biological diversity than has that of the United States, the protection of remnant tropical forests will prove increasingly difficult in the face of human population pressures. Although Costa Rica has made great progress in reducing its birthrate, the Costa Rican population is still growing at a rate which (if that rate continues) will double the nation's population in another 28 years.

The decline of migratory songbirds dependent on forests may be matched by a decline in migratory shorebirds dependent on a few "refueling" points along their extended routes. Ornithologist Pete Myers and his colleagues have concluded that even shorebirds that are still "abundant," like Sanderlings, Ruddy Turnstones, Dunlins, and Western Sandpipers, may be in jeopardy because of their dependence on a few sites that provide superabundant food resources. Just five key feeding grounds—the beaches of Delaware Bay, the Cheyenne Bottoms of Kansas, Washington's Gray's Harbor, the Bay of Fundy on the Atlantic coast of southeastern Canada, and the Copper River Delta of southeastern Alaska—collectively support over 5 million shorebirds each year. And each of these feeding grounds may be critical to more than 80 percent of the breeding population of one or more species of shorebird.

Myers and his colleagues pointed out the vulnerability of some of those critical migratory sites to oil spills, writing in 1987 that "the Copper River Delta lies immediately south of Valdez, Alaska, the southern terminus of the Alaska oil pipeline."

Just after midnight on March 24, 1989, their fears were realized when the *Exxon Valdez* ran aground on Bligh Reef in Prince William Sound, about 100 miles northwest of the Copper River Delta; the spill was a disaster for the local avifauna, but fortunately the oil did not reach the Delta, though it spread hundreds of miles in the opposite direction.

The outlook is the same elsewhere in North America: resort development and beach erosion threaten Delaware Bay; dredging may destroy key feeding grounds at Gray's Harbor; and two-thirds of the coastal wetlands that existed in California in 1900 have already been lost. Similarly, crucial migratory sites in Latin America are in danger, and shorebirds' wintering grounds have also been degraded. Even the "abundant" Sanderling has shown a drop in numbers of as much as 80 percent along the U.S. East Coast in recent years. One factor in the decline of the Eskimo Curlew has been the conversion of its upland winter habitat to cropland and pastures. The same difficulties face the Buff-breasted Sandpiper, which somehow was spared the full impact of whatever decimated the Eskimo Curlew but whose population may now be as few as 10 to 15 thousand birds.

Nor have grassland birds escaped the woes of their brethren in forests and on shorelines. Many species of sparrows, longspurs, and meadowlarks east of the Rockies are in serious decline. The reasons for these declines are not clear, but Northern Flickers, for example, may be suffering because they so often feed on the ground in agricultural fields, perhaps ingesting pesticide residues. Expanding human populations require expanding food supplies, and the way agricultural systems are operated these days, that means an expanding misuse of pesticides. The impact of that misuse on bird populations in the United States was presented so dramatically in Rachel Carson's *Silent Spring* that many people date the genesis of the environmental movement from that book's publication in 1962. Peregrine Falcons, for example, were wiped out east of the Mississippi and in southern California because of eggshell thinning traced to prey tainted with DDT. Ospreys, Bald Eagles, and Brown Pelicans are among other species that suffered heavily from pesticide poisoning.

A decade after *Silent Spring* was published, DDT was almost entirely banned in the United States, and bird populations that had suffered from eggshell thinning began to recover. Unfortunately, levels of DDT in the environment are again increasing, because it occurs as a contaminant in the widely used pesticide Kelthane. Worse yet, large quantities of many pesticides banned in the United States are still being sprayed in tropical countries, and the migrants from North America are thus exposed on their wintering grounds. Peregrines have been reestablished over much of their range in North America, thanks largely to the efforts of raptor expert Tom Cade (the founder of the Peregrine Fund) and his associates. But some Peregrine populations remain in trouble because of residues of chlorinated hydrocarbons (the group of synthetic compounds to which DDT and many other pesticides belong), apparently picked up south of the border.

Aside from direct habitat destruction and the purposeful spreading of toxins such as DDT, the greatest threat to birds from human population growth lies in the inadvertent release of nitrogen and sulfur oxides, chlorofluorocarbons (CFCs), carbon dioxide, and methane. These are the gases that are chiefly responsible for acid precipitation, depletion of the ozone layer, and

global climate change. And each of these effects is a monumental—potentially even terminal—threat to life on the planet.

Acid precipitation appears to be implicated in the declines of Common Loons and American Black Ducks in some areas of North America, since the acidification of lakes devastates populations of the fish and aquatic invertebrates that these birds depend on to feed their young. Acidification is a widespread problem. In Britain, breeding Dippers are absent from acidified sections of streams; the insect larvae they dine on are gone as well. An even more ominous development, in the Netherlands, is eggshell thinning, attributed to acid rain, in various birds from titmice to woodpeckers. And what may be happening in eastern and northeastern Europe, where pollution controls have been nonexistent, scarcely bears thinking. Apparently, acidification impairs calcium uptake by trees, leads to calcium-deficient insect prey, and thus affects eggshell development in much the same way that the chlorinated hydrocarbons do.

Indeed, it is entirely possible that in the coming decades the major threats to birds will shift away from the sorts of factors discussed in the species accounts in this book, toward global environmental changes. What imperils today will not necessarily be what imperils tomorrow—and it behooves us to be on guard. It is too soon to know what the impact of the thinning of Earth's ozone shield is likely to be. Life on Earth was confined to the sea until several hundred million years ago. By then, algae and other marine photosynthesizers had placed enough oxygen in the atmosphere to form the shield, and organisms could then survive on land. But as the ozone layer thins (ozone is a form of oxygen), the amount of deadly ultraviolet radiation from the Sun reaching Earth's surface increases, and that

increase will affect birds at least indirectly, through its impacts on plants, insects, and mammals, all of which will suffer. The birds themselves may find their immune systems impaired and thus become more susceptible to disease; they may also develop cataracts and carcinomas.

But the greatest potential danger from the gaseous effluents of humanity is posed by those (chiefly carbon dioxide, methane, nitrous oxide, and CFCs) that contribute to the greenhouse effect. One possible consequence, a rapid rise in sea level, would destroy complex coastal wetland ecosystems, depriving shorebirds, herons, rails, and other birds of critical habitat. Wetlands can "keep up" with sea-level rise only if it is gradual, and if there are no barriers to prevent their "migration" inland. Current estimates of sea-level rise over the next century are about 2 feet, which is thought to be the maximum rate at which most coastal wetlands can retreat and survive. In areas where dikes, roads, or other human-made obstructions block their retreat from the deepening waters, and where, predictably, people will resist the loss of valuable real estate, the survival of the wetlands may be touch-and-go.

If, however, the climate changes at an unprecedented pace, the results could be far worse. Much of the habitat that birds now depend on occurs in nature-reserve "islands" that are surrounded by seas of human development. When the climatic conditions required by the vegetation in those islands begin to shift too rapidly, there will be no way for the vegetation to follow, nowhere for it to spread. Saplings, for example, that happen to begin life in cow pastures or parking lots, and thus to represent movement into the islands' frontier, usually fail to survive. There is also evidence that bird species dependent on boreal lakes for food resources for their young may find the fauna of those lakes changing dramatically with just one or two degrees of warming. In general, rapid climate change could lead to the extinction of a significant portion of Earth's avifauna. At the least, many populations can be expected to disappear *even if* no dramatic evidence of habitat disturbance is seen.

All of these atmospheric threats to birds are tied to the size of the human population. Even the CFCs, the easiest of the lot to control by substituting newer technologies, would be only half the threat they currently pose if the human population were only half as large (and everything else were equal). But the connections between human population size and emissions of carbon dioxide, methane, and nitrous oxide will not easily be broken—so here also human numbers are likely to determine the numbers of birds for decades to come.

One might be tempted to say, "What the hell, people are more important than birds, so why care?" But the choice is not that simple, for what threatens birds also threatens people: rapid climate change will hammer our agricultural systems; ozone depletion will give us cancers and other ailments and impact food production; acid rain has already ruined local fisheries and forests; coastal marshes essential to marine fish production, already reduced by other forces, could be wiped out by sea-level rise; misuse of toxic substances directly threatens human health; and so on.

In the last century, coal miners took canaries into the mines with them because, if poisonous gases were present, the birds would give warning by succumbing first. Now birds are serving as miner's canaries for us once again, warning us that too many people, profligate consumption, and faulty technologies threaten not just birds but ourselves and all other living things as well.

The ecologist Jared Diamond, widely respected for his research on bird communities in New Guinea and adjacent islands, summarized the situation very well (in a piece in *Natural History* in 1990): "The Maoris who arrived in New Zealand 1,000 years ago had no annual Christmas bird counts, no tables of moa reproductive rates, and no books on previous extinction holocausts elsewhere. They can hardly be blamed for having precipitated extinctions. We, who exterminate today with full knowledge of what we are doing, have no such excuses."

So when birders you meet comment that it is harder and harder to find certain warblers in their local woodlot, remind them that part of the reason is that it's *easier* to find house cats there. Corner your congressional representative or write to your senators or the President, and ask why the U.S. lags behind most of the rest of the world in dealing with human population problems. If you are Canadian, write your M.P. or Prime Minister and ask why the decimation of the northwestern forests is allowed to continue. Press those politicians, especially your local politicians, to deal effectively with critical environmental problems. You will be helping not only the birds that tragically have had to be portrayed in this book, but many other species (of birds *and* other organisms) that may soon be jeopardized as well. And you'll also be helping tomorrow's kids, the birdwatchers (and scientists and politicians) of the future.

SCOPE AND ORGANIZATION
OF THE BOOK

Birds in Jeopardy treats four main groups of species and subspecies: first, the 70 birds in the 50 United States, Puerto Rico, and Canada currently considered by the U.S. Fish and Wildlife Service (and, in many cases, by the Canadian Wildlife Service) to be imperiled; second, eleven birds not listed in the U.S. that illustrate the spectrum of vulnerability of North American birds; third, the 70 birds on either the National Audubon Society's "early-warning" Blue List or the Society's auxiliary lists of birds warranting Special Concern or Local Concern, which identify species or subspecies undergoing general or regional decline; and fourth, birds that are already extinct. Lists of imperiled birds, by their very nature, are tentative, open for debate, and undoubtedly soon to be modified—hopefully by removing names from lists as populations recover, but far more likely by *adding* names as more population declines become apparent.

Birders have, of course, always shown an interest in the North American birds that travel to the tropics for the winter. Today, however, increasing attention is being directed toward the tropical birds that live year-round within the United States or its jurisdiction. For that reason, we include separate sections on the imperiled and extinct birds of Hawaii and Puerto Rico. Hawaii, in particular, has been the locus of so many extinctions that the islands have become a laboratory for the study of the impact of people on birds. Fully half of the birds officially listed by the USFWS as Threatened or Endangered are found in Hawaii or Puerto Rico, but not on the U.S. mainland. With this book, we hope to encourage support for increased protection of these island birds.

We have excluded birds imperiled in Mexico, on other Caribbean islands, and in other U.S. territories. We do this not because they are exempt from declines (35 birds in Mexico alone were listed by the International Council for Bird Preservation (ICBP) as Threatened in 1988), but to restrict the scope of the book to those birds for which there is relatively more ecological information available, and to those areas where Americans and Canadians can significantly influence legislation aimed at conserving the imperiled species.

In the text accounts, those birds listed as Threatened or Endangered by the USFWS (and therefore eligible for special protection and federal dollars) are given first. The accounts of imperiled *species* precede those of *subspecies,* since the extinction of an entire species constitutes a more serious biological loss than does the extinction of a subspecies. To those familiar with birds and their classification, this separation of species and subspecies treatments may seem cumbersome and unnecessary. For other readers, however, we wish to emphasize the difference between the two. We feel that it is important to dispel any misconception that once a bird such as the Northern Spotted Owl is listed, *all* Spotted Owls are automatically ushered into a net of greater safety. When the Northern Spotted Owl was listed in 1990, the media failed to emphasize that the bird is but one of three Spotted Owl subspecies in serious decline, and that the other two subspecies receive no benefits at all from the Northern's listing. Indeed, the Spotted Owl is also in trouble in Texas, Colorado, Utah, New Mexico, Arizona, and Mexico, yet the owls there represent only one candidate among 51 others awaiting possible future listings that would confer on them special federal protection—hopefully before their numbers drop too low to permit recovery.

We have accordingly chosen to supply separate accounts for each species and subspecies individually listed by the USFWS. For example, Peregrine Falcons are treated not only as an endangered *species,* but also as two Peregrine *subspecies,* the American Peregrine Falcon and the Arctic Peregrine Falcon. Since all three of these are ranked by the USFWS independently (two are Endangered, one is Threatened), we have provided three separate accounts. (The same rule of thumb was followed for the Least Tern and the California Least Tern.) The decision to treat the peregrines (or the terns) separately was not an obvious choice—some degree of reader confusion was likely either way—but we chose in favor of repetition over omission. It should be remembered that even if both listed Peregrine subspecies recover and are removed from listing, the Peregrine Falcon *as a species* will remain listed, in compliance with efforts to control illegal international trade in endangered species (see CITES, p. 12).

The accounts of Threatened and Endangered species and subspecies of Hawaii and Puerto Rico are presented in like fashion. In two cases (the Kauai 'O'o and the Kauai 'Akialoa), we have chosen to include a spe-

cies among the extinct birds even though it is still officially listed as only Endangered. We do this because the ornithologists most familiar with Kauai's avifauna consider the two species more likely to be extinct than to be surviving in small numbers in remote localities overlooked by birders and researchers taking censuses. Although the same case could be made for the Ivory-billed Woodpecker (on the U.S. mainland) or Bachman's Warbler (which also has not been seen in the U.S. for decades), the ornithological community still considers their persistence possible (a few small islands are more easily surveyed for rare birds than is a substantial region of a continent).

A list of the birds treated in *Birds in Jeopardy* is printed on the endpapers. Each group is presented essentially in taxonomic order (that is, in the order that ornithologists feel represents evolutionary relationships). Note that the process of becoming *officially* listed as Threatened or Endangered by the USFWS is a political one, not one that is based solely on biological data. Thus, receiving the special federal protection that comes with listing does demonstrate in some measure a bird's biological vulnerability, but does not necessarily measure the bird's *relative* vulnerability, as contrasted with other imperiled species.

Birds recognized *unofficially* as imperiled have been ranked by the National Audubon Society according to its Blue List (and its auxiliary lists; see p. 119). The Blue List, last compiled in 1986, does not now represent an exhaustive summary of the imperiled birds that have yet to receive USFWS listing, and it did not then. For that reason and others, the Blue List is not without its critics: some consider it already out of date; others are skeptical because its listings rely on data collected by a vast pool of birders of varying skills rather than solely

on single-species (or subspecies) surveys by trained field biologists. But until the pool of biologists expands to cover all aspects of conservation, we must rely upon—and indeed are indebted to—this army of volunteers who have shouldered the responsibility of keeping track of their local avifaunas. Moreover, we contend that as more birders become more actively involved in local censusing and local conservation issues, the more likely that future editions of books like this will hold not only fewer errors but also fewer—not more—treatments of species and subspecies.

Some notable aspects of bird conservation—indeed, some declining birds—are not included in this book. With the exception of Hawaiian birds experiencing island-by-island losses of entire subspecies, local extinctions are not covered. For example, the Bank Swallow, which has been extirpated from southern California and is threatened in northern California by plans to channelize the Sacramento River (now its primary breeding habitat), but persists elsewhere, has neither been granted federal protection, nor recognized as a candidate for listing, nor included on the National Audubon Society's lists, nor treated in *Birds in Jeopardy.* To have treated all cases of widespread birds that are in local or regional difficulty would have been to greatly expand the book.

Similarly, not all aspects of a bird's habitat requirements are noted in its account, and exceptions to the descriptions of nesting and foraging resources that we have reported here are inevitable, because birds are highly variable across their range. We suggest that you refer to *The Birder's Handbook* for a detailed explanation of behavioral variation and further information about any of the North American species.

Here are the topics covered in the individual accounts, and an indication of how we cover them:

NESTING: What materials and circumstances does the bird require for successful nesting? In what sorts of habitats? Such information often helps explain a bird's decline. Have woodpeckers abandoned habitat known formerly to have supported woodpeckers simply because snags have been felled? Is an area formerly known to have supported rails now vacant because the marsh has been drained?

FOOD: What is the bird's usual diet? What does it feed its young? Are food supplies in the breeding areas adequate? This information, too, may shed light on factors contributing to the bird's decline. For example, if a species feeds its young fish, then the acidification of lakes, which depresses fish populations, may be a major threat to the bird's survival. Food supplies located away from nesting grounds may also be critical: most Bristle-thighed Curlews rely on a single site on the southwestern Alaskan coast for "refueling" before their transoceanic flight to Hawaii; American White Pelicans nesting at a major U.S. breeding site in Nevada must now fly 60 miles one way to forage.

RANGE: What is the bird's worldwide breeding range? **WINTERS:** Where does the bird spend the winter? **IN PERIL:** In what portions of its range is the bird imperiled? And (for those birds formally designated as Threatened or Endangered by the USFWS) what is the current estimated total population? This information identifies those birds that are endemic (restricted) to North America, those that may be jeopardized south of the U.S. in winter, those populations that are in decline or already extirpated, and how far the bird's total population has declined from former levels.

Species range maps, often compiled from thousands of bird sightings recorded by birders and reported in birding publications, are found in standard field guides, including the National Geographic Society's *Field Guide to the Birds of North America*; Roger Tory Peterson's *A Field Guide to the Birds East of the Rockies* (fourth edition) and *A Field Guide to Western Birds* (third edition); and C. S. Robbins, B. Bruun, and H. S. Zim, *A Guide to Field Identification of Birds of North America* (revised edition). Most of these maps, though they are broadly useful and more or less dependable, are reproduced at very small scale and do not provide information on the distribution of subspecies.

NOTES: Are there any easily observed behaviors or other special factors pertinent to the bird's conservation?

JEOPARDIZED: What former and/or current threats are thought to be responsible for the bird's decline? Here is where we discuss *why* particular avian populations are threatened. We list factors such as the loss of habitat due to the drainage of wetlands, the fragmentation of forests, coastal development, urbanization, road-building, and many of the other costs attendant on human economic and population growth, such as persecution and killing of adult birds, collecting of eggs, misuse of pesticides, habitat degradation from air pollution, oil discharges and spills, the use of lead shotgun pellets, and so on.

LISTING: What actions have been prompted by concern for the bird's conservation? Is the bird on the USFWS List of Threatened and Endangered Wildlife and Plants (known for simplicity as the Endangered Species List)? If not, is it, or one of its subspecies, a candidate for future federal listing? Is it on Canada's list of Threatened, Endangered, or Vulnerable species? Or is it perhaps included on the National Audubon Society's Blue List (or its auxiliary lists of birds that are of Special or Local Concern)?

RECOVERY PLANS: What are some of the goals the USFWS has announced to encourage a Threatened or Endangered bird's recovery and eventual removal from listing? We offer only a sample of the steps taken toward recovery, since plans change in accordance with changes in conditions, federal funding, and public support.

EXTINCTION: When was the last sighting?

The book concludes with a number of commentaries and reference materials. Among the **Commentaries** is an overview of the general threats facing avian populations, and information on how you can help to protect birds. Much of this material has been adapted from *The Birder's Handbook*. Next is a **Quick Check of Birds in Jeopardy,** a summary (extracted from the "Listing" sections of the accounts) noting region by region where particular birds are in jeopardy. Included with this Quick Check is a map identifying the U.S. states and Canadian provinces (or parts of states or provinces) included in each region. The major works from which we have drawn information are discussed under **Sources.** A **Bibliography** lists all other references used in the preparation of this book, including all those cited specifically in the text. A brief closing piece offers information about the **Center for Conservation Biology,** at Stanford University. Finally, the **Index** lists both common and latinized ("scientific") names of all the birds mentioned in the book, whether species or subspecies, and whether fully treated or simply mentioned in passing (as an example of the latter case, the European Starling—scarcely imperiled!—may be said to compete with a particular imperiled bird for scarce resources).

BIRDS THAT ARE
OFFICIALLY THREATENED
OR ENDANGERED

As passed by the U.S. Congress, the 1973 Endangered Species Act stated that the U.S. Fish and Wildlife Service (USFWS) may classify a species as Endangered when it is in danger of extinction throughout all or a significant part of its range, and may classify it as Threatened if it is likely to become Endangered within the foreseeable future. The Act required that all federal agencies undertake programs for the conservation of listed species, and that they prohibit "authorizing, funding, or carrying out any action that would jeopardize" a listed species or modify critical habitat (if the listing specifies habitat). It also made possible cooperative agreements with the states, provided matching federal funds for these agreements, and extended the Service's authority to acquire land for species listed under the CITES agreement. (CITES, the Convention on International Trade in Endangered Species of Wild Fauna and Flora, is an international cooperative agreement designed to regulate the trade of over 30,000 animal and plant species by implementing a system of import and export permits and limitations.)

Amendments to the Endangered Species Act followed in 1978, 1982, and 1988. Provisions in the 1978 amendment allowed federal agencies to "undertake an action that would jeopardize listed species if the action were exempted by a cabinet-level committee convened for this purpose." The amendment also made it possible to designate critical habitat at the time of a bird's listing, extended authority to acquire land within the natural distribution of any listed species, and restricted the Act's broad definition of "species" (with respect to "subspecies" or "populations") to vertebrates (that is, a vertebrate population or subspecies could *legally* be defined as a species). Provisions in the 1982 amendment required that decisions on listing be limited to information on biology and trade, not on possible economic (or other) effects. It required the Service to make a determination whether to list or not to list, in response to an external petition, within a year of receiving the petition. It also made it possible to designate populations of a listed species that could be "subject to lessened restrictions." Provisions in the 1988 amendment required, among other things, the monitoring of species that were *candidates* for listing, as well as species that had recovered and had been removed from the list, allowed emergency listing when evidence warranted it, and required that reports of state and federal expenditures, status lists, and recovery plans be submitted to Congress. The Act is currently authorized through 1992, with renewal at five-year intervals. (Interestingly, in 1988 the Senate reauthorization vote passed 93 to 2.)

Canadian wildlife in danger of extinction has been accorded legal protection since the signing of the Canada Wildlife Act in 1973. In general, the provincial legislators are legally responsible for the regulation of the wildlife within their borders (except, for example, species found on federally regulated land, migratory species that cross borders, and species regulated by international agreements). By 1984, however, only Ontario, Manitoba, Alberta, British Columbia, the Yukon, and the Northwest Territories had specific legislative or regulatory provisions for the protection of vulnerable wildlife (Newfoundland, Prince Edward Island, Nova Scotia, Quebec, and Saskatchewan had none), and only New Brunswick had both an Endangered Species Act and an Ecological Reserves Act. By 1991, further provisions had been established in some of the provinces, but imperiled birds were still not accorded legal protection everywhere.

To rank Canada's vulnerable species, the Committee on the Status of Endangered Wildlife in Canada (COSEWIC) was formed. COSEWIC, which includes federal, provincial, and territorial representatives along with three representatives of wildlife conservation organizations, solicits expert opinions on jeopardized indigenous wildlife, commissions scientific status reports on these organisms, draws on the results to specify degree of imperilment in each case, and then recommends action to the provinces and other jurisdictions. As of 1991, COSEWIC had classified 38 birds— 17 as Vulnerable, eight as Threatened, nine as Endangered, one as Extirpated, and three as Extinct—and had identified a number of other species as in need of study.

All of Canada's officially listed birds are given in the Regional Quick Check (see p. 239) and reflected in the text treatments. (See the endpapers.)

The Endangered Species Act of 1978 was not the first piece of legislation in the U.S. to identify species in danger of extinction. The 1966 Endangered Species Preservation Act allowed listing of native animal species as "endangered" and provided some means to protect those listed. The departments of Interior, Agriculture, and Defense were assigned responsibility for protecting listed species and, where appropriate, preserving their habitat. As such, they were authorized to acquire land. Three years later, in 1969, the Endangered Species Conservation Act provided additional protection to species in worldwide danger of extinction, and prohibited their importation or sale within the United States. It also set the stage for a meeting to adopt CITES (the convention restricting the international trade of species that would, or could, be harmed by the trade; see above). Within four years, CITES was signed. Later that same year the Endangered Species Act of 1973 was also signed.

Successful protection has depended, of course, on coordination and compliance, but more significantly on the flow of money, which, unfortunately, has yet to match the flow of extinction-bound species. In part, this has been because too few of the original budget-makers appreciated the severity of the problems at hand. In 1973,

fewer than 200 animal and plant species were listed; by 1990, 554 were listed and an additional 3,650 "candidates" (organisms petitioned to qualify for Threatened or Endangered status) were awaiting their turn. Some candidates have been waiting a decade already, and in the past ten years 34 have been declared extinct *while still awaiting listings*. (Although the USFWS has sufficient data to list 950 of its 3,650 candidates, it has the resources to cover only about 50 additions annually.) Today, 70 birds in the continental U.S., Hawaii, and Puerto Rico are listed as Threatened or Endangered, with the Golden-cheeked Warbler and Northern Spotted Owl, both named in 1990, being the most recent additions. An additional 52 birds (from within the same geographic area) are candidates for listing.

The USFWS identifies candidates as either Category 1 or Category 2 (technically as "Category 1 and 2 notice of review species"). Category 1 candidates are those for which the Service has substantial biological information to support listing. Category 2 candidates are those whose listing is *possibly* appropriate (but for which the Service requires further information), or those the Service ranks behind other organisms awaiting their turn to be listed, or those that are held up by bureaucratic inertia or overload. There is also a Category 3, which embraces those organisms removed from the active list either because they are thought to be already extinct, or because they have been found in fact not to be distinct species or subspecies, or because they have been found to be more abundant than previously thought.

Plants make up the bulk of the Category 1 and Category 2 candidates (about 2,180). Plants' dominance in the listings is in part an artifact of the early days of the Act; initially, the Smithsonian Institution, on a request by Congress, created two lists of plants that were treated simply as petitions. Animals make up the remaining 1,470 or so candidates; of these, 75 are Category 1 candidates, and four of those are birds, including two from the areas covered by this book, the California Black Rail and the Appalachian Bewick's Wren. (The other 50 bird candidates fall into category 2.)

The Endangered Species Act of 1973 requires an annual report of federal expenditures for conservation. According to the 1988 amendment, the report should be limited to only those expenditures that are "reasonably identifiable" as having been applied to the needs of particular organisms. As a result, the annual report represents an incomplete picture: many expenditures are not funded on an organism-by-organism basis, and there is a good deal of variability among the reporting methods used by the various federal agencies. Nonetheless, the report does provide an overview of conservation priorities.

In the latest report available (for 1989), reasonably identifiable expenditures totaled almost $44 million. These expenditures were apportioned among two-thirds (347) of the 554 listed organisms. Interestingly, half of the total was spent on only 12 organisms (3 percent of the list), and nine-tenths of the total was spent on just 60 organisms.

How well did birds do? The Bald Eagle led the entire list of 554, receiving more than $3 million. In fact, of the top 12 organisms noted above, six were birds (Bald Eagle, Red-cockaded Woodpecker, American Peregrine Falcon, Whooping Crane, Piping Plover, and Kirtland's Warbler). The Red-cockaded Woodpecker and Peregrine Falcon each received more than $2 million, and the others received more than $1 million apiece. At the other end, however, were 16 birds that received nothing: Maui 'Akepa, Kauai 'Akialoa, Molokai Creeper, Oahu Creeper, Crested Honeycreeper (or 'Akohekohe), Puerto Rican Nightjar, Nukupu'u, Maui Parrotbill, Po'o-uli, Newell's Shearwater, San Clemente Sage Sparrow, Large Kauai Thrush (or Kama'o), Molokai Thrush (or Oloma'o), Small Kauai Thrush (or Puaiohi), Inyo California Towhee, and Kauai 'O'o.

The goal, of course, for every organism listed as Endangered is that it recover sufficiently to be reclassified as Threatened and ultimately to be removed from the list altogether. Our few textbook examples of rebounding species include the Brown Pelican (with populations recovered along the U.S. Atlantic coast and in Florida and Alabama), the Bald Eagle, the Whooping Crane (just barely), and the Peregrine Falcon (in parts of its North American range).

But despite the Endangered Species Act, there have been more failures than successes. The years since its enactment in 1973 have seen 18 listed organisms go to extinction, including the Dusky Seaside Sparrow, Texas Henslow's Sparrow, Santa Barbara Song Sparrow (listed too late to be saved), and the possible (if not probable) loss of, among others, Bachman's Warbler, Ivory-billed Woodpecker, Eskimo Curlew, Kauai 'Akialoa, Kauai 'O'o, and Molokai Creeper. These birds are reminders that legislating safeguards is sometimes impossible, no matter how much information, public good will, or money is available.

Not surprisingly, a gap persists between public understanding of the threats to a declining avifauna and public understanding of the laws that protect birds. For example, one difficulty in interpreting the Endangered Species Act involves its use of the term "species." Unlike the scientific definition, the Act uses the word to mean a "species," a "subspecies," or even a "population." In this book we have made an effort to minimize the confusion by using the term "species" only in its biological sense; that is, with reference to organisms that are distinctly different from others *and do not ordinarily interbreed* with individuals of other species (see p. 35). Public interest in imperiled organisms continues to climb, as does public awareness of scientific practice, and we await a simple terminology and explanatory style that will work in the public, scientific, and legal arenas alike and eliminate unnecessary confusion about what it is that is at risk.

Moreover, with so many people strongly supporting the protection of species, why is so little said about all the other federal laws and international treaties that have been enacted to protect birds? The Lacey Act of 1900, which was written to regulate the harvest of birds, helped make the preservation of species a national concern. The Migratory Bird Treaty Act of 1918 implemented the 1916 treaty between the U.S. and Great Britain (on behalf of Canada) to protect 832 species of North American birds. Additional migratory bird treaties were signed with Japan (1972) and the Soviet Union (1976).

The Endangered Species Act has been law for nearly 20 years; hopefully, it will be reauthorized in 1992 or replaced with something that affords greater protection. The current bind is increasingly clear: on the one hand, we remain wrapped in a listing process that identifies those organisms most likely to become extinct; on the other hand, managers attempt to save those species most likely to recover. There can be little doubt that, given the severity and complexity of the problems, protecting biological diversity on a species-by-species basis is a far less effective strategy than is protecting entire ecosystems.

No level of protection, in fact, can guarantee the persistence of any particular species, and even the Office of Technology Assessment (OTA) agrees that ecosystem preservation is the best, and perhaps only, tactic that has a hope of ensuring species preservation. According to OTA estimates, up to one-half of the major land-based ecosystems in the U.S. are not under federal control and are subject to jurisdictional disregard or interplay. The problems this book identifies will only increase as efforts to save critical habitats and maintain corridors between them become complicated by the effects of global warming, acid precipitation, and other global and regional problems. Clearly, the smaller a remaining population and the longer the timeframe, the more likely that extinction will be its fate. Threats to our imperiled birds increase as forests, wetlands, and other key habitats shrink, fragment, and degrade, and as the distribution of bird populations alters accordingly.

Aside from reauthorization of the Endangered Species Act, in 1992, the next major piece of legislation could be the National Biological Diversity Conservation and Environmental Research Act, which was introduced in March 1988. The Reagan administration consistently opposed its passage, and at this writing, so does the Bush administration. So we wait.

Meanwhile, one development in avian conservation looks more hopeful. A new program has been initiated by the U.S. Fish and Wildlife Service to assess the changing status of migratory forest birds, more specifically forest birds that migrate to the tropics. With research and monitoring programs as its primary aims, it is expected to help North American bird species in general. And even as it gets under way, more information on migratory birds is now available from other sources. As required by Congress, the Office of Migratory Bird Management (of the Fish and Wildlife Service) has released a nongame-bird management plan that is available to the public (see Bibliography, under Office).

For further information concerning birds on the federal list of Threatened and Endangered Wildlife and Plants, contact the appropriate Regional Office of the U.S. Fish and Wildlife Service.

In California, Hawaii, Idaho, Nevada, Oregon, and Washington:

(for all six states)
Regional Office of Endangered Species
U.S. Fish and Wildlife Service
Lloyd 500 Building, Suite 1692
500 N.E. Multnomah Street
Portland, OR 97232

(for Hawaii, also try)
Office of Environmental Services
U.S. Fish and Wildlife Service
300 Ala Moana Boulevard
P.O. Box 50167
Honolulu, HA 96850

In Arizona, New Mexico, Oklahoma, and Texas:

Regional Office of Endangered Species
U.S. Fish and Wildlife Service
P.O. Box 1306
Albuquerque, NM 87103

In Illinois, Indiana, Iowa, Michigan, Minnesota, Missouri, Ohio, and Wisconsin:

Regional Office of Endangered Species
U.S. Fish and Wildlife Service
Federal Building
Fort Snelling
Twin Cities, MN 55111

In Alabama, Arkansas, Florida, Georgia, Kentucky, Louisiana, Mississippi, North Carolina, South Carolina, Tennessee, Puerto Rico, and the Virgin Islands:

(for all these states and territories)
Regional Office of Endangered Species
U.S. Fish and Wildlife Service
The Richard B. Russell Federal Building
Suite 1276
75 Spring Street, S.W.
Atlanta, GA 30303

(for Puerto Rico, also try)
Caribbean Field Office
U.S. Fish and Wildlife Service
P.O. Box 491
Boqueron, Puerto Rico 00622

In Connecticut, Delaware, District of Columbia, Maine, Maryland, Massachusetts, New Hampshire, New Jersey, New York, Pennsylvania, Rhode Island, Vermont, Virginia, and West Virginia:

Regional Office of Endangered Species
U.S. Fish and Wildlife Service
Suite 700
One Gateway Center
Newton Corner, MA 02158

In Colorado, Kansas, Montana, Nebraska, North Dakota, South Dakota, Utah, and Wyoming:

Regional Office of Endangered Species
U.S. Fish and Wildlife Service
P.O. Box 25486
Denver Federal Center
Denver, CO 80225

In Alaska:

Regional Office of Endangered Species
U.S. Fish and Wildlife Service
1011 East Tudor Road
Anchorage, AK 99503

For further information concerning birds on Canada's list of Endangered, Threatened, and Vulnerable species of wildlife, contact the following:

Committee on the Status of Endangered
    Wildlife in Canada (COSEWIC)
Secretariat
Canadian Wildlife Service
Ottawa, ONT K1A OH3

World Wildlife Fund Canada
90 Eglinton Avenue, East
Toronto, Ontario M45 2Z7

REFERENCES: Blockstein, 1988; Canadian Wildlife Service, 1991; Ehrlich, Dobkin, and Wheye, 1988; Office of Migratory Bird Management, 1987; U.S. Fish and Wildlife Service, 1990a, b.

BROWN PELICAN
Pelecanus occidentalis

NESTING: Usually in coastal areas, generally on islands, with abundant, long-term food supplies nearby. In the southeastern U.S., the Brown Pelican nests most often in the tops of mangroves (also in Australian pines, red cedars, live oaks, redbays, and sea grapes), where it can construct its saucer of sticks, reeds, feathers, bones, grass, seaweed, and similar materials. When nesting on islands that are free of mammalian predators, as is common in the West, it may nest on the ground or in low bushes.

FOOD: Mostly midwater fish during breeding; sometimes invertebrates such as euphausiids (shrimplike crustaceans). While hunting, the Brown Pelican dives, dropping from height into the water and employing its pouch as a flexible scoop or "net." Upon surfacing, it points its bill down to drain, and then up to swallow the catch. It regurgitates food for its young.

RANGE: In the West, breeds from Anacapa Island, California (formerly from Point Lobos, Monterey County), south to Chile. In the East, from North Carolina and the north shore of the Gulf of Mexico south to Venezuela and Trinidad. **WINTERS:** After breeding, some western birds disperse as far north as southern British Columbia before retreating south along the coasts of the Americas for the winter. Most birds seen along the Pacific Coast in late summer through late fall have migrated north from nesting colonies in Mexico. **IN PERIL:** Throughout its range except along the U.S. Atlantic Coast and in Florida and

Alabama. Perhaps 50,000 pairs once nested in Texas and Louisiana, but by the 1950's and 1960's most nesting on the Texas coast, and all nesting on the Louisiana coast, had ended. By 1989 the Texas colonies were down to about 500 pairs; those in Louisiana (stocked in the meantime with Florida birds) numbered more than 1,000 pairs. In the West, in 1970, the 550 nesting pairs of the Anacapa Island colony produced a single fledgling. Two years later, DDT was banned in the U.S. and endrin use also declined. These changes proved to be instrumental in the recovery of this species: today perhaps 3,000 pairs nest in the East, about 6,000 in southern California, and about 45,000 on Mexico's west coast.

NOTES: Eastern and western populations are different subspecies. Brown Pelicans usually seek salt water but are seldom found more than 20 miles out to sea. Because ground-nesting birds may switch sites when the colony site suffers erosion and flooding, empty rookeries need not indicate declines.

JEOPARDIZED: Mainly by eggshell thinning from pesticides (particularly DDE), direct poisoning (by endrin, for example), habitat loss, and various forms of human disturbance. Losses to disturbances are reported particularly for the California and Sea of Cortez populations, which are also threatened by reduced fish supplies resulting either from weather or, more likely, from excessive commercial fishing.

LISTING: Listed as **Endangered** in Texas,

Louisiana, and California in October 1970. The species was also included on the **Blue List** in 1972 because of declines along the Atlantic coast, the Gulf of Mexico, and the Pacific coast. Subsequent increases in fledging success led to the removal of the populations along the Atlantic coast of Florida and in Alabama from the federal list, and those in the western U.S. are now being considered for downlisting to **Threatened.**

RECOVERY PLANS: Publicity encouraged people to visit the Brown Pelican's nesting sites, reducing fledging success; access to nesting sites on federally owned land is now restricted. Eastern and California birds have separate recovery plans.

WOOD STORK

Mycteria americana

NESTING: In the southeastern U.S., usually requires the horizontal top limbs of large cypress in marshes and swamps, less often in mangroves and adjoining stream habitats. The nest is a flimsy platform of large sticks. The Wood Stork is highly colonial; 5 to 25 nests, some touching, may be supported by a single tree.

FOOD: Mostly fish; also reptiles (including snakes and small alligators), amphibians, and aquatic invertebrates. While foraging, the Wood Stork usually moves its 9-inch touch-sensitive bill through the water column until contact with prey triggers a swift (25-millisecond) bill-snap reflex. Foot shuffling apparently flushes prey. Because foraging waters are usually muddy, which conceals prey, the storks require dense concentrations of fish. Flights to feeding grounds (using thermals) may extend 80 miles, one way. The Wood Stork regurgitates fish to feed its young.

RANGE: Breeds from southern Sonora, the north coast of the Gulf of Mexico, and South Carolina south to Ecuador and northern Argentina. Some birds, especially young ones, disperse north after the breeding season. **WINTERS:** Largely within the breeding range. **IN PERIL:** In Florida, Georgia, and South Carolina. The population of about 16,000 to 20,000 pairs in the 1930's fell to about 11,000 by the 1960's, fewer than 6,000 in the 1970's, and fewer than 5,000 in 1980. The number of breeders fluctuates year-to-year, but the Wood Stork's population appears to have stabi-

lized in the early 1990's at between 7,000 and 10,000 pairs.

NOTES: The Wood Stork's unfeathered head probably saved the species from decimation by plume hunters, and its unpalatable flesh saved it from the cook pot. The Wood Stork evolved a boom-or-bust cycle: colonies skip breeding if food is low, and they desert their nesting grounds or broods if persistent rains keep the water level too high for prey to be concentrated.

JEOPARDIZED: Mainly by habitat loss and modification: cypress trees in which the storks nest have been cut for lumber, and foraging swamps have been drained for agriculture, industry, and housing. One-third of the foraging habitat in southern Florida has been lost since 1900, and habitat surrounding protected rookeries in the Everglades and the Corkscrew Swamp Sanctuary has been modified by development. The water-control system in the Everglades, completed in the 1960's, forced birds to begin nesting later in the year, leaving too little time for pairs to fledge their young before the rains raised water levels and ended the concentration of prey in pools. The mean number of pairs attempting to breed in the Everglades dropped from 1,800 pairs in the 1960's to 400 pairs in the 1980's. No longer the primary breeding site, the Everglades remains a critical foraging habitat; during dry years, up to 70 percent of the North American population uses the area. Heavy metals, especially mercury, have been found throughout the Ever-

WHOOPING CRANE

Grus americana

glades, and phosphorus run-off from agricultural areas is causing deleterious changes in plant communities. Low water levels lead to significant nest predation by raccoons.

LISTING: **Blue-Listed** from 1972 to 1981 and warranted of **Special Concern** in 1982. Increased concern prompted federal listing as **Endangered** in February 1984.

RECOVERY PLANS: South Carolina's Silverbluff Plantation Sanctuary's artificial habitat at Kathwood Lake, a dry lake bed, was a model for foraging habitat design, and was discovered by Wood Storks in 1986. Florida's Panther National Wildlife Refuge (1989) also protects this species. Restoration efforts under way there include renewing the flow of water that had been impounded to the north and avoiding unnatural pulses of water. Integrating the restoration and maintenance programs of the various agencies involved in the recovery is imperative.

NESTING: Requires freshwater marshes and sloughs around potholes and lake margins and in wet prairies of wilderness wetlands. The cranes build a tight, heaping saucer of soft grass on a pile of coarse grass, reeds, or sod near or within the water.

FOOD: Mostly crustaceans, fish, small vertebrates, and insects; also roots, berries, and grain. While foraging, the Whooping Crane usually probes beneath the surface of mud or sand in or near shallow water, takes prey from within the water column, or picks items from the substrate.

RANGE: Breeds now only in and near Wood Buffalo National Park, southwestern Mackenzie and northern Alberta, Canada; formerly south to North Dakota and Iowa and along the coast of Texas and Louisiana. Whooping Crane eggs introduced into the nests of "foster-parent" Sandhill Cranes at Gray's Lake, Idaho, hatched and the young fledged, but these young birds have not yet bred. **WINTERS:** On the coast of Texas, in and near Aransas National Wildlife Refuge, Texas, formerly also east to Louisiana and south into Mexico. The birds from Gray's Lake winter mostly in the Bosque del Apache National Wildlife Refuge, along the Rio Grande in New Mexico. **IN PERIL:** Throughout its range, including stopover sites in Saskatchewan, Colorado, and Utah. Numbers increased from 15 birds in 1941 to 160 (including captives) by 1986. The total current population is assumed to be about 200 individ-

uals, about half in the Canadian population and the remainder divided more or less evenly between the Idaho population and three captive flocks (those responsible do not make actual counts, because their presence during the counting would disturb the birds). The viability of the Canadian population is at risk of oil and chemical contamination along the small Texas winter range.

NOTES: Decades of census data at Aransas National Wildlife Refuge show a ten-year cycle in the size of overwintering flocks (cause unknown).

JEOPARDIZED: Whoopers have been in decline for more than 50 years because of habitat loss (especially conversion of the prairie wetlands to farm fields), over-hunting (1870's–1920's), and collisions with power lines, the number one known cause of death in fledged birds. The wintering grounds at Aransas, once degraded by oyster dredging, are now undergoing slow, chronic erosion. The Whooping Crane is extremely sensitive to intrusion and human disturbance, especially during breeding.

LISTING: Listed as **Endangered** in the U.S. in March 1967 and listed as **Endangered** in Canada in 1978.

RECOVERY PLANS: Wood Buffalo National Park and Idaho's Gray's Lake National Wildlife Refuge harbor wild flocks, and experimental captive breeding populations have been established at the Patuxent Wildlife Research Center, Laurel, Maryland, the International Crane Foundation, Baraboo, Wisconsin, and the San Antonio Zoo, Texas. In cooperation with the Patuxent center, the Canadian Wildlife Service prepared a captive breeding program that began in 1990. Reintroductions using sub-adult birds are scheduled for 1992 at Florida's Kissimmee Prairie.

NESTING: Usually on sandy beaches, sometimes on gravelly or pebbly beaches, well above the tide line, particularly in areas of sparse grass cover. The Piping Plover will also place its highly exposed nest on undisturbed gravel pits, on salt-encrusted spits along alkali lakes, or on natural alluvial river islands and those built up from the spoils of dredging operations.

FOOD: Mostly aquatic invertebrates (and their eggs), including marine worms, crustaceans, and mollusks, as well as insects. While foraging, the Piping Plover usually picks the substrate, and occasionally probes beneath the surface of sand or mud.

RANGE: Bred originally from Alberta and eastern Montana across the northern Great Plains to the shores of the Great Lakes; also along the Atlantic coast from Newfoundland to North Carolina. Now absent from many parts of this range. **WINTERS:** Mainly along the coast of the southeastern U.S. from Texas to South Carolina, occasionally in the Greater Antilles and Bahamas. **IN PERIL:** Essentially throughout its range. The population is estimated at about 3,500 to 4,200 individuals.

NOTES: More than 80 percent of the known breeding of this species occurs in Massachusetts, New York, New Jersey, and Virginia. Because 70 to 80 percent of the Piping Plover's annual cycle is spent away from its breeding areas, the protection of wintering habitat is also essential to recovery efforts.

JEOPARDIZED: First by overhunting (from which the species recovered during the 1920's), now by widespread habitat loss and degradation. Construction of homes and roads encroaches onto the Piping Plover's habitat, beach visitors disturb and trample nests, unleashed pets taken to beaches kill chicks and destroy eggs, debris and garbage attract mammalian predators (including foxes, feral dogs and cats, opossums, skunks, and rats), off-road vehicles destroy nests, and inland water projects alter sites. By around 1986 the large Ontario population was gone, perhaps only 20 percent of the nesting sites in Manitoba were in use, some 2,500 plovers were left in the Prairie Region, a couple of dozen were left around the Great Lakes, and fewer than 1,500 remained in the Atlantic Coast Region.

LISTING: Blue-Listed from 1972 until December 1985, when the U.S. Fish and Wildlife Service listed it as **Endangered** in the Great Lakes watershed of Illinois, Indiana, Michigan, Minnesota, New York, Ohio, Pennsylvania, Wisconsin, and Ontario and as **Threatened** elsewhere. The Piping Plover was also listed as **Endangered** in Canada in 1985.

RECOVERY PLANS: Include closing critical beach habitat in Massachusetts, Rhode Island, Connecticut, New Jersey, and Virginia during breeding, increasing public information programs, including public service announcements, and displaying plover-alert posters in stores selling and renting beach recreational equipment. The aim is to establish 1,200 breeding pairs for the Atlantic Coast population, 1,300 pairs for the U.S. Great Plains population, 2,500 pairs for the Canadian Great Plains population, and 150 pairs for the Great Lakes. Public education, monitoring, management programs, protection from disturbance, and predator control are all part of the recovery plan.

ESKIMO CURLEW
Numenius borealis

NESTING: In wetlands of open tundra. The Eskimo Curlew makes a simple depression on the ground, which may include a few intended or inadvertent decaying leaves.

FOOD: Mostly insects, particularly crickets and grasshoppers; also berries, snails, and other invertebrates. While foraging, the Eskimo Curlew usually picks items from the substrate, probes beneath the surface of sand or mud either near or in shallow water, or takes prey from within the water column.

RANGE: Bred originally at least in northwestern Mackenzie, Northwest Territories, and probably in northern Alaska. **WINTERS:** In South America, mainly in Argentina. Its migration route from the Arctic ran southeast across Canada, with a stopover in Labrador or at other sites on the east coast of Canada, then south along the U.S. and across the Caribbean to Venezuela and the Guianas and on to Argentina. Its return route led through Central America, Texas, and the Plains States to the Canadian tundra. **IN PERIL:** Throughout whatever range the species may still occur in. Estimating the size of the population would be pure guesswork, since there have been no confirmed sightings in 30 years, but if the Eskimo Curlew is not already extinct, there are probably fewer than 50 birds remaining. The last confirmed sighting was in 1962.

NOTES: Because the Eskimo Curlew was decimated so long ago, in the late 1800's, little information on its biology is available. It was well-known in its heyday, however, and the crowberries with which it fueled its migration came to be known as curlewberries.

JEOPARDIZED: By overhunting for commercial markets. Formerly the Eskimo Curlew was relatively abundant and was referred to as the "doughbird" from the substantial layer of fat it added prior to migration. The fat raised its weight to a marketable 1 pound, and the birds were preserved for winter stores in Labrador, one of the species' migration stop-over points. The Eskimo Curlew is an upland wintering species; loss of wintering habitat to pasture and agriculture may pose a major problem.

LISTING: Listed as **Endangered** in the U.S. in March 1967, and listed as **Endangered** in Canada in 1978.

RECOVERY PLANS: Recent unconfirmed sightings led to the formation of an Eskimo Curlew Advisory Group. It recommended, among other things, management of staging areas along migration routes if such areas could be located.

LEAST TERN
Sterna antillarum

NESTING: Usually on open, level beaches or the borders of rivers or lakes, where colonies of the terns lay their eggs in simple scrapes in the sand. Along the coasts, especially in the East, preferred colony sites provide pebbles or shells amid short, sparse vegetation on sand. The Least Tern also selects barren salt flats and, although rarely, flat rooftops.

FOOD: Mostly fish; also aquatic invertebrates, particularly crustaceans and insects. While foraging, the Least Tern hovers (for longer than do other terns), then drops from height into the water.

RANGE: Breeds along the Pacific coast from San Francisco Bay south to southern Mexico, along large rivers in the central U.S. as far north as South Dakota and Ohio, and along the Atlantic, Gulf of Mexico, and Caribbean coasts from Maine south to Venezuela. **WINTERS:** Along the coasts of Central and northern South America; details of the winter range are still poorly known. **IN PERIL:** Throughout most of the species' North American breeding range. In 1987 the population of interior Least Terns was estimated at about 4,500 individuals (that total excludes the California subspecies; see p. 43).

NOTES: In North America, three Least Tern subspecies are recognized, but the division between them remains controversial. Currently, the California Least Tern (a subspecies) and the interior population of the Least Tern (not designated as a distinct subspecies) are Endangered. This is North America's smallest tern, smaller than a robin. It forms colonies of varying sizes, now usually of no more than 20 widely spaced nests, but sometimes of up to 75 nests, and occasional terns are solitary.

JEOPARDIZED: Once by plume hunters, who almost annihilated the species (by 1900 a typical seasonal kill would bring down 100,000). Now, in inland areas, by the channelization and damming of rivers, which eliminate the sandbars and beaches on which the terns nest. Declines continue in most areas, and losses to cats, rats, and humans often lead to colony desertion. The inland population is limited to some 12 main areas along major rivers. For the many threats to the Least Tern in California, see p. 43.

LISTING: Blue-Listed from 1972 until May 1985, when it was federally listed. By 1982, reports from the East (from the Northeastern Maritime to the Central Southern regions) voiced increasing concern about its status, leading the U.S. Fish and Wildlife Service finally to list it as **Endangered** in 1985.

RECOVERY PLANS: Bare or nearly bare alluvial islands or sandbars, appropriate water levels during nesting, and sufficient food are essential to the Least Tern's survival and recovery. The birds will nest on artificial sites, and snowfencing placed around nests offers chicks shade and shelters them from predators.

CALIFORNIA CONDOR
Gymnogyps californianus

NESTING: In the wild, the California Condor nested on spacious cliff ledges with an area of cushioning coarse gravel on which it placed a few twigs or leaves to accommodate its single egg. It also nested in shallow caves or (probably rarely) in holes in giant sequoias.

FOOD: Mammalian carrion, nearly entirely: deer, elk, pronghorn, livestock, and probably smaller species such as gophers and rats. Also salmon. The condor searched while soaring at high altitude, regularly using the presence of eagles or ravens to locate prey.

RANGE: Fossil evidence indicates that prehistorically the condor inhabited most of the U.S.; in the 1800's it ranged at least from the Columbia River to northern Baja California and east to Arizona. By the close of the nineteenth century, the condor had been driven from the Pacific Northwest, by the 1930's it was gone from northern Baja California, and by 1950 it was already confined to the mountains surrounding the south end of the San Joaquin Valley, California. **WINTER:** Condors dispersed great distances in search of food, but apparently did not undertake any regular migration.

IN PERIL: None remain in the wild. By the 1960's the remaining population had been reduced to 60 birds; by the early 1980's, to 25 birds; and by 1984, to just 15 birds (including five breeding pairs). By 1986 only three males remained in the wild, and all three were captured in 1987. At that time, just 27 of the birds existed, all of them in

captivity, but by 1991 the captive population had risen to 52 individuals, half at the San Diego Wild Animal Park, half at the Los Angeles Zoo. There are plans to release the first individuals in the fall of 1991, possibly to establish two populations, one in California and one in Arizona (or perhaps New Mexico).

NOTES: Condors ordinarily breed in alternate years, although they are capable of nesting yearly and can produce a replacement clutch if the first is destroyed or removed. On average, however, they do well to produce two surviving young every four years, when factors such as post-fledging mortality are considered. A condor requires eight years to reach sexual maturity and may live to be 45. It can fly at speeds of 45 to 60 miles per hour, and was known to travel up to 140 miles daily between its roost and its foraging grounds.

JEOPARDIZED: Recently, by lead from bullets in carcasses, poisoned bait (intended for coyotes), food contaminated with DDT, other pesticides, collisions with power lines, hunters, general harassment, and habitat destruction.

LISTING: Listed as **Endangered** in March 1967.

RECOVERY PLANS: The first chick conceived in captivity was hatched in 1988, and four were hatched in 1989. Eight more hatched in 1990, from 16 eggs laid. A dozen pairs may breed in 1991. Returning condors to the wild requires both effective breeding programs and effective reintroduction strategies. Experimental reintroductions using captive-bred Andean Condors are being conducted in southern California: several birds released in 1989 adjusted well and have since been recaptured. The six birds released in 1990 are roosting, soaring, and feeding together.

BALD EAGLE
Haliaeetus leucocephalus

NESTING: On a platform of large sticks and vegetation built in a tall tree or on a cliff ledge in open areas along coasts, rivers, or large lakes. Cliff nests vary from a few sticks to massive structures. Nests may be used for 35 years or more.

FOOD: Mostly fish, particularly salmon (weighing up to 15 pounds and often dying or already dead); also small mammals (particularly rabbits), seabirds, waterfowl, carrion, and rarely other vertebrates. While hunting, the Bald Eagle soars at high altitude, seeks prey in a low searching flight, or swoops down from a perch to snatch prey from the ground in its talons.

RANGE: Bred originally from central Alaska and northern Canada south to Baja California, central Arizona, and the Gulf of Mexico. Now extirpated from large areas in the southern part of this range. **WINTERS:** Mostly from southern Alaska and southern Canada south through the remainder of the breeding range. **IN PERIL:** In most of the lower 48 states and the western provinces of Canada. By 1981 about 90 percent of the nesting pairs in the U.S. were limited to ten states, and by 1982 the breeding population in the lower 48 states had fallen to fewer than 1,500 pairs, but it rose to some 2,400 in 1988. A census that year showed some 11,000 birds wintering within the U.S. The Chilkat Bald Eagle Preserve, not far from Glacier National Park, supports the largest wintering population in the world and is threatened by a proposed copper mine.

PEREGRINE FALCON
Falco peregrinus

NOTES: The Bald Eagle was adopted in 1782 as the national emblem of the U.S. even though the bird is primarily a somewhat timid carrion-feeder.

JEOPARDIZED: By habitat destruction (including the cutting of suitable nesting or roosting trees), reproductive impairment from exposure to pesticides and heavy metals, collisions with high power lines, shooting, and human encroachment. The banning of DDT has been instrumental in the Bald Eagle's recovery.

LISTING: Listed as **Endangered** in most of the U.S. and as **Threatened** in Washington, Oregon, Minnesota, Wisconsin, and Michigan in March 1967. The species remains unlisted in Alaska.

RECOVERY PLANS: Widespread efforts to restore and protect breeding populations have been generally successful. In fact, some states now support (with the help of desert reservoirs, effective nest-monitoring, and programs to release young birds into the wild) more Bald Eagles than ever before recorded. At the federal level, efforts toward recovery have involved monitoring populations, improving protection, setting up captive-breeding programs, relocating wild birds, and establishing a wide-ranging public-information program. Additional efforts include tax-supported state programs to monitor nests and to help fund reintroduction projects, acquisition of important habitat by conservation organizations, and agreements of private landholders to cooperate with conservation efforts. Reintroductions have proved successful, changes in powerline designs have been beneficial, and rehabilitation centers for injured birds are available. Reclassification of the Bald Eagle from Endangered to Threatened in many areas is expected, but illegal shooting, while declining, remains the most commonly recorded means of death.

NESTING: Usually uses cliff ledges in open habitats, from tundra, savanna, and sea-coasts to high mountains, on which it makes a well-formed scrape in piled debris. Rarely does the Peregrine Falcon use abandoned cavities or tree nests; now, in places, it nests also on ledges on tall buildings and bridges.

FOOD: Mostly birds, particularly doves or pigeons, but also waterfowl, shorebirds, and passerines. While hunting, the Peregrine Falcon often chases and catches prey in midair, dropping on flying birds from above at speeds exceeding 100 miles per hour, killing them in flight with a blow from the feet. It also often attacks passing birds from a perch or after circling, and will flush ground birds into flight. Flight speeds of more than 200 miles per hour have been recorded during stoops on prey.

RANGE: Almost worldwide. **WINTERS** (North American populations): South through Central America and the Caribbean to southernmost South America.

IN PERIL: In the lower 48 states. In the 1930's and 1940's there were at least 210 active nests and 350 pairs in the eastern U.S., but by the mid- 1960's all breeders had left or died; an estimate of 250 to 350 active nests in the western U.S. in 1973 dropped to 200 by 1983. Today in the U.S., some 100 breeding pairs are found in the East, nearly 20 in the Midwest, and 400 in the West. Eggshell thinning due to chemical contamination is once again appearing in some parts of the eastern U.S.

NOTES: As with other falcons, pairs may hunt cooperatively, although more often each bird is a solitary hunter. Females are larger, and tend to take larger prey. Nest sites on cliffs are often used for many years. The worldwide range of this magnificently adapted predator is the most extensive of any bird's.

JEOPARDIZED: By eggshell thinning caused by pesticide and PCB poisoning, with severe population losses since the 1940's. The banning of DDT has been instrumental in the recovery of this species.

LISTING: The Peregrine Falcon is listed worldwide as **Endangered** (by CITES; see p. 12). In 1970, the most widespread subspecies, the American Peregrine Falcon, was federally listed as **Endangered,** and the Arctic Peregrine Falcon (see p. 49) was listed as **Threatened.** Peale's Peregrine Falcon was listed as **Vulnerable** in Canada in 1978. When discussing future downlisting or de-listing of the Peregrine Falcon as a species, some suggest keeping it listed regionally along the Pacific coast and on the northern prairie, and considering it recovered in the southwest and Threatened in other parts of the interior. De-listing of the Arctic subspecies is currently under consideration.

RECOVERY PLANS: In the East, plans center on reestablishing the extirpated populations; in the West, on protecting existing aeries; in the northern Rockies, on augmenting existing populations with introduced individuals; in the central Rockies, on monitoring; and in the Southwest, on providing protection. The captive breeding and release program is well established; since the 1970's, some 3,000 captive-bred Peregrine Falcons have been released, through an effort spearheaded by the Peregrine Fund in conjunction with state and federal agencies.

THICK-BILLED PARROT
Rhynchopsitta pachyrhyncha

NESTING: Requires naturally occurring or woodpecker-excavated tree cavities in highland pine–oak forests. In Arizona, Thick-billed Parrots were reintroduced at elevations between 6,500 and 10,000 feet, where oak–conifer forests dominate the lower elevations and mature pine, fir, spruce, and aspen dominate the upper ones.
FOOD: Mostly conifer seeds, with pine seeds making up 80 to 90 percent of the diet; also juniper "berries" and acorns.
RANGE: Bred originally at least in the Sierra Madre Occidental in Chihuahua and Durango, Mexico; dispersed to southern Arizona and to the states of Michoacán and Veracruz. The species was last seen in the U.S. in 1935, until reintroduced in Arizona in 1986. **WINTERS:** The introduced flock (13 birds) migrates (six birds were fitted with radio transmitters) 250 miles between the Mogollon Rim in central Arizona and the Chiricahua Mountains in southeastern Arizona. Mexican populations wander widely. **IN PERIL:** Throughout its range; fewer than 30 individuals make up flocks of fewer than ten individuals each. At last count (in the 1970's) only some 55 nests remained in Mexico.
NOTES: Very little is known about the Thick-billed Parrot's breeding biology. "Operation Psittacine," an investigation conducted from 1986 to 1988 by the U.S. Fish and Wildlife Service, indicated that up to 26,000 parrots (including some Thick-billeds) are annually smuggled from Mexico and Central and South America across the U.S. border near Brownsville, Texas, alone.

JEOPARDIZED: Possibly by overhunting, certainly by deforestation by the lumber and mining industries. The Mexican population is threatened by the pet trade and continued habitat destruction.
LISTING: Listed as **Endangered** in June 1979, *but only in Mexico.* (The Endangered Species Act limited listing to native species until 1969; after that, the listing of foreign species was permitted, and the Thick-billed was added. Today, although Mexican birds are listed as Endangered, U.S. birds are still not protected under the Act.) The critically imperiled Short-tailed Albatross (*Diomedea albatrus*) is another species that is not protected here; the taking of a Short-tail by a fisherman off the U.S. coast is not a violation of the Act. (Because this bird does not breed here, it is not listed and we have not treated it.)
RECOVERY PLANS: The current Arizona population originated from 29 captives confiscated from smugglers. New releases have been added to make up for those lost to raptors. As of 1988, at least one pair had successfully bred in the wild. One result of this experiment is the discovery that only parent-reared birds will join flocks and survive. Because confiscated birds tend to be weak, a steady supply of new captive-bred, parent-reared birds from private breeders and zoos is needed for further releases.

RED-COCKADED WOODPECKER

Picoides borealis

NESTING: Requires dead, resin-free heartwood of mature trees in open pine woodlands, especially pines infected with heart fungus, which eases excavation of a cavity. Still, excavation may require more than a year. The woodpeckers depart when their forest is logged or the understory gets tall enough that predators can climb through it to reach the nest.

FOOD: Mostly insects, particularly wood-boring beetles and grubs; also some fruit, berries, and seeds. While foraging, the Red-cockaded Woodpecker drills and gleans trunks and branches, especially of large, living pines; males forage mostly at mid-trunk and higher, females lower.

RANGE: Bred originally from eastern Oklahoma, southeastern Missouri, eastern Kentucky, and probably Maryland south to the Gulf of Mexico and Florida; now limited to about 30 isolated populations within this range. **WINTER:** Resident.

IN PERIL: Throughout its range. Prior to Hurricane Hugo, the entire Red-cockaded population comprised 2,000 active groups. About 560 groups, constituting three main population centers and containing about one-fourth of the entire wild population, were in South Carolina's Francis Marion National Forest. Hugo destroyed 100,000 acres of that forest, including the cavity trees of half the resident clans (only 1 percent of the clans were left completely unscathed). As a result, the largest population center is now found in Apalachicola National Forest in northern Florida, and that

population, representing more than one-third of the remaining Red-cockadeds, shows disturbing signs of imminent collapse. The species' total population is now estimated at about 7,400 individuals.

NOTES: Strongly territorial family groups (male, female, young, and occasional male helpers) defend territories of 100 to 200 acres, occasionally up to 1,000 acres, which may contain dozens of cavities (often 50 or more), each cooperatively excavated and maintained for generations. Scaling loose bark and drilling holes to maintain a resin barrier around the nest hole deters predators, especially rat snakes.

JEOPARDIZED: By agriculture, by forestry policies that prevent fire (which keeps down underbrush and hardwoods) or encourage the harvest of immature trees, by nest-site competition from Red-headed Woodpeckers and flying squirrels, and by predators (snakes and small mammals; the flying squirrels may also prey on the Red-cockaded Woodpecker's eggs and young). The longleaf pine forest ecosystem, crucial for Red-cockadeds, has been reduced to some 10 percent of its original acreage. Now, with the population concentrated in so few sites, storms like Hugo are even more threatening than before.

LISTING: Listed as **Endangered** in October 1970.

RECOVERY PLANS: Saving this species depends on increasing scarce nesting habitat, setting incentives to encourage the perpetuation of old-growth pine (tagging trees

IVORY-BILLED WOODPECKER

Campephilus principalis

against cutting is only a start), and maintaining corridors between sites. This means 75- to 90-year cutting rotations in some areas, a plan the forest industry does not support. More than 85 percent of the colonies are on federal land, and more than one federal recovery plan has been implemented, but critics complain of too many concessions to the timber industry, minimal rather than optimal protection, poor implementation of weak guidelines, too little money, too little expertise, and too many mistakes being made. A moratorium on clear-cutting within three-fourths of a mile of most active colonies, longer rotations between timber harvests, the control of hardwoods that compete with the pines, and efforts to keep cavities free of competitors and predators are central to the Red-cockaded Woodpecker's survival.

NESTING: Usually in mature deciduous forest swamps or riverine bottomlands, sometimes cypress swamps or mountain pines. The Ivory-billed Woodpecker excavates its nest cavity in large deciduous trees, sometimes dead oaks or pines. Excavation may take 8 to 14 days.

FOOD: Primarily wood-boring insects, especially beetle larvae; also seeds, nuts, and berries. While foraging, this woodpecker usually drills and gleans tree trunks and branches or picks items from the ground. It frequently forages by prying off loose bark.

RANGE: Bred formerly from southeastern Oklahoma, southeastern Missouri, southern Indiana, and North Carolina south to the Gulf of Mexico and Florida; also in Cuba. Now known to persist only in the mountains of eastern Cuba, in very limited numbers. **WINTER:** Resident. **IN PERIL:** Wherever the species may survive. It apparently was never common.

NOTES: North America's largest woodpecker, the Ivory-billed remains within several miles of its natal cavity. The U.S. and Cuban populations are separate subspecies, and unless documented proof of its existence is produced by 1992, the U.S. subspecies will be declared extinct.

JEOPARDIZED: By large-scale logging of bottomland and virgin cypress forests (each pair of Ivory-billed Woodpeckers requires up to 2,000 acres), by loss of foraging habitat (stands of dead, often fire-killed trees), and by hunting. In 1948, the 120-square-mile "Singer (Sewing Machine Company)

Tract" along the Tensas River in Louisiana held the last known population; it was cleared for soybean production.

LISTING: Listed as **Endangered** in March 1967.

RECOVERY PLANS: The last confirmed U.S. sighting, in Louisiana's Tensas River National Wildlife Refuge, was more than 40 years ago; more recent supposed sightings are thought to be of misidentified Pileated Woodpeckers, but an ongoing survey (to be completed by 1992) holds out hope that Ivory-billed Woodpeckers may yet be found in Louisiana's Atchafalaya Basin or along South Carolina's Santee River, Georgia's Altamaha River, Mississippi's Hyazoo or Pascagoula rivers, or Florida's Suwannee, Withlacoochee, or Ochloconee rivers. There were confirmed sightings in the mountains of Cuba in 1986, and should the Cuban population prove sufficiently large, reintroduction of the Ivory-billed Woodpecker from Cuba to the U.S. may one day be attempted.

BLACK-CAPPED VIREO
Vireo atricapillus

NESTING: In oak–juniper woodland or scrub maintained by wildfires or grazing. The nest, a cup of bark strips, coarse grass, and leaves, wrapped with silk and fibrous materials, is suspended amid the dense foliage of a scrub oak or other small tree.

FOOD: Mostly insects and spiders; also seeds and fruit. While foraging, the Black-capped Vireo usually gleans foliage and branches, moving restlessly in dense cover.

RANGE: Bred formerly from Kansas, now from Oklahoma, south through central Texas to Coahuila, Mexico. **WINTERS:** On the Pacific slope of Mexico from Sonora to Oaxaca, but mostly in Sinaloa and Nayarit. **IN PERIL:** Throughout its range; by 1954 it had already been extirpated from Kansas. Recent reports indicate that the U.S. population ranges between 250 and 500 birds, most of which are found near Austin, Texas; fewer than 110 are in Oklahoma. The Mexican population is little known; population estimates are steeped in controversy and range from fewer than 50 birds to more than 3,000.

NOTES: Males tend to return to their former breeding territory, often selecting clumped vegetation on steep ravine slopes in rugged terrain.

JEOPARDIZED: By habitat (particularly nesting) losses to development, by the grazing of sheep and goats, and by range management that involves removal of low, broad-leaved, woody vegetation. Cowbird parasitism of the Black-capped Vireo is heavy; by the time the vireo eggs hatch, the

cowbird chicks outweigh the vireo chicks tenfold, and nestling vireo survival is zero (see pp. 219–20). Almost 90 percent of the entire U.S. population is immediately threatened by housing development and road construction, and the species is expected to be lost within the decade.
LISTING: Listed as **Endangered** in October 1987. The decline of the Black-capped Vireo had been overlooked completely and it was never nominated for entry onto the Blue List.
RECOVERY PLANS: Cowbird control is being undertaken in Texas and Oklahoma, where cowbird parasitism of the species is approaching 100 percent. Changes in land management are also essential for successful conservation of this species, but the prospects for either are bleak.

BACHMAN'S WARBLER
Vermivora bachmanii

NESTING: In a vine tangle, brambles, cane thicket, or other undergrowth in palmetto or cypress swamps, where it builds a cup of dried leaves and stalks of grasses and weeds.
FOOD: Presumably, mostly insects and spiders. While foraging, Bachman's Warbler usually hunts by slow and deliberate gleaning of foliage.
RANGE: Bred formerly in the southeastern U.S. at least from southeastern Missouri, Kentucky, and South Carolina south to Louisiana and southern Alabama. **WINTERS:** In mainland Cuba and the Isle of Pines. **IN PERIL:** Throughout its range, wherever the species may survive. Now possibly extinct; the last confirmed sighting of a territorial bird was in 1962.
NOTES: The rarest native U.S. songbird, Bachman's Warbler is thought to have been limited to bamboo thickets ("canebrakes") during nesting. Its tendency to be irruptive (that is, to wander widely and unpredictably) may have been a response to the bamboo's irregular reproductive cycle of slow growth followed by synchronous flowering and death. Interestingly, Hurricane Hugo increased suitable Bachman's Warbler habitat in the southeastern U.S.
JEOPARDIZED: By the loss of the extensive canebrakes of the southeastern U.S. (which have been converted for agricultural development and modified by flood-control programs), loss of the Caribbean wintering habitat, and, in earlier times, plume harvesting. Bachman's Warbler's reputed sta-

GOLDEN-CHEEKED WARBLER

Dendroica chrysoparia

tus at the turn of the century as the seventh most common migrant along the lower Suwannee River suggests that its historic range might have extended throughout the swampy forests of the Southeast, but the species has been generally considered very rare.

LISTING: Listed as **Endangered** in March 1967.

RECOVERY PLANS: The species is so rare and poorly known that no plans have been formulated or put into action.

NESTING: Requires stands of mature Ashe juniper ("cedar" brakes) in forks of which the bird places its compact nest of peeled Ashe juniper bark strips, bound in spider web and grass. (Young trees do not provide the bark strips, nor do any other Texas junipers.)

FOOD: Insects and other arthropods.

RANGE: Breeds on the Edwards Plateau, central Texas, and in scattered areas north to near Dallas. **WINTERS:** In highland pine—oak forests of Mexico (Chiapas), Guatemala, Honduras, and Nicaragua.

IN PERIL: Throughout its limited range. The population in 1974 was estimated at 15,000 individuals, but as of 1990, only an estimated 2,200 to 4,600 birds remained.

NOTES: The Golden-cheeked Warbler was first discovered in Guatemala in 1859 and later (1864) was found in Texas. It is an extreme habitat specialist, and both male and female usually return to the same territory to breed. Nest-building is carried out solely by the female. Most migrating birds pass through a narrow Mexican cloud-forest along the eastern slope of the Sierra Madre Oriental.

JEOPARDIZED: Primarily by habitat loss to the cities of Austin, San Antonio, and Waco; also by industrial development, habitat conversion for grazing sheep and goats, logging of juniper (mostly for fence posts), and by very heavy cowbird parasitism (see p. 219).

LISTING: Listed as **Endangered** in May 1990.

KIRTLAND'S WARBLER

Dendroica kirtlandii

RECOVERY PLANS: The species' survival requires protection of private, state, and federal land. Conservationists have identified 80,000 acres of critical habitat that can be purchased for about $10 million. Apparently, the federal government holds title to a portion of formerly private habitat (thousands of acres) obtained from failed savings and loan associations. In addition to habitat protection, much research on the biology of the species is needed.

NESTING: Requires extensive thickets of young jack pine covering at least 80 acres of porous Grayling sand. Such soil drains quickly, keeping rainwater from flooding the warbler's nest, which is made of grass or other plant fibers and is usually hidden near the base of a tree.

FOOD: Mostly insects; also tree sap (particularly pine) and berries (especially blueberries). While foraging, Kirtland's Warbler usually gleans foliage and branches, picks items from the substrate, or captures flying insects while sallying from a perch on a short flight, or while hovering.

RANGE: Breeds only in central Michigan, near the Au Sable River. **WINTERS:** Almost exclusively in the Bahamas, with a few reaching the Dominican Republic. **IN PERIL:** Throughout its very limited range. The number of territorial males (which sing, and are thus more easily counted than are females) has increased steadily in recent years, from 167 in 1987 to 347 in 1991. Current numbers have brought the population to a level not seen since 1961.

NOTES: The eggs of Kirtland's Warbler take an unusually long time to incubate— longer than those of any other North American warbler, making this species unusually susceptible to nest predators and cowbird parasitism (see p. 219).

JEOPARDIZED: Largely because of the bird's extremely specific habitat requirements for breeding. Forest management policies that reduce the size and frequency of fires and replace jack pines with red pines or hardwoods have worked against the species. Today only about 4,500 acres suitable for breeding remain, only about one-third of what had been available in the 1950's and 1960's. Within the past 100 years, cowbirds have expanded their range into Kirtland's Warbler's breeding habitat and frequently parasitize the warblers' nests. As a result, egg losses of at least 40 percent were common in the 1970's (see p. 220). Despite intensive trapping, the number of cowbirds trapped continues to rise; in 1989, 8,000 cowbirds were trapped, twice the total of the preceding year. Global warming may rapidly destroy the remaining habitat and force Kirtland's Warbler to extinction.

LISTING: Listed as **Endangered** in the U.S. in March 1967, and as **Endangered** in Canada in 1979.

RECOVERY PLANS: Include the planting of trees to provide suitable habitat (1.3 million were planted in 1991), the use of fire to maintain and encourage favorable habitat, and prevention of hunting, logging, and other activities in Kirtland's Warbler's breeding habitat until September 15, when the birds have departed for the winter. Cowbird removal is a major part of the effort to save Kirtland's Warbler: by 1980, 40,000 cowbirds had been trapped. Before trapping began, 75 percent of the warbler's nests were parasitized; now only 6 percent are.

Just as a full species may be designated by the U.S. Fish and Wildlife Service as Endangered, so may a subspecies. The Endangered Species Act can grant protection for a subspecies (or even a population) even in cases where the species as a whole does not qualify. (A subspecies is a group of actually or potentially interbreeding populations within a species that is considered different enough morphologically (from other subspecies of that species) to be given a scientific name.) Subspecies with only a single, sparse population, such as the San Clemente Loggerhead Shrike (see p. 55) or the San Clemente Sage Sparrow (see p. 61), exemplify legally protected subspecies, but ones that are so highly vulnerable to human-induced disturbance that listing is unlikely to save them in the long run.

The division of species into subspecies is based traditionally on visible characteristics such as wing length or plumage color. Today, genetic techniques permit another perspective on relationships among populations, and some of the laboratory findings have caught taxonomists by surprise. For example, the Dusky Seaside Sparrow (*Ammodramus maritimus nigrescens;* see p. 199)—a bird afforded legal protection under the Endangered Species Act, to no avail—turned out to be, on a genetic basis, less clearly a subspecies than had been thought.

The Dusky Seaside Sparrow had an extremely limited range within the salt marshes of central coastal Florida. By the late 1980's, not even a 5-million-dollar purchase of remaining habitat by the USFWS was able to save it. Its Merritt Island *Spartina* marsh habitat, for example, had been destroyed when developers of the space-program facilities flooded it for mosquito control. By the time the Dusky habitat was finally acquired, it had been so severely modified that restoration adequate for the sparrows would have taken ten to twenty years. Similarly, a Dusky population at St. John's was discovered when privately held habitat was drained and biologists walked into the site; but within two to three years that population, too, was extirpated. In addition, by the time salvaging programs got under way, the number of available Dusky Seaside Sparrows was already very small, making the enterprise extremely vulnerable to a single accident. The captive breeding program, which involved the mating of the five remaining male Duskys with females of the closely related Scott's Seaside Sparrow (*Ammodramus maritimus peninsulae*), did, however, show the potential for preserving genetic diversity by "re-establishing" the subspecies through backcrossing. The hybrids produced were fertile, and three-quarters or more "pure" Dusky. Unfortunately, however, because the hybrids were not *legally* Dusky Seaside Sparrows, the Service slashed funds for protecting the habitat needed for reintroducing the hybrid birds back into the wild.

It was some time later that DNA analyses suggested that the Dusky was genetically almost identical to three other Atlantic Coast "subspecies" of Seaside Sparrow. The difference was no more than a single melanistic gene. The discovery that the Dusky was closely related to Atlantic subspecies but not to the Gulf subspecies (Scott's) meant that the last Duskys had been bred to the "wrong" subspecies—not to the one that would have kept the offspring most closely similar to the Dusky's original strain. Debate continues over the eligibility of hybrids (between species, subspecies, or populations) for protection under the Endangered Species Act.

The failure to save the Dusky Seaside Sparrow also added fuel to the debate over how much money should be spent on captive breeding programs for Endangered subspecies. Funds available for conservation are limited, and dollars to be spent on captive breeding cannot be spent on habitat preservation. With habitat destruction and degradation the major threat to Earth's avifauna, the question of allocating funds for other aspects of species conservation—including captive breeding programs—will be raised repeatedly as we try to protect increasing numbers of individual species, subspecies, and populations on fewer, smaller plots of land to which they are not optimally adapted.

Clearly, the key to saving species is saving subspecies, and the key to saving subspecies is saving populations. Diverse populations help to ensure against an entire subspecies—or species—being wiped out

by a single calamity that destroys a few of its populations. Saving populations also conserves genetic diversity, which can be critical to the ability of a subspecies or species to evolve in response to environmental changes such as global warming.

The U.S. Fish and Wildlife Service currently lists 22 continental subspecies as either Endangered or Threatened, three of which are also listed in Canada.

REFERENCES: Avise and Nelson, 1989; Diamond, 1985; Ehrlich, Dobkin, and Wheye, 1988; Soulé, 1986; Soulé and Wilcox, 1980.

ALEUTIAN CANADA GOOSE

Branta canadensis leucopareia

NESTING: Usually in inland meadows or marshes, sometimes near inlets and in bushy habitat near the sea. The goose makes its nest by scraping a depression, then incorporating dry grass, other herbaceous plants, moss, sticks, and aquatic vegetation.

FOOD: The diet of the Aleutian Canada Goose is similar to that of other Canada Geese and includes a wide variety of marsh vegetation, algae, seeds of grass and sedges, grain (especially in winter), and berries, as well as insects and other terrestrial invertebrates, crustaceans, and mollusks. The bird forages on the water, taking items from the surface or below, and gleans items from the ground when feeding on land.

RANGE: Breeds on Alaska's Aleutian Islands; formerly also on Bering Island and in the Kurile Islands, Soviet Union. **WINTERS:** Now mostly in California and Oregon; historically in Japan and from British Columbia to California. **IN PERIL:** In the Aleutian Islands. Its population in 1975 was estimated at 790 individuals, but by 1991 the population had grown to more than 6,000.

JEOPARDIZED: Mainly by predation from Arctic Foxes introduced onto the Aleutian Islands in the 1830's, but also through hunting and loss of wintering habitat. Commercial fox farmers released animals from 1836 to 1930. By the late 1930's, surveys showed that where foxes had been introduced, the geese had been extirpated. Today, less than 15 percent of historic breeding habitat has been cleared of foxes; and on one such island, Amukta, a nesting pair was discovered in 1989 (foxes had not been introduced to Buldir, which had been considered by the fox farmers to be too small). Wintering geese are subject to outbreaks of disease, owing to changes in agricultural practices and to urban development that concentrates their numbers in fewer remaining areas.

LISTING: Listed as **Endangered** in March 1967. In 1989 it was proposed for downlisting to **Threatened** (fox removal, geese reintroductions, hunting restrictions during migration and wintering, and monitoring would also continue after downlisting).

RECOVERY PLANS: Arctic Foxes were eliminated from the Aleutian Islands National Wildlife Refuge in 1965, and the removal of foxes from many of the islands has continued, with the goal of eventual complete elimination from the primary nesting islands. Geese have been reintroduced successfully on fox-free islands, and a captive breeding program was begun in 1963. Programs identifying and protecting key migration and wintering sites, providing hunter-education programs, and changing hunting regulations were implemented in Oregon and California. As a result of these efforts, the wild population has increased since 1975 by an average of 16 percent per year.

CALIFORNIA CLAPPER RAIL

Rallus longirostris obsoletus

NESTING: Requires cordgrass, pickleweed, gum-plant, and salt-grass in tidal marshes. The nest is made of pickleweed and other aquatic vegetation and materials left behind by the tide, arranged into a dome over a platform of similar material that both protects the nest from aerial predators and retains eggs during tidal flooding.

FOOD: Mostly mussels, clams, small crabs, and spiders. While foraging, the California Clapper Rail either probes beneath the surface of mud or sand, in or near shallow water, or picks items from the substrate.

RANGE: Tidal marshes of San Francisco Bay, California. **WINTER:** Resident. **IN PERIL:** Throughout the Bay Area. Initial population estimates in the mid-1970's indicated 4,000 to 6,000 birds, but intensive winter surveys found only 1,000 birds a decade later. The most recent surveys put the population at fewer than 500 individuals.

NOTES: The California Clapper Rail was classified as a distinct species in 1880, then reclassified as a Clapper Rail population in 1926, and finally recognized in 1977 as one of numerous Clapper Rail subspecies.

JEOPARDIZED: Early on by hunting, now by habitat loss, non-native predators, and environmental pollution. Hunting was controlled with the signing of the Migratory Bird Treaty of 1918. Wetlands have been drained for agriculture, urban development, airports, and commercial salt evaporation sites. The approximately 300 square miles of tidal marsh originally present in the California Clapper Rail's range have been reduced to only 50 today, much of which is leveed or in other ways degraded. The birds are restricted mainly to remnant salt marshes in the counties of San Mateo, Alameda, and Santa Clara, but other small populations and scattered individuals dot the San Francisco Bay Area. Norway rats, feral cats, raccoons, and, especially, red foxes take the young and eggs; foxes also take adult birds. Elevated levels of mercury and selenium are appearing in rail eggs.

LISTING: Listed as **Endangered** in October 1970, as were the Light-footed and Yuma Clapper Rails (see pp. 39–41). As of 1990, the U.S. Fish and Wildlife Service considers the Mangrove Clapper Rail (*R. l. insularum*), found in Florida, a Category 2 candidate for adding to the federal list. After years of reported declines, the Clapper Rail (as a species) was listed as of only **Special Concern** by the National Audubon Society in 1986.

RECOVERY PLANS: Include primarily the acquisition of critical habitat, but also restoration programs instituted at the local, state, and federal levels. Acquisition continues generally through conservation organizations, and restoration has been carried out by local parks departments and the California Department of Fish and Game. The U.S. Fish and Wildlife Service has also established a national wildlife refuge on a section of San Francisco Bay that includes appropriate rail habitat. Recovery efforts are not likely to succeed without an effective program to control red foxes and other introduced predators.

YUMA CLAPPER RAIL
Rallus longirostris yumanensis

NESTING: Although little-studied, probably on dry hummocks or low shrubs within dense, mature cattails and bulrushes along the edges of shallow ponds in freshwater marshes with stable water levels. The nest is constructed of either sticks and dead leaves or finer stems of dried materials and is placed above the water level.

FOOD: Mostly small fish, crayfish, clams, and insects. The Yuma Clapper Rail probably hunts like the California Clapper, mostly by probing beneath the surface of mud or sand, either in or near shallow water, and picking items from the substrate.

RANGE: The valleys of southeastern California: Imperial, Salton Sea, lower Colorado River, Gila River, and lower Salt River; also southern Arizona and extreme northwestern Mexico, including the Colorado River delta. **WINTER:** Most birds are resident, as demonstrated by radiotelemetry. **IN PERIL:** Throughout its range. In 1969 and 1970 the population was estimated at about 700 breeding birds; more recent surveys have put it at 1,700 to 2,000 within the area bounded by Mexico's Colorado River delta, California's Salton Sea, Topock Marsh on the Arizona side of the Colorado River, and near Tacna, Arizona, along the Gila River.

NOTES: Over the last century, Yuma Clapper habitat has expanded and contracted: California's Salton Sea (and its Clapper habitat) was created in 1905 when the Colorado River overflowed its banks and moved through newly built irrigation works; more recently, flow control of the Colorado slowed its currents, permitting the emergence of new marshes upstream of dams and the inundation of other suitable habitat. Mexican populations are often found in brackish marshes.

JEOPARDIZED: By the loss of wetlands.

LISTING: Listed as **Endangered** in March 1967.

RECOVERY PLANS: Yuma Rail populations are tied tightly to development projects along the Colorado River and the maintenance of shallow-water areas that support the early stages of cattail marshes.

LIGHT-FOOTED CLAPPER RAIL

Rallus longirostris levipes

NESTING: Requires saltwater or brackish marshes with vegetation sufficient for foraging, cover, and nest-building. Nests are placed in patches of pickleweed or in stands of cordgrass at ground level or built up to just above ground level.

FOOD: Mostly crabs; also other crustaceans, small fish, tadpoles, snails, insects, and some plants. The Light-footed probably hunts like other Clapper Rails, that is, by probing beneath the surface of mud or sand in or near shallow water and picking items from the substrate.

RANGE: Some 21 Pacific Coast tidal marshes from Santa Barbara, California, to San Quintín, Baja California. **WINTER:** Resident. **IN PERIL:** Throughout its range. Some 90 percent of the U.S. population is concentrated in just five marshes: Carpinteria Marsh in Santa Barbara County, Upper Newport Bay (which contains the greatest number of individuals) and Anaheim Bay in Orange County, and Kendall-Frost Reserve (Mission Bay) and Tijuana Marsh in San Diego County. The California population was estimated at 500 to 750 pairs in the early 1970's, but this unrealistic estimate was corrected to 300 in 1974; populations crashed in 1984 and 1985, and by 1986 fell to 143. The U.S. population was estimated at about 190 pairs in 1990, with 70 percent concentrated at Upper Newport Bay. In 1981 the Mexican population was estimated at roughly 1,600 individuals, but a thorough analysis is yet to be done, and current estimates place the number at about the size of the U.S. population.

NOTES: The Light-footed Clapper Rail will use artificial nesting sites. Despite its habit of clappering at dawn and dusk in the early spring, its furtive behavior makes accurate censusing difficult.

JEOPARDIZED: By wetland loss and degradation. Less than 25 percent of the southern California wetlands that existed in 1900 remain today. Severe losses have occurred around San Diego and in the Los Angeles–Long Beach area. The remaining inhabited marshes are susceptible to violent storms, storm-driven tides, and excessive runoff that is greatly exacerbated by the paving over of watershed and by siltation caused by the exposure of vast areas of bare dirt with grading for housing tracts. In the meantime, predators pose a serious threat to ground-nesting clappers in general, particularly where the marshes are isolated and disrupted by introduced predators. The two principal colonies in Baja California, at El Estero de Punta Banda and Bahía de San Quintín, are also threatened by proposed developments.

LISTING: Listed as **Endangered** in October 1970.

RECOVERY PLANS: Wetlands protected since 1979 include Anaheim Bay and Upper Newport Bay, Goleta Slough, and San Diego County's South Bay Marine Reserve, Tijuana Marsh, and Kendall-Frost Ecological Reserve. Marsh restoration has begun in Orange and San Diego counties. Artificial floating platforms for nesting proved successful and are being implemented at several California locations. Concern is high because the birds are concentrated in so few sites. The revised recovery plan aims for 1,600 individuals in 20 secure marshes, protecting and improving all existing habitat, creating new habitat, stocking habitat where needed, securing the Mexican Light-footed population, and continual study and monitoring to refine management techniques. A captive breeding program is planned for 1991.

MISSISSIPPI SANDHILL CRANE

Grus canadensis pulla

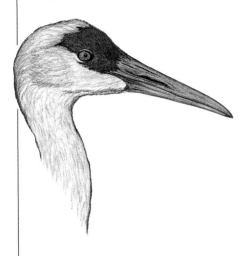

NESTING: In open wetlands in savannas or young pine plantations; also along swamp margins or the edges of sodden pine forests. The Mississippi Sandhill Crane places (occasionally conceals) its bulky saucer of dead sticks, moss, reeds, and grass amid longleaf or slash pine, bald cypress, gallberry, wax myrtle, black gum, sweet bay, or yaupon. Nesting territories, of 90 to 500 acres, are defended, and tend to be used year after year.

FOOD: Aquatic invertebrates, reptiles, amphibians, insects, and aquatic plants. While foraging, this crane often probes with its bill, digging when necessary to extract buried items, but mostly it feeds on food visible on the surface. In winter it may feed on grain remaining in the fields after harvest.

RANGE: Southern Jackson County, Mississippi. **WINTERS:** Mainly in Mississippi's Bluff Creek, Bayou Castelle, and Paige Bayou marshes. **IN PERIL:** Throughout its restricted range. Since 1984, with the help of captive-bred cranes, the population has risen from some 22–38 to about 60.

NOTES: This subspecies is darker than other Sandhill Cranes. It is a gregarious bird, flying and roosting in groups.

JEOPARDIZED: Mainly by habitat loss from timber harvesting and drainage, which accelerated in the 1950's with the establishment of pine plantations and their requisite drainage ditches, fire breaks, and access roads. The decline continued with the construction of three highways crossing the habitat and the ensuing commercial and residential development that the highways prompted. Periodic floodwaters from hurricanes also reduce nesting success.

LISTING: Listed as **Endangered** in June 1973.

RECOVERY PLANS: Habitat recovery requires additional open areas, plugging of ditches, digging of small ponds, encouraging the growth of plants on which the cranes forage, and the control of predators. With the help of the Nature Conservancy, 18,000 acres have been set aside as the Mississippi Sandhill Crane National Wildlife Refuge. Administered by the U.S. Fish and Wildlife Service, the Refuge has been improved since the 1970's, when part of it was closed to deer hunting. Three eggs (on average) are removed each year and raised in the U.S. Fish and Wildlife Service's laboratory in Patuxent, Maryland. The captive population of three in 1966 rose to 40 by 1986. Since 1970, 178 fertile eggs have been produced—all but three using artificial insemination. Of releases since 1981, almost half survived. Fertile captive eggs have been successfully substituted in infertile wild nests. Ten captives are released yearly, with the aim of achieving a wild population of 100, of which 60 would be breeding pairs.

CALIFORNIA LEAST TERN

Sterna antillarum browni

NESTING: Usually on open, flat beaches along lagoon or estuary margins, but sometimes on mud or sand flats a distance from the ocean or on artificial islands created from dredge spoils. The California Least Tern lays its eggs in a shallow depression in sand or dried mud, lined at most with a few fragments of shells.

FOOD: Fish, especially anchovy, topsmelt, surf-perch, killifish, and mosquitofish. The bird usually hunts by hovering (longer than do other terns) and then dropping from height into the water.

RANGE: Breeds in colonies scattered along the Pacific coast from Alameda, California, south through Baja California, including its east coast. **WINTERS:** Possibly along the Pacific coast of Central America, at least from Colima, Mexico, south, but its precise winter range is largely unknown.

IN PERIL: Throughout its range. The California Least Tern was once abundant along the southern California coast: an estimated 600 pairs were sighted on one beach in the San Diego area in 1909. From 1973 to 1975, population estimates for the U.S. averaged 600 pairs; in 1988, about 1,250 pairs. The known Baja California population is estimated at about 800 individuals.

NOTES: In 1988, red foxes killed 75 percent of the nesting terns in Orange County, California.

JEOPARDIZED: By human encroachment, especially after construction of the (California) Coast Highway in the early 1900's provided access to previously inaccessible beaches. Nesting areas, especially sandy ocean beaches, have been disturbed, and feeding sites have been modified or polluted. These impacts have left the terns confined to very few of their former nesting sites, and the option of shifting from site to site—an essential element of the species' anti-predator strategy—is no longer available to it.

LISTING: Listed as **Endangered** in October 1970.

RECOVERY PLANS: Include restoring degraded wetlands by improving tidal circulation to increase fish populations, providing sufficient resting sites, expanding nesting areas with artificial islands, providing adequate protection from predators (especially red foxes, but also ravens, shrikes, even Northern Harriers and meadowlarks), and erecting protective fences and posting public information notices around the colonies.

ROSEATE TERN

Sterna dougallii dougallii

NESTING: On offshore islands with sandy, pebbly, or rocky beaches or open, bare, or grassy areas. The nest is a scrape concealed within beach grass, vines, or herbaceous plants, or the eggs are simply laid amid rocks or on the sand.

FOOD: Mostly fish, especially sand eels, and some aquatic invertebrates, including mollusks. While hunting, it usually hovers, then drops from height into the water; sometimes it pirates the catch of other birds, and often gathers where large fish force small fish to the surface.

RANGE: Breeds at scattered sites along the Atlantic coast from Quebec and New Brunswick south to the Caribbean, with population centers in Connecticut, Maine, Massachusetts, New York, Nova Scotia, the Magdalen Islands of Quebec, Florida, Puerto Rico, the U.S. Virgin Islands, and the Bahamas; also locally in western Europe and northern Africa. **WINTERS** (North American populations): From the West Indies south to eastern Brazil. **IN PERIL:** Along the northern Atlantic coast (especially from Maine to New Jersey), in Florida, and on some Caribbean islands, including Puerto Rico. The combined U.S. and Canadian population is estimated at 6,650 birds, the Caribbean population at 6,000 birds.

NOTES: The Roseate Tern nests colonially, does not breed until it is three or four years old, and is often found with other terns, especially Common Terns. Fledging rates in the Northeast have not dropped, though population declines continue, indicating that mortality on the wintering grounds may have increased. Sixty percent of nesting birds in the Northeast occur on one Massachusetts island where gulls have been removed.

JEOPARDIZED: By plume hunters (formerly), loss of nesting habitat to development, and predation by gulls (especially Herring and Greater Black-backed), Great Horned Owls, Black-crowned Night Herons, and others, and by depleted sand eel populations. After the plume trade decimated U.S. populations, the Migratory Bird Treaty Act of 1918 enabled the numbers to rise. They dropped again at mid-century, to 4,800 pairs by 1952 and 2,500 by 1977.

LISTING: Blue-Listed in 1972 and from 1979 to 1986. (The species was mentioned as down in numbers in 1982 but inadvertently not listed.) The U.S. Fish and Wildlife Service qualified the Roseate Tern for Category 1 status (see p. 99) and listed it as **Endangered** in the northern part of its range in November 1987. In Florida, Puerto Rico, and the U.S. Virgin Islands, it is listed as **Threatened.** The species was listed as **Threatened** in Canada in 1986.

RECOVERY PLANS: Have been carried out mostly by private conservation groups. Until lighthouses were automated, human presence kept competing gulls away from some critical breeding habitat; now gull-removal programs are needed. Caribbean island habitats tend to be gull-free, but humans and other nest-robbing mammals must be dissuaded.

AUDUBON'S CRESTED CARACARA

Polyborus plancus audubonii

NESTING: The Crested Caracara in general nests in desert scrub, dry prairies with patches of wetlands, pastures, or even sparsely wooded areas if interspersed with expanses of open grassland. Its nest is a massive, loose, and deeply scooped platform built of sticks, vines, and twigs. The low, flat, grassy Kissimmee Prairie (north of Florida's Lake Okeechobee, and the U.S. population center of this subspecies) has scattered ponds and sloughs; nests there are usually built in cabbage palms.

FOOD: Mostly carrion; also small mammals, birds, lizards, snakes, small turtles (and their eggs), and frogs, as well as insects and other invertebrates. While foraging, the Crested Caracara walks along picking prey from the ground, and seeks prey while flying low, or while soaring. Its long legs and flat claws allow the caracara to chase down quick prey or to rake the ground in search of more sluggish prey. It often feeds with vultures, or harasses them until they disgorge their food. Pairs may hunt together.

RANGE: Breeds from Baja California, southern Arizona, Texas, and Florida south to western Panama and Cuba. **WINTER:** Resident. **IN PERIL:** In Florida, where the population is estimated at about 500 individuals. In 1900 the population was estimated at more than 1,500; by 1987 it had been reduced to 300 adults and 200 immatures.

NOTES: Not much of the Crested Cara-

EVERGLADE SNAIL KITE
Rostrhamus sociabilis plumbeus

cara's breeding biology has been documented, even though the species is the national bird of Mexico. It is known by many common names, including Caracara Eagle, Mexican Eagle, Mexican Buzzard, and King Buzzard.

JEOPARDIZED: Primarily by conversion of its habitat to agriculture (especially citrus groves), residential development, and illegal shooting and trapping (it was mistakenly thought to kill calves). The subsequent increase in roads has led to increased mortality from increased traffic, because the Crested Caracara feeds on roadkills. Its range and population continue to decrease.

LISTING: Placed on the **Blue List** from 1972 to 1979 and in 1981; the species warranted **Special Concern** from 1982 to 1986. In 1986 the Florida population was listed as a Category 2 species by the U.S. Fish and Wildlife Service (see p. 99), and the subspecies was formally listed as **Threatened** in Florida in July 1987.

RECOVERY PLANS: Include efforts by the U.S. Fish and Wildlife Service to persuade local governments and private organizations to purchase critical habitat. Special protection is needed for a primary portion of Caracara range that lies within the U.S. Air Force's Avon Park Bombing Range in Florida.

NESTING: The Everglade Snail Kite builds a flimsy platform of sticks, leafy twigs, and green leaves in a low tree, on a hummock of marsh grass, or in a flooded bush, in subtropical freshwater marshes.

FOOD: Almost entirely freshwater apple snails of the genus *Pomacea*, which the kite usually seeks in a low, searching flight over marshes or snatches in its talons after swooping down from a perch. Alternative foods (turtles, other snails, freshwater crabs, and so forth) are, like the apple snails, animals that have shells and move slowly. The kite's long bill and long toes facilitate the removal of snails from their shells.

RANGE: Breeds in the Lake Okeechobee area and the Everglades; formerly bred more widely in Florida. **WINTER:** Resident. **IN PERIL:** Throughout its limited range. Relatively common in the 1920's, but by 1964, shooting and marsh draining, especially at Lake Okeechobee, had reduced the Florida population to only 25 to 60 individuals. The population climbed to some 700 birds by 1983, dropped in 1984 to 670, and after the drought of 1985, dropped again to about 400. The 1986 Snail Kite Survey found 560 individuals.

NOTES: This is the northernmost population of a tropical species that is widespread in Central and South America. The Everglade Snail Kite forms loose colonies of a few pairs. It reaches sexual maturity within only 10–12 months and is often not monogamous. In contrast to the Wood Stork's, the kite's nesting success increases with higher water levels, which promote greater snail abundance. In years of high rainfall, breeding may continue 10 months or more, with the male or female commonly deserting the nestlings and remating. Seasonal movements in Florida are poorly understood, but some birds banded in Florida have later been found in Cuba (150 miles away). An 18-year study found very low nesting success because of nest collapse, predation, nest desertion, and frequent multiple broods with renesting after failure. Under good conditions, however, there was superior juvenile and adult success. The study also found that in dry years low nesting success occurred in part because nests were placed in unsuitable habitat. Drought conditions force birds to disperse, and finding safe areas is increasingly difficult for them.

JEOPARDIZED: By wetland degradation and loss to agricultural and residential development, human demands for fresh water, and pesticides flowing in from orchards and accumulating in snails. Drought–flood cycles have been shortened from at least ten years to five or six. Introduced dense-growing aquatic plants such as the water hyacinth may impair the kite's hunting, and Australian punktrees colonize and dry up marshes. The effects on snail prey of Velpar, an herbicide used to control the invasive punktrees, remain unknown.

LISTING: Listed as **Endangered** in March 1967.

RECOVERY PLANS: The National Audubon Society leases about 28,000 acres containing breeding habitat on western Lake Okeechobee and has relocated nests to artificial structures. Restoration plans for the eastern Everglades provoked long debate among biologists interested in serving the best interests of all species in jeopardy, species whose needs are not necessarily congruent. Florida's new 30,000-acre Panther National Wildlife Refuge also protects kite habitat. According to the 1986 revised Recovery Plan, when a population of 650 has stabilized for 10 years, the species can be reclassified as Threatened.

AMERICAN PEREGRINE FALCON

Falco peregrinus anatum

NESTING: Usually on cliff ledges with open habitats from tundra, savanna, and seacoasts to high mountains, on which the falcon makes a well-formed scrape in piled debris. Rarely, the Peregrine Falcon will use abandoned tree nests or cavities; now, commonly, it places its nest on ledges of tall buildings and bridges.

FOOD: Birds, particularly doves and pigeons, but also waterfowl, shorebirds, and passerines. While hunting, the Peregrine Falcon usually chases and catches prey in midair, dropping on flying birds from above and killing them in flight with a blow from the feet, or flushes them from their perches. In level flight the Peregrine Falcon can reach 60 miles per hour, and in a stoop on prey it can reach speeds exceeding 200 miles per hour.

RANGE: Bred originally over most of North America from the tree line south (excluding the coasts of Alaska and British Columbia) to Baja California, Sonora, Texas, and Georgia. Now absent from large areas, including the entire eastern U.S., except where successfully reintroduced.

WINTERS: Largely within its breeding range. **IN PERIL:** In the lower 48 states. In the 1930's and 1940's there were at least 210 active nests and 350 pairs in the eastern U.S., but by the mid-1960's all breeders had left or died; an estimated 250 to 350 active nests in the western U.S. in 1973 dropped to 200 by 1983. Today there are some 100 breeding pairs in the East, about 20 in the Midwest, and 400 in the West.

NOTES: As with other falcons, pairs occasionally hunt cooperatively; females are larger, and tend to take larger prey. Nest sites on cliffs are often used for many years. For further information about North American Peregrine Falcons, see p. 48.

JEOPARDIZED: By eggshell thinning caused by pesticide and PCB poisoning, with severe population losses since the 1940's.

LISTING: Listed as **Endangered** in the U.S. in October 1970, and **Endangered** in Canada in 1978.

RECOVERY PLANS: In the East, plans center on reestablishing the extirpated populations; in the West, on protecting existing aeries; in the northern Rockies, on augmenting existing populations with introduced individuals; in the central Rockies, on monitoring; and in the Southwest, on providing protection. The captive breeding and release program is well established; some 3,000 captive-bred Peregrine Falcons have been released since the 1970's, through an effort spearheaded by the Peregrine Fund in conjunction with state and federal agencies.

ARCTIC PEREGRINE FALCON

Falco peregrinus tundrius

NESTING: Requires cliffs (presumably the Arctic Peregrine Falcon faces much the same constraints as the American Peregrine Falcon).

FOOD: A wide variety of birds. Like the other races of the Peregrine Falcon, this one usually hunts by chasing and catching prey in midair, dropping on flying birds from above and killing them in flight with a blow from the feet.

RANGE: Breeds on the North American tundra from northern Alaska east to Greenland. **WINTERS:** From the southern U.S. south to southern South America. **IN PERIL:** Throughout its range. By the mid-1970's the number of nesting pairs had decreased some 30 percent from an estimated high of 150 pairs. By 1985, 85 nesting pairs were known, and from this figure an estimated population of at least 150 to 175 breeding pairs was extrapolated.

NOTES: This subspecies is lighter in color than the American or Peale's Peregrine Falcons, the other two North American subspecies, and has white underparts. For further information about North American Peregrine Falcons, see pp. 26 and 48.

JEOPARDIZED: Mainly by pesticides and eggshell thinning.

LISTING: Listed as **Threatened** in the U.S. in October 1970, and as **Threatened** in Canada in 1978.

RECOVERY PLANS: Appear to be succeeding, and, as the estimated number of breeding pairs continues to increase and approaches its historic level, the U.S. Fish and Wildlife Service is evaluating the delisting of this subspecies.

NORTHERN APLOMADO FALCON

Falco femoralis septentrionalis

NESTING: The Aplomado Falcon in general requires open country—usually semi-arid grasslands or savannas with a few oaks, acacias, or palms. In the U.S., it sought coastal prairies adjacent to sand ridges, woodlands along desert streams, or desert grasslands with scattered mesquites and yuccas. Rather than building its own nest, the Aplomado Falcon usually adopts the abandoned twig platforms of ravens or hawks.

FOOD: Mostly birds, which constitute over 90 percent of the diet by bulk; also rodents, bats, reptiles, frogs, and large insects. While foraging, the Aplomado Falcon usually chases prey, catching it in midair (dropping on flying birds from above, killing them in flight with a blow from the feet), or forces it to the ground. It also captures flying insects after sallying from a perch on a short flight.

RANGE: Breeds now primarily in Mexico; formerly north to southern Arizona, New Mexico, and Texas. **WINTER:** Resident.

IN PERIL: Occasional nests were found in New Mexico until 1952, after which the species was extirpated from the U.S. Declines may have begun as early as 1905 to 1909, but the Northern Aplomado Falcon was not considered rare until the 1930's. A small population of captive-bred individuals is now being reintroduced.

JEOPARDIZED: By habitat conversion for agriculture, habitat degradation due to desertification through overgrazing, by shooting, and by eggshell thinning from exposure to pesticides. Channelization of desert streams and loss of riparian habitat have had major impacts on local fauna, and much of the Aplomado Falcon's former grassland and savanna habitat in the southwestern U.S. is now too overgrown with mesquite for successful hunting by the falcon. Grazing cattle degraded habitat, particularly grassland, leading to declines in the birds that served as prey for the falcons. Mexican populations are stable, although DDT and DDE continue to be used in Mexico and falcons from Veracruz have been found to be severely contaminated.

LISTING: Listed as **Endangered** in February 1986.

RECOVERY PLANS: Include reintroducing the subspecies into its historic range in the southwestern U.S. From 1983 through 1988 a captive breeding program in Santa Cruz, California, reared 20 birds, some of which were released in Texas. Releases in Arizona were planned for 1991. Prescribed burns and brush-removal programs have been recommended in the Southwest. The U.S. Fish and Wildlife Service will reclassify the Aplomado Falcon as **Threatened** if a population of 100 breeding pairs is maintained in the U.S. for three years. Elimination of DDT and DDE within the Mexican breeding range may be necessary to stabilize a population of 200 breeding pairs.

ATTWATER'S GREATER PRAIRIE-CHICKEN

Tympanuchus cupido attwateri

NESTING: Requires open coastal prairies, where tall dropseed, little bluestem, sumpweed, broomweed, ragweed, and big bluestem dominate the habitat. The birds seek taller grasses in which to conceal their shallow scrape.

FOOD: Mostly plants, seeds, and, seasonally, insects. From October to April, Prairie Chickens take, in general, mostly seeds and some waste grain, acorns, and fruit; the rest of the year about one-third of their diet is insects, primarily grasshoppers. While foraging, the bird picks items from the substrate.

RANGE: Bred originally in coastal Texas and southwestern Louisiana; now restricted to a narrow band along the Texas coast and a few offshore islands. **WINTER:** Resident. **IN PERIL:** Throughout its range. Although these birds were abundant in the 1800's, by 1940 there were fewer than 9,000. Nearly half of the birds that remain today live in Aransas, Goliad, and Refugio counties, Texas. The total population was about 1,280 in 1982, and it continued to decline through the 1980's. The 1990 spring census was up 14 percent to 494 birds, but the apparent increase may have been an artifact of a more intensive survey effort.

NOTES: Winter flocks may be all male, all female, or combined. The subspecies' "booming grounds" (traditional courtship areas called "leks") occur on natural grass or deserted roads, airport runways, or oil-well pads.

JEOPARDIZED: By habitat loss to agriculture, residential development, and oil and gas development.

LISTING: Concern for conservation was too late for the eastern subspecies of the Greater Prairie Chicken, the Heath Hen, but the Attwater's survives and was listed as **Endangered** in March 1967. The Greater Prairie-chicken was listed as **Endangered** in Canada in 1978; by 1990, Canadians officially considered the species **Extirpated** (extinct within Canadian borders).

RECOVERY PLANS: Habitat purchased in Colorado County, Texas, in the 1960's, and transferred acreage from the neighboring Aransas National Wildlife Refuge became the Attwater's Prairie-Chicken National Wildlife Refuge in 1972. The refuge has since been enlarged by several thousand acres. Suppression of woody plants through moderate cattle grazing and prescribed burning may help protect this subspecies against habitat degradation, but habitat loss and fragmentation continue elsewhere, and populations in Galveston, Harris, and Brazoria counties are likely to be lost to urban development. One study recommends that a captive breeding stock be established.

MASKED BOBWHITE

Colinus virginianus ridgwayi

NESTING: Requires grasslands, sparsely studded or bordered by mesquite, in which it weaves a concealing arch in the thick cover over its shallow scrape.

FOOD: Mostly greens and insects in the summer and early fall, legume and weed seeds in the autumn, winter, and early spring. While foraging, the Masked Bobwhite picks items from the substrate.

RANGE: Originally, south-central Arizona and eastern Sonora, Mexico. **WINTER:** Resident. **IN PERIL:** Throughout its range. The Masked Bobwhite was extirpated from the U.S. by about 1900. By 1985, drought and cattle grazing led to the near-complete crash of the Sonoran population. Captive-bred birds are being reintroduced into the subspecies' former range in southern Arizona. Between 1985 and 1987, 4,500 quail were released. The total population size is uncertain, and overgrazing of native grasslands presents a perhaps insurmountable problem for the continued existence of this subspecies.

NOTES: The Masked Bobwhite has a short lifespan and a short interval between generations. When not nesting, two or more family groups gather in coveys of up to about 20 individuals. Coveys begin assembling when the young reach the age of 3 weeks and begin disbanding by late June, the onset of the next breeding season. Nesting may be skipped if July rains are delayed or absent.

JEOPARDIZED: Primarily by the rapid expansion of cattle grazing in Arizona from 1870 to 1890. As the cattle depleted native grasses and herbaceous plants (needed for nesting, cover, and food), woody plants invaded and eliminated grasslands, so that by the turn of the century the habitat was occupied by other species of quail.

LISTING: Listed as **Endangered** in March 1967.

RECOVERY PLANS: Efforts at reintroduction in Arizona and New Mexico and restoration in Mexico from 1937 through 1950 proved unsuccessful because releases were made outside the subspecies' historic range in unsuitable habitat. A successful captive-breeding program was established in 1966. From an original base of four birds from breeders and 57 wild birds taken from Mexico in 1968 and 1970, 3,000 chicks are produced annually at Patuxent, Maryland, then released into family groups. An additional 18 Mexican birds were added to the captive flock in 1986 to ensure genetic variability. Success will depend on the restoration of suitable grassland habitats. Releases from 1985 to 1990 are under evaluation. The Buenos Aires Ranch (Altar Valley, Arizona) was purchased in 1985 by the U.S. Fish and Wildlife Service and became the Buenos Aires National Wildlife Refuge.

NORTHERN SPOTTED OWL

Strix occidentalis caurina

NESTING: Requires dense old-growth conifer (especially redwood and Douglas fir) and some deciduous forests, a high, multi-layered, multi-species canopy, and large trees with cavities, broken tops, or (sometimes) dense growth of mistletoe. The Spotted Owl may also scrape a depression in the debris found within abandoned platform nests of ravens, eagles, or hawks.

FOOD: Mostly flying squirrels, voles, other rodents, rabbits, and hares; also some birds, but mammals comprise more than 90 percent of the prey. While foraging, the Spotted Owl swoops down in a spreading-wing descent from a perch, snatching up prey from the ground in its talons. It caches excess prey.

RANGE: Breeds from southwestern British Columbia south through western Washington and western Oregon to Marin County, California, possibly to Monterey County.

WINTER: Resident or altitudinal migrant.

IN PERIL: Throughout its range. The population on federal land is estimated at about 3,000 pairs; the population on private land is unknown, but is believed to be quite small.

NOTES: The Northern Spotted Owl is nocturnal, and does not tolerate even moderately high temperatures; it selects cool daytime summer roosts, preferring those on north-facing slopes under a dense canopy. Three subspecies (the Northern Spotted Owl, California Spotted Owl, and Mexican Spotted Owl) are found in North America (see below).

JEOPARDIZED: By habitat loss to logging and forest fragmentation. The closely related Barred Owl is expanding into the Northern Spotted Owl's range, and the Great Horned Owl has expanded into clearcut areas and forest edge and preys on fledgling Spotted Owls. By 1990 the Northern Spotted Owl's preferred Pacific Northwest habitat had been reduced to an estimated 10 percent of its original extent. Acute political and economic considerations precluded federal protection until 1990.

LISTING: Blue-Listed since 1980. By 1982, concern in the Northern and Middle Pacific Coast regions centered on accelerated habitat loss and competition from Barred Owls, which had begun to expand into Oregon. Apparent increases in census reports seemed to be the result of better surveys, particularly of private timberlands. By 1986, reports on the two more-southern subspecies were lacking, but the U.S. Fish and Wildlife Service qualified them for Category 2 status. Reports for the northern subspecies, which was listed as **Endangered** in Canada in 1986, indicated serious declines in the Northern Pacific Coast Region and declines in the Middle Pacific Coast Region, but in 1987 the U.S. Fish and Wildlife Service decided it did not warrant listing. In response to a legal challenge, however, the Northern Spotted Owl was listed as **Threatened** in June 1990. Two subspecies, the California Spotted Owl (*S. o. occidentalis*) and the Mexican

53

Spotted Owl (*S. o. lucida*), found from southeastern Utah and central Colorado south through the mountains of Mexico, were the subjects of a petition for listing in 1989. As of this writing, the Service has not decided on a response to this petition.

RECOVERY PLANS: Involve a well-coordinated two-part strategy to protect sufficient habitat and to carry out research and monitoring to test the adequacy of the strategies adopted. These strategies include the isolation of 80 acres around each pair's nest, the protection of larger blocks (up to 600,000 acres) of habitat capable of supporting multiple pairs, a ban on logging and the control of other silvicultural activities in protected areas, and the dedication of corridors between conservation areas. Concern continues despite listing, owing to the emotional issues surrounding the debate over jobs vs. the environment.

FLORIDA SCRUB JAY
Aphelocoma coerulescens coerulescens

NESTING: The Florida Scrub Jay prefers post-fire scrub on ancient dunes. There it uses dense thickets of scrub oaks (myrtle, sand live, and Chapman) under 10 feet tall interspersed with bare patches of fine porous sand (for foraging and burying acorns) in areas less than half-sheltered under a canopy. It builds a cup of grass supported on a platform of twigs, occasionally moss.

FOOD: Mostly lizards and arthropods in spring and summer, acorns in fall and winter. It caches acorns in the sand.

RANGE: Central Florida. **WINTER:** Resident. **IN PERIL:** Throughout its limited range. Some 40 percent of the Florida Scrub Jay's initially patchy habitat is now gone, and at the current rate of decline, only a small population of jays will remain by the early 1990's. The subspecies has already been eliminated from Broward, Dade, Duval, Pinellas, and St. John's counties, and counts have dropped radically overall, with losses since 1900 believed to exceed 50 percent. In 1990 the population was estimated at about 10,000 individuals. Eighty percent are confined to two main sites: the Merritt Island National Wildlife Refuge/Cape Canaveral area and the Ocala National Forest.

NOTES: Acorns cached and forgotten by the jays likely help to disperse oaks. This subspecies breeds cooperatively, and young birds, even if sexually mature, often remain in their natal territory as helpers at older birds' nests for several years (males up to six). Predation, a major threat to nesting success, is lower when helpers attend the nesting pair. Because the Florida Scrub Jay differs so much from other subspecies of the Scrub Jay in behavior, patterns of reproduction, and plumage, it may well be a distinct species.

JEOPARDIZED: By habitat loss to beachfront development and, in the interior, to citrus groves, residential development, and habitat degradation brought on by the suppression of fires. The Florida Scrub Jay can persist only where burning keeps the oak scrub community at the proper stage of succession. By 1984 most of the population was located on public lands, and in anticipation of future land-use restrictions, the developers are moving in quickly.

LISTING: Blue-Listed since 1973 and listed as **Threatened** in June 1987. By 1982, populations were already reported in trouble from habitat clearing, orange-grove development, and suspected competition with an expanding Blue Jay population.

RECOVERY PLANS: At Merritt Island National Wildlife Refuge, controlled burns of all scrub have been implemented to maintain suitable habitat. Habitats on other public lands must maintain low-growing oaks if they are to support jay populations.

SAN CLEMENTE LOGGERHEAD SHRIKE

Lanius ludovicianus mearnsi

NESTING: Requires shrubs over 7 feet high for its ample, well-formed cup of twigs and forbs. Sites providing a significant canopy are preferred.

FOOD: Large insects and smaller vertebrates, including mice, birds, and lizards; also other terrestrial invertebrates. While foraging, shrikes sally from a perch on short flights or chase and catch prey in midair. They kill with a lightning-fast bite on the neck while holding the prey with their feet, though they lack the strong talons of raptors. Often called "butcher birds," shrikes often impale prey on a plant spine or barbed wire to help them tear it apart or to advertise their territory.

RANGE: San Clemente Island, California.

WINTER: Resident. **IN PERIL:** Throughout its limited range, and on the verge of extinction. Documentation for the years prior to 1973 was poor, but records in 1917 suggested no need for concern. By the 1970's, about 30 individuals remained. By 1985 that had dropped to about 11 pairs; and by 1988, to about five pairs.

NOTES: The shorter bill, wings, and tail and the lighter underparts differentiate this subspecies from the subspecies found on the nearby mainland. Of the Channel Islands, San Clemente has the most endemic plants, but feral sheep and goats foraging on fruit and seeds have prevented the reproduction of woody plants, and today two-thirds of the plant cover in the shrike's foraging areas consists of exotic species.

Goats, introduced in the 1800's, peaked at 12,000 in the 1970's. The island supports Navy-built roads, rifle ranges, an airstrip, and a ship-to-shore gunnery site. Bald Eagle, Peregrine Falcon, Osprey, Rufous-sided Towhee, Song Sparrow, and extinct San Clemente Bewick's Wren all formerly bred there.

JEOPARDIZED: Primarily by the grazing and browsing of feral goats, which nearly denuded the island of vegetation and led to increased predation. The shrike has been eliminated from many parts of the island that it inhabited in the early 1900's, and its nests are subject to predation by ravens, foxes, and feral cats.

LISTING: The species as a whole has been **Blue-Listed** since 1972, and this subspecies was declared **Endangered** in August 1977. As of 1990 the Migrant Loggerhead Shrike (on the mainland) remains a Category 2 candidate for federal listing (see p. 99).

RECOVERY PLANS: Are contingent on the eradication of goats from the island, begun in 1972 and nearly complete by 1991. The delay, in part the result of propagandizing and intrigue by a group intent on protecting goats, may have allowed the degradation of the remaining shrike nesting habitat beyond the point of return. Restoring large native shrubs to denuded northern canyon habitat and protecting nests and young from predators, especially cats, are required. Shrike productivity is low, and the rearing of chicks in captivity from eggs taken from the wild is under way at the San Diego Zoo and Wild Animal Park.

LEAST BELL'S VIREO
Vireo bellii pusillus

NESTING: Usually in dense thickets of riparian woodland vegetation with a well-developed shrub layer beneath or adjacent to a canopy of willow/cottonwood trees. The nest is a rounded, deep cup of dried leaves, shredded bark, plant fibers, and spider silk suspended from twigs about 3 feet off the ground.

FOOD: Mostly insects. While foraging, the vireo gleans foliage and branches.

RANGE: Formerly bred throughout California's Central Valley (then the center of its abundance), the Sierra Nevada foothills, and in the Coast Ranges from Santa Clara County to northwestern Baja California. Populations were also found in Owens Valley, Death Valley, and the Mojave Desert. Currently restricted to localities from the Santa Ynez River, Santa Barbara County, through southern California and northwestern Baja California at least to Mission San Fernando, but probably to Cataviña.

WINTERS: In the Cape region of Baja California, with stragglers in southern California. **IN PERIL:** At least in the U.S. and probably in most of its range in Mexico. Since 1977 most or all of that range has been surveyed. The U.S. population is estimated at about 385 pairs, of which 80 percent are found along just five drainages: 168 pairs along the Santa Margarita River, 41 along the Sweetwater River, 34 along the San Luis Rey River, 25 on the San Diego River, and 42 on the Santa Ana River (Prado Basin). Several hundred additional breeding pairs probably persist in northern Baja California, where critical riparian habitat is also disappearing.

NOTES: This is one of four subspecies of Bell's Vireo. The Least Bell's Vireo has undergone one of the most dramatic declines of any California passerine in recent times, and has been eliminated from 95 percent of its former U.S. range, including California's Sacramento and San Joaquin valleys.

JEOPARDIZED: By the destruction of riparian woodlands (the result of flood control and water-development projects, agricultural development, highway construction, livestock grazing, invasive exotic plants, off-road vehicles, urban development, and the proliferation of golf courses) in combination with cowbird parasitism. (Rare or absent from the Least Bell's range before 1910, the cowbird is now a common parasite of this species; see p. 219).

LISTING: The Bell's Vireo was **Blue-Listed** from 1972 to 1982, and warranted of **Special Concern** in 1986. The Least Bell's Vireo was listed as **Endangered** in May 1986 (but see the Bell's Vireo, p. 137).

RECOVERY PLANS: Periodic flooding perpetuates a mosaic of canopy and shrubby thickets of vegetation, which the vireo uses for nesting. Water-control programs are thus potentially threatening. Programs to control cowbirds and prevent habitat loss have been credited with increasing vireo numbers, but the threats remain.

INYO CALIFORNIA TOWHEE

Pipilo crissalis eremophilus

NESTING: Requires dense thickets, almost invariably of willows, around desert springs and streams in rocky canyons. The nest is a bulky cup made of plant materials.

FOOD: Mostly seeds; also insects. While foraging, the Inyo California Towhee picks items from the substrate, after scanning the bare ground from rocks. The birds feed primarily or exclusively on the rocky slopes near the canyon-bottom thickets where they nest. They feed their young only insects, so far as is known.

RANGE: Restricted to the southern part of the Argus Range, southwestern Inyo County, California (thus in the western extremity of the Mojave Desert). **WINTER:** Resident. **IN PERIL:** Throughout its very limited range. The total population is estimated at fewer than 150 individuals.

NOTES: Formerly called the Brown Towhee. Because western populations (in Oregon, California, and Baja California) differ in skeletal anatomy, wing structure, egg color, behavior, vocalizations, and genetics from populations to the east, the species was recently split into two separate species, the western California Towhee (of which the Inyo is a subspecies) and the more eastern Canyon Towhee (*P. fuscus*).

JEOPARDIZED: By low numbers, a restricted range, habitat alteration stemming mainly from water diversion, and mining. Located near scarce water, some of this towhee's habitat has been trampled and grazed by cattle, horses, and feral burros. In 1987, three-fourths of the population in-habited an area 11 miles in diameter in the China Lake Naval Weapons Center, and the remainder was on either Bureau of Land Management land or 190 acres of privately held land.

LISTING: Listed as **Threatened** in August 1987, but being considered for reclassification as **Endangered.**

RECOVERY PLANS: Cattle grazing was stopped in 1981, and 8,000 horses and burros were removed from sensitive habitat; the vegetation appears to be recovering. The Navy, which controls much of the Argus Range, will keep critical habitat clear of horses and burros, and plans no weapons testing in the areas in question. The Bureau of Land Management has produced a management plan for the portion of the habitat under its supervision; it permits hiking, camping, hunting, and off-road vehicle use in the area but, by law, must consider the towhee when leasing mineral rights. Threats to the water supply and streamside vegetation equate to threats to the subspecies.

FLORIDA GRASSHOPPER SPARROW

Ammodramus savannarum floridanus

NESTING: Usually in poorly drained, frequently burned-over scrub land with fire-maintained stunted saw palmetto, dwarf oaks, bluestems, and wiregrass interspersed with low, sparse tufts of grass. The Florida Grasshopper Sparrow will also conceal its cup nest of dried grass in pastures if some native vegetation remains. Overhanging grass and other herbaceous plants may help to conceal the nest, which is sunk in a shallow depression and arched or domed at the rear.

FOOD: Mostly insects and other terrestrial invertebrates; also seeds of grass and other herbaceous plants. While foraging, the bird usually picks items from the ground.

RANGE: Central peninsular Florida.

WINTER: Resident. **IN PERIL:** Throughout its limited range. The population is estimated at fewer than 250 individuals in nine scattered sites.

NOTES: The Florida Grasshopper Sparrow nests in small semicolonial groups. It is isolated from other Grasshopper Sparrows by more than 300 miles. Local population sizes fluctuate greatly from year to year.

JEOPARDIZED: By conversion of habitat to pastureland. The sparrows are driven out when fields are cleared of shrubs and saw palmetto. Nests of the species as a whole are often destroyed by the mowing of fields. Those birds remaining after mowing has stripped away their cover are highly vulnerable to predators.

LISTING: The Grasshopper Sparrow has been **Blue-Listed** since 1974; this sub-species was listed as **Endangered** in July 1986.

RECOVERY PLANS: Much of the Florida Grasshopper Sparrow's current distribution is limited to a few large, private ranches that could improve their pastureland management, but landowners may be unfamiliar with the bird and its requirements. One useful management technique is to burn the prairie scrub in winter, maintaining it at an early successional stage. The Air Force has been working with the U.S. Fish and Wildlife Service toward an effective management program for its 100,000-acre Avon Park Bombing Range, which contains 5,000 acres of critical habitat sheltering this and other Threatened and Endangered species.

CAPE SABLE SEASIDE SPARROW

Ammodramus maritimus mirabilis

NESTING: Requires salt marsh with moderately dense clumped grasses, rushes, and sedges. The sparrow weaves a canopy into the encircling grass to cover its cup nest of dried grasses and sedges.

FOOD: Mostly insects, especially beetles, and other invertebrates, including spiders, amphipods, and mollusks; also the seeds from a variety of marsh plants. While foraging, the Cape Sable Seaside Sparrow usually picks items from the substrate or gleans them from low foliage.

RANGE: Extreme southern Florida. **WINTER:** Resident. **IN PERIL:** Throughout its limited range. The population is estimated at fewer than 6,600 individuals.

NOTES: This sparrow was described as a species in 1919 and, until reclassified as a subspecies of the Seaside Sparrow, was famous as the most recently discovered bird in the continental U.S. Males defend nest-centered territories year-round. The Seaside Sparrow, in general, nests in loosely defined, often isolated colonies.

JEOPARDIZED: Mainly by the destruction of its salt-marsh breeding habitat. Draining, development, DDT, and flooding for mosquito control led to the extinction of another subspecies of the Seaside Sparrow (the Dusky; see p. 199) and the extreme endangerment of this one. Rice rats prey upon many Seaside Sparrow nests in the South. This subspecies' salt-marsh habitat is subject to occasional flooding, which can severely affect nesting. The Cape Sable Seaside Sparrow remains widely distributed within its historic range, inhabiting 278 of 864 sites surveyed in 1981, with the greatest number found in the Big Cypress Swamp and Taylor Slough in the East Everglades.

LISTING: Listed as **Endangered** in March 1967.

RECOVERY PLANS: The focus is on avoiding programs that would alter the East Everglades (the only portion of the sparrow's range not under U.S. Park Service management) by lowering the water levels and degrading nesting habitat. Although the Cape Sable Seaside Sparrow is adapted to periodic fires, the timing of burns is important. If habitat degradation and nesting failures are to be minimized, burning must not be too frequent or carried out too late in the dry season. State or federal agencies' purchasing and managing of remaining habitat, zoning changes to prohibit development, and maintaining water levels have been identified by the U.S. Fish and Wildlife Service as preservation options.

SAN CLEMENTE SAGE SPARROW

Amphispiza belli clementeae

NESTING: In low, fairly dense, deciduous maritime desert scrub, primarily of box-thorn, ragwort, and cactus. In this scrub the bird builds a cup of twigs, grass, forbs, and bark. It uses the shrub canopy for cover, roosting, song perches, and nesting, although it nests on the ground also.

FOOD: Probably similar to that of other Sage Sparrows, which take mostly insects and spiders, although this subspecies takes more seeds and other plant material than do mainland subspecies. While foraging, it usually picks items from the substrate or gleans them from foliage and branches. It feeds its young insects.

RANGE: San Clemente Island, California, where the bird is now restricted to a strip only a few hundred yards wide at lower elevations on the west side. **WINTER:** Resident. **IN PERIL:** Throughout its tiny range. The population is estimated at about 265 to 300 adults.

NOTES: The San Clemente Sage Sparrow's larger bill differentiates it from mainland Sage Sparrows. Of the Channel Islands, San Clemente (about 65 miles from San Diego, California) has the most endemic plants, but feral sheep and goats foraging on fruit and seeds have prevented the reproduction of woody plants. Goats, introduced in the 1800's, peaked at 12,000 in the early 1970's. In the 1950's, pigs and deer were introduced for sport hunting; most are now gone. San Clemente supports Navy-built roads, rifle ranges, an airstrip, and a site for ship-to-shore gunnery practice. The Bald Eagle, Peregrine Falcon, Osprey, Rufous-sided Towhee, Song Sparrow, and the extinct San Clemente Bewick's Wren all formerly bred on San Clemente.

JEOPARDIZED: By a reduced food supply, due in large part to habitat degradation by feral goats and pigs. The San Clemente Sage Sparrow seems to find marginal habitat useless. Predation by feral cats, foxes, and raptors may be significant.

LISTING: Listed as **Endangered** in August 1977.

RECOVERY PLANS: The Navy, which administers San Clemente Island, has developed a management plan and has been removing introduced feral cats, goats, and pigs from the island. Now that the removal of goats is nearly complete, the island's native vegetation is beginning to recover.

THREATENED AND ENDANGERED
HAWAIIAN SPECIES

It is a sobering thought that Hawaii, which occupies 1/550 of the land area of the United States, is home to 28 of the 70 U.S. birds currently listed under federal protection as Threatened or Endangered. The threats that these 28 native Hawaiian birds face have been carefully detailed in numerous books, most recently in *Forest Bird Communities of the Hawaiian Islands* (Scott et al., 1986). The threats include habitat loss and degradation; the effects of introduced species, including competing plants and animals (which reduce critical resources); introduced predators and pathogens (which attack species more directly); and disregard of the legal protection afforded the birds. Underlying what we have wrought, directly or indirectly, is the threat of natural calamity: events such as fires, hurricanes, and (on the island of Hawaii) volcanic eruptions can work more swiftly and prove quite as disastrous as human interventions.

A significant amount of original habitat below about 3,800 feet elevation has been lost or degraded since humanity's arrival in 400 A.D., with the most pervasive damage having occurred prior to the arrival of the Europeans in 1778. The Europeans, however, introduced highly destructive animals (particularly goats and European pigs) and plants (intentionally or otherwise) that have massively altered the native ecosystems. Goats arrived 200 years ago, and by 1850 were common. They compacted the soil, encouraged erosion by their overgraz-ing, and discouraged or prevented the regeneration of native plants from seed or rootstock.

Sheep were introduced in 1793, and today are feral on the island of Hawaii, where their tendency to flock, roam over familiar trails, and overbrowse the mamane forests continues to threaten habitat critical to birds. The mouflon, another and larger sheep introduced to the island of Hawaii in 1954, hybridizes with feral sheep and also threatens the mamane. Fencing and systematic hunting have been used to reduce or eradicate the goats and to control the sheep and mouflon.

Cattle have also played a role in destroying native Hawaiian ecosystems. Many native bird populations became isolated as forests were fragmented and modified for the establishment of pastureland, and domestic herds continue to threaten a number of bird species. Feral cattle, eradicated from Kauai by the 1930's but still found on Hawaii and Maui, degraded the forest, opening it up to invading plants capable of outcompeting the native flora in the disturbed areas.

Axis deer, which were introduced on Molokai in 1868, on Lanai in 1920, and on Maui in 1960, compacted the soil and overbrowsed the native vegetation. Black-tailed deer, released on Kauai in 1961, must now be hunted to prevent them from invading the Alakai Swamp—the last retreat of many of that island's imperiled birds.

Pigs, introduced by the Polynesians, escaped and can be found wild on all the main islands except Lanai. And since the arrival of European pigs, the populations of wild pigs have increased substantially. As they root, pigs destroy vegetation, altering the composition of the understory and inhibiting forest regeneration. The disturbance encourages invasion by introduced plants and even damages the structure of the soil, especially in steep terrain. Pigs ingest many seeds of introduced plants, which germinate in their dung. They also trample ground nests and burrows and prey upon shearwater eggs and adults.

When habitat disturbance opens the door for introduced plants, the invaders, once established, may fundamentally alter the ecosystem. Plants imported for agriculture and horticulture, weed seeds contaminating feed imported for livestock, and trees imported for reforestation or horticulture have each played a role in displacing native flora, altering the soil, changing the water and nutrient cycling, and in some cases encouraging the success of imported animals. Among the worst plant pests are vegetation-smothering banana poka, some guavas and gingers, and fire-adapted plants such as the fire tree, which alters the nitrogen content of the soil. Despite the success of the introduced flora, however, it is thought that most native Hawaiian plant communities could hold their own if guarded from humanity (and humanity's hoofed animals).

But people will not curb their intrusions.

Prime old-growth rainforests continue to be harvested, and large tracts of vegetation continue to be cleared for housing and agricultural development. There are no economic incentives to encourage ranchers to manage their land with conservation as a paramount concern, or to discourage developers from altering critical, unprotected habitat. Many people realize the value of Hawaii's native birds, but adequate legal protection still needs to be enacted and enforced.

In the forest, where the majority of the jeopardized birds live, predation is thought to be most severe among the birds, such as thrushes (Oloma'o, Kama'o, Puaiohi), Maui Parrotbill, and Po'o-uli that dwell in the understory. Introduced black rats inhabit all eight main Hawaiian islands and were partly responsible for the extinction of several denizens of the understory. Black rats not only prey upon nests, but also compete with some fruit eaters for food and occasionally kill critically important koa trees by tearing away bark. Polynesian rats also inhabit the forested Hawaiian islands, and although their effect on birds has not yet been determined, they are considerably less common than black rats at elevations above 5,000 feet.

Cats, too, accompanied the Europeans, and feral cats have been common on the islands since the 1860's. Like the small Indian mongoose, which was introduced in 1883 and is established on the islands of Hawaii, Maui, Molokai, and Oahu, cats

are most dangerous to ground-nesting species and birds of the understory.

The role of introduced birds has not been thoroughly investigated, and a number of introductions are too recent to permit an evaluation of how well the native birds have adapted to their presence. Many introduced birds thrive in areas where the habitat is disturbed, a circumstance that provides another compelling reason to preserve unbroken tracts of forest. The Japanese White-eye, the most common and most widely dispersed avian invader, appears to have a greater effect on native forest birds than they do on it. This omnivore forms flocks, an asset for moving into areas that have been disturbed but are reverting to forest. Common Mynas compete for sites with native hole-nesting species and prey on the eggs and young of other birds. Feral parrots (escapees from cages) spread avian diseases. The Red-billed Leiothrix and perhaps the Melodious Laughing Thrush may also compete with native forest birds or spread diseases, and the ground-nesting Chukar and Ring-necked Pheasant may exploit some of the resources used by the Nene.

Losses to disease may also have been significant, and are frequently cited in the literature, but their incidence is poorly documented. The two most important diseases appear to be avian malaria and avian pox. Mosquitoes, first released in Hawaii in 1826 (sailors are said to have emptied larva-laden water casks into a Maui stream), transmit avian malaria, which was probably introduced through infected birds between 1865 and 1871. Avian pox, an imported virus that appears in several strains, is contagious and is spread by infected individuals, contaminated objects, or (possibly) mosquitoes. Many Hawaiian forest birds are now absent from (or found in very low numbers in) mosquito-infested areas and persist largely at elevations beyond the range of mosquitoes, but whether the insects have been responsible for the birds' retreat is not clear. It is quite likely that losses of lowlands to sugar cane (which took 250,000 acres) and other forms of encroachment are more responsible.

Many of humanity's assaults on Hawaii's ecosystems can still be minimized, and in some cases reversed, but delays in protecting what remains (we can be certain that *some* measures *will* be delayed) will be devastating. The ravages of nature—volcanic activity, fire, hurricanes, and even aseasonal rains—over which we have no control, can pose a far greater threat to populations already reduced in size and increasingly restricted to relatively small patches of often marginal habitat, than they can to large, widespread populations.

On the Hawaiian Islands, Western civilization has proved once again that it is far easier to damage the environment than it is to repair it. At least 23 Hawaiian birds have long since been driven to extinction, and of the 28 currently listed as Threatened (1) or Endangered (27), twelve number between 1,000 and 20,000 individuals in the wild, nine number between 100 and 1,000, five number between 10 and 100, and two consist of fewer than 10 individuals and may be extinct. Two birds, the Kauai 'O'o and the Kauai 'Akialoa, are officially listed as Endangered, but ornithologists working closely with them consider these two species already lost. Accordingly, treatments for these two birds are found with the group of extinct Hawaiian birds.

How many imperiled Hawaiian birds can hold on until adequate protection is provided is, for the most part, up to us. Some of these battles, regretfully, are all but over. Hawaii, where the native flora and fauna have been so egregiously decimated, demonstrates the extreme vulnerability of island organisms to the arrival of predators, diseases, and competitors against which they have not evolved defenses. The story is the same on other islands around the world, as we are reminded by the fates of the Dodo, many species of flightless rails, most of the avifauna of Guam (eaten by a single species of introduced snake), and the Santa Barbara Song Sparrow.

REFERENCE: Scott et al., 1986.

NEWELL'S SHEARWATER, or 'A'O

Puffinus auricularis

NESTING: Now restricted to mountainous terrain between 500 and 2,300 feet elevation, where it digs its perennial burrow near dense, soil-stabilizing ferns on cliffs or above an open, downhill flight path.

FOOD: Fish, plankton, and occasionally ship wastes.

RANGE: Breeds on Kauai, the island of Hawaii, Molokai, and perhaps Oahu.

WINTER: Remains in Hawaiian waters from April through October but migrates elsewhere for the rest of the year. Its dispersal requires study. **IN PERIL:** On all the islands where it nests. Considered extinct in 1931, Newell's Shearwater was rediscovered in 1954. When its breeding grounds were discovered in 1967, its population was thought to be in the thousands and declining. Its current breeding population is estimated at 8,000, and an additional 2,000 nonbreeders are generally at sea.

NOTES: This is a medium-sized, gull-like species whose classification remains somewhat controversial. It has also been called *Puffinus newelli* and *P. puffinus newelli,* and *P. auricularis newelli.* The similar Townsend's Shearwater nests in the Revillagigedo Islands off western Mexico.

JEOPARDIZED: By predation from introduced black rats, pigs, cats, and mongooses (the introduction of mongooses to Kauai seems increasingly probable), and by artificial lights, which induce night blindness and accidental crashes into trees, poles, utility wires, autos, and buildings (rainy nights and new moon pose the highest risk). Many birds fall on Kauai's highways, since they come ashore only at night. Attracted to light, fledglings follow river valleys to the sea, confusing electric lights and car headlights with stars. Confused fledglings land before reaching the sea and are killed by dogs, cats, and autos. These birds cannot take off from level ground, and in October 1987, as the young departed for the sea, 200 per day were turned in to aid stations. On Kauai, the species is also vulnerable to fire.

LISTING: Listed as **Threatened** in September 1975.

RECOVERY PLANS: A "Save-Our-Shearwaters" campaign was set up in 1978 to encourage residents to take fallen birds to aid stations, where injured individuals could be tended and released. More than 20,000 shearwaters have been rescued and released since 1978, with 1,500 fledglings (poorer flyers than adults, and more sensitive to light) recovered annually. Efforts to design streetlights that will not attract the night-flying birds continue. Breeding colonies located near developed areas require protection from trespassing. At Kilauea Point National Wildlife Refuge and Mokuaeae Islet, Newell's eggs are placed in the nests of Wedge-tailed Shearwaters in the hope of establishing a colony on a predator-free offshore islet, but Newell's Shearwater will not likely recover without effective control of the feral pigs, which continue to prey upon eggs, trample burrows, and take some adults.

NENE,
or HAWAIIAN GOOSE
Nesochen sandvicensis

NESTING: Now restricted to sparsely vegetated, rugged-upland volcanic slopes. The nest is a down-lined saucer often concealed beneath bushy vegetation surrounded by barren lava.

FOOD: Green vegetation, including the leaves, buds, flowers, seeds, and fruits of native plants.

RANGE: The islands of Hawaii and Maui. The reintroduced Maui population dates to 1962. **WINTER:** Resident. **IN PERIL:** Throughout its shrinking range (the Nene was previously found on all of the larger Hawaiian islands). Portions of the Hawaii population are protected within Hawaii Volcanoes National Park and four sanctuaries covering almost 60,000 acres. The Maui population is contained within the Haleakala National Park. The wild population, although holding steady with continued releases of captive-bred recruits, is estimated at only about 390 to 425 birds.

NOTES: This heavily barred goose is Hawaii's state bird.

JEOPARDIZED: By habitat loss and a scarcity of food plants, low reproductive rate, introduced competitors, hunting (begun in earnest in 1850), poaching, and egg collecting. Introduced predators, including mongooses and feral cats, are especially dangerous to the young, which remain flightless for about 11 to 14 weeks after hatching. Goats and pigs may also affect the population. Captive-bred recruits from Slimbridge (see below) may bring parasites.

LISTING: Listed as **Endangered** in March 1967.

RECOVERY PLANS: In 1918 a captive breeding program was begun on the island of Hawaii. By the early 1950's another was established, in Slimbridge, England, and reintroductions were begun. In 1972, enclosures were placed around nests in Hawaii Volcanoes National Park, and a similar program has begun at Haleakala National Park. A predator-control program is in place, food and water are provided in key areas, exotic vegetation is being replaced by native food plants and cover, and radiotelemetry has been used to monitor the movements of individuals, but survival depends on the continued success of the captive breeding programs, and competition with introduced gamebirds needs to be eliminated.

KOLOA,
or HAWAIIAN DUCK

Anas wyvilliana

NESTING: Requires wetlands, such as freshwater marshes, flooded grasslands, bogs, forest swamps, coastal ponds, mountain pools, or streams, from sea level to 8,000 feet elevation. The Koloa's nest is a down- and feather-lined saucer.

FOOD: Snails, insects (including dragonfly larvae), earthworms, grass seeds, and other plant matter.

RANGE: Kauai, Oahu, and the island of Hawaii, formerly also on Maui and Molokai, where it is now extinct; the populations on Oahu and the island of Hawaii are the result of reintroductions. **WINTER:** Resident. **IN PERIL:** Throughout its shrinking range. Total population, according to an estimate made in the 1960's, numbers some 2,000 to 3,000 birds.

NOTES: This fairly sedentary, very wary, dark-brown duck is closely related to the Mallard, and viewed by some taxonomists as a subspecies of the Mallard. The species may also be cited as Koloa maoli.

JEOPARDIZED: By wetland loss (especially from the conversion of flooded taro fields to dry sugar-cane acreage), habitat degradation (the encroachment of introduced plants), hunting, predation by introduced mongooses and cats (the young remain flightless for nine weeks), and hybridization with feral Mallards.

LISTING: Listed as **Endangered** in March 1967.

RECOVERY PLANS: Hunting was curtailed on Kauai in 1925. In 1972 a portion of Kauai's Hanalei Valley became Hawaii's first national waterbird refuge, and four more wetlands have since been set aside. As soon as populations on Oahu and the island of Hawaii become self-sustaining at 500 birds, the U.S. Fish and Wildlife Service plans to downgrade the Koloa from Endangered to Threatened status.

LAYSAN DUCK

Anas laysanensis

NESTING: In a hypersaline lake with some densely vegetated edges, where the duck conceals its nest.

FOOD: Insects, especially brine flies, noctuid "miller" moths, and their cutworm larvae, as well as small crustaceans.

RANGE: Laysan Island (northwestern Hawaii). **WINTER:** Resident. **IN PERIL:** Everywhere, but the population is stable; as of a 1989 estimate, 500 birds remain.

NOTES: The Laysan Duck is active at night. Although a strong flyer, it does not often fly. It is also called the Laysan Teal.

JEOPARDIZED: By the cumulative effects of 30 years of habitat degradation from introduced rabbits (now gone) that stripped the ground cover and led to erosion of the duck's restricted habitat, and by nest predation by introduced rats. The Laysan Duck was also hunted for food and feathers.

LISTING: Listed as **Endangered** in March 1967.

RECOVERY PLANS: In the 1950's, individuals captured on Laysan were taken to the Honolulu Zoo and then shipped to other zoos and breeders to establish captive breeding stocks. To maintain genetic diversity, trading among breeders has been encouraged. Habitat on Laysan (open only to researchers) is managed by the Hawaiian Islands National Wildlife Refuge, is internationally recognized as a Research Natural Area, and has been nominated for listing in the National Wilderness Preservation System. Control of introduced plants and predators is considered essential.

'IO, or HAWAIIAN HAWK

Buteo solitarius

NESTING: At elevations from 3,000 to 8,500 feet, usually in open savanna, dense rainforest, or agricultural areas bounded by large trees. In such trees the hawk places its large nest of twigs, sticks, and leaves. Although widespread and adaptable, the 'Io tends to avoid the driest areas and is usually absent from areas with few or no trees.

FOOD: Introduced and native birds, small mammals (including rodents), insects, and spiders.

RANGE: Breeds only on the island of Hawaii, but wanders to Maui and Oahu.

WINTER: Resident. **IN PERIL:** Throughout its limited range. The population is estimated at 2,000 birds.

NOTES: The 'Io, Hawaii's only hawk, is a very territorial, strong-flying buteo. It is usually solitary or seen in pairs, often soaring over forests or fields. It occurs in light and dark color phases.

JEOPARDIZED: By nest disturbance, illegal shooting and nest harassment, deforestation of lowlands, loss of prime old-growth forest, and forest degradation (especially by the invasion of non-native plants). Pesticide contamination from agriculture poses a potential threat. Cats probably compete in some areas for rodent prey.

LISTING: Listed as **Endangered** in March 1967.

RECOVERY PLANS: Koa and ohia rainforest is protected in the Hakalau Forest National Wildlife Refuge, on the northwestern slope of Mauna Kea. Systematic studies, not initiated until the early 1980's, have shown that the greatest losses are now due to human disturbance during nesting, and to hunting. With populations stable for the moment, the 'Io's Endangered status may be reassessed.

'ALALA,
or HAWAIIAN CROW

Corvus hawaiiensis

NESTING: Now restricted to open ohia or mixed ohia–koa forests (at elevations of 3,000 to 6,000 feet) that have a fruit-producing understory of native shrubs and plants. The 'Alala prefers closed-canopy forest, selecting sites high in ohia trees for its nest. 'Alala nests, built from branches and twigs, are apparently used over long periods by generations of birds.

FOOD: Half of the diet is fruit and flower nectar; the remainder is largely spiders and isopods.

RANGE: The island of Hawaii. **WINTER:** Resident. **IN PERIL:** Throughout its range. In 1980 there were about 200 individuals; in 1989 only nine birds were seen (and are the subject of a current lawsuit), and fewer than a dozen were held in captivity.

NOTES: This stocky, fairly furtive omnivore is Hawaii's largest passerine and flies in family groups. It is easily disturbed during nesting. During breeding, pairs defend large territories, excluding even their young of previous years. Females are not sexually mature for two to three years; males, four. Its loud wailing was probably responsible for early Hawaiian lore that 'Alala were spirits.

JEOPARDIZED: By human settlement (habitat losses to subdivisions and agriculture), hunting (a shooting campaign by Kona farmers was waged in the 1890's), changes in native forests due to browsing and grazing by cattle, horses, sheep, and goats (domestic stock continues to be a ma-

jor threat), degradation and fragmentation of the koa–ohia forest in Kona (on the island of Hawaii), fire and the spread of the fire-adapted fountain grass and fire tree, potential pesticide contamination from agricultural practices, competition for food with black rats, poor reproduction (complete reproductive failure is common), and, possibly, insect-borne diseases that may have contributed to restricting the species' range. Young birds incapable of flight fall prey to mongooses and cats.

LISTING: The 'Alala was granted complete legal protection in 1931, and was listed as **Endangered** in March 1967.

RECOVERY PLANS: In 1984 the Hawaii Board of Land and Natural Resources established a sanctuary on Hualalai (a volcano northwest of Mauna Loa) to protect various species, including the crow, but as of 1990 the only available habitat for this bird consisted of degraded vegetation. The Board's captive breeding program, begun in 1976, comprised nine birds, including two active breeding pairs, by 1983; only three young (all from one nest) were produced by the captive flock in ten years (there are very few females). Concern for the few captives continues because breeding is very difficult and the gene pool is extremely limited. Captive propagation is nonetheless considered essential to the survival of the species. For years the captive breeding facility (originally developed for the Nene) was unsuitably located in dry habitat at high elevation, and near high-intensity military

NIHOA MILLERBIRD

Acrocephalus familiaris

training. Its new facility, at an abandoned prison, is far superior, but establishment of a viable captive population and protection of suitable habitat for reintroduction are still lacking. The few remaining wild birds are on private land that is threatened with habitat destruction.

NESTING: In areas supporting dense shrubs, which hold the nest of grass and rootlets.

FOOD: Insects gleaned from leaves, bush stems, leaf litter, and soil surface in dense brush.

RANGE: Nihoa (northwestern Hawaiian Islands). **WINTER:** Resident. **IN PERIL:** Throughout its tiny range. As of a 1986 estimate, almost 600 birds remained.

NOTES: This is a secretive, sedentary, inconspicuous ground bird. The name "millerbird" is derived from the bird's habit of feeding on large "miller" (noctuid) moths. The Nihoa Millerbird is actually a subspecies (*Acrocephalus familiaris kingi*), but because the only other subspecies, formerly found on Laysan Island, has been extinct since at least 1917, the endangerment of the Nihoa endangers the species as a whole, by definition.

JEOPARDIZED: By its limited range. The Nihoa Millerbird requires protection from the increasingly probable introduction of rats and other predators and disease-carrying insects, exotic birds, predatory insects (such as ants that could reduce the Millerbird's food supply), and exotic plants (that could out-compete preferred native species). Fire also poses a constant threat on the island.

LISTING: Listed as **Endangered** in March 1967.

RECOVERY PLANS: Nihoa has been protected since 1909, when President Theodore Roosevelt created the Hawaiian Islands Reservation. By 1940 the island had been designated as a wildlife refuge, and it is now qualified as a Research Natural Area, with access permitted only to scientific researchers. Whether the Nihoa Millerbird should be introduced to some of the other islands as a safeguard against catastrophic events on Nihoa is under consideration. Sea vessel inspection and habitat monitoring to detect the invasion of exotic species is essential.

KAMA'O, or LARGE KAUAI THRUSH

Myadestes myadestinus

NESTING: Now restricted to higher elevations in the largest remaining tracts of wet ohia forests.

FOOD: Primarily fruit, occasionally insects and snails.

RANGE: Kauai. **WINTER:** Resident. **IN PERIL:** The Kama'o is on the verge of extinction. As of a 1981 estimate, 24 birds remained, having retreated to the remote southern portion of the Alakai Swamp.

NOTES: Like the other Hawaiian thrushes, this melodious, large-bodied bird is noted for shivering its wings while perched. In 1891 it was Kauai's most common forest bird, but by 1928 it was gone from the lower forests.

JEOPARDIZED: Primarily by introduced insects transmitting avian diseases (including avian pox and malaria), which appear responsible for the decline this century, but also by general habitat degradation (especially that caused by pigs), the introduction of black rats (which compete for food, especially fruit), and predation by cats (mostly in the understory). The Kama'o will also be jeopardized by the introduction of the mongoose, which is considered highly probable.

LISTING: Listed as **Endangered** in October 1970.

RECOVERY PLANS: Kauai's Alakai Wilderness Preserve, established in 1964, protects almost 10,000 acres. Another 19,500 acres of forest on the island, most of it now administered by the Hawaii Division of Forestry and Wildlife, has been identified in

OLOMA'O,
or MOLOKAI THRUSH
Myadestes lanaiensis

the recovery plan for forest bird populations as crucial habitat, but lack of habitat is not the problem. Survival of the species depends upon a successful captive breeding program (which is not in place), because this species has suffered the most significant recent decline of any Hawaiian bird.

NESTING: Now restricted to wet montane ohia forest (above 3,000 feet elevation) with a dense understory.
FOOD: Fruit, berries, insects, and snails taken under the forest canopy.
RANGE: Molokai; formerly Lanai and Maui as well. **WINTER:** Resident. **IN PERIL:** The subspecies on Lanai is already extinct; the Maui population, known only from bones, was extirpated before the arrival of Europeans. The Oloma'o was considered abundant and widespread in the Molokai forest 100 years ago, but by the 1930's its range had declined and its numbers were reduced. Surveys in the late 1970's and early 1980's indicated that some 20 birds remained, but that estimate was probably optimistic. The species is on the verge of extinction.
NOTES: This reclusive, heavy-bodied bird has been scarcely studied. The name "Oloma'o" may also refer to the Lanai Thrush (see p. 211).
JEOPARDIZED: In addition to the general problems caused by deforestation, habitat degradation, and diseases, this bird competes with black rats for food (particularly fruit) and is subject to predation by cats (especially in the understory). In the area where these birds have been seen most recently, there are large numbers of the introduced Japanese Bush-warbler, which might be a competitor.
LISTING: Listed as **Endangered** in October 1970.

PUAIOHI,
or SMALL KAUAI THRUSH
Myadestes palmeri

RECOVERY PLANS: In 1903 the State Forest Reserve System was established to protect habitat, control feral animals, and eliminate introduced plant species. The System now manages one-third of Hawaii's forests. Seemingly suitable habitat is abundant, but because the Oloma'o chooses not to use it, the long-term outlook for the species is bleak.

NESTING: Now restricted to gulches at higher elevations and dense ohia forests in the Alakai Swamp. The Puaiohi's nest is placed in a cavity or on a platform. It was only in 1983 that nests (two of them) were first discovered; one had been constructed beside a stream on a shelf of a cliff.
FOOD: Insects and fruit, including that of the olapa.
RANGE: Kauai. **WINTER:** Resident. **IN PERIL:** Between 1968 and 1973 the Kauai population was estimated to be about 175 birds, but in 1983 the estimate had fallen to between 20 and 100 birds, with only 13 individuals actually seen during intensive surveys of the Alakai Swamp.
NOTES: This rare, small, secretive thrush may also be referred to in the literature as Palmer's Thrush. Its biology is little known.
JEOPARDIZED: Primarily by introduced insects transmitting avian diseases (including avian pox and avian malaria), but also by habitat degradation (especially the encroachment of introduced plants encouraged by the damage wrought by feral pigs), competition with introduced black rats for food, especially fruit, and predation by cats. Managers anticipate that the Puaiohi will also be jeopardized by the introduction of the mongoose, which seems increasingly probable.
LISTING: Listed as **Endangered** in March 1967.
RECOVERY PLANS: Kauai's Alakai Wilderness Preserve, established in 1964, protects almost 10,000 acres. Another 19,500

acres of forest on the island, most of it now administered by the Hawaii Division of Forestry and Wildlife, have been identified in the recovery plan for forest bird populations as crucial habitat.

LAYSAN FINCH

Telespiza cantans

NESTING: In dense vegetation, typically shrubs and low, tangled ground cover. The Laysan Finch prefers nesting in clumps of bunchgrass.

FOOD: Mostly seeds and other plant matter, including tender shoots and flowers; also seabird eggs, insects (including fly larvae found on dead seabirds), carrion, and fruit.

RANGE: Laysan Island (northwestern Hawaiian Islands). **WINTER:** Resident. **IN PERIL:** Throughout its limited habitat. By 1923 (when rabbits introduced in 1903–4 were eradicated from Laysan Island), about 100 Laysan Finches remained. Recent estimates indicate that about 10,000 birds are now found on Laysan. An introduced population established on Pearl and Hermes Reef, 310 miles northwest of Laysan, in 1967, numbers 500 to 700 individuals.

NOTES: This songbird was considered a good cage bird by early explorers. Bunchgrass grows to about 3 feet and offers cover, nesting sites, and food. The introduced population uses alternative vegetation and debris, since bunchgrass on Pearl and Hermes Reef is uncommon. Because it will not use artificial nestboxes, conservation requires the maintenance of bunchgrass habitat. The two Laysan Finch populations are the only passerines on their islands.

JEOPARDIZED: By introduced plants, rabbits (which had earlier denuded the habitat and led to the extinction of the Laysan Rail [see p. 202], the Laysan Millerbird [see

p. 210], and the Laysan Honeycreeper [see p. 213]), insects transmitting avian diseases, and natural disasters (hurricanes and tidal waves). The accidental introduction of black rats is held responsible for the failure of a population introduced on Midway Island.

LISTING: Listed as **Endangered** in March 1967.

RECOVERY PLANS: Laysan Island has been protected since 1909, when President Theodore Roosevelt created the Hawaiian Islands Reservation. By 1940 the island was designated as a wildlife refuge, and it is now qualified as a Research Natural Area, administered by the U.S. Fish and Wildlife Service, with access permitted only to scientific researchers.

NIHOA FINCH
Telespiza ultima

NESTING: In holes in rocky outcroppings. The Nihoa Finch prefers sparsely vegetated, open habitat.

FOOD: A wide variety of plant seeds and flowers; also bird eggs, carrion, and small invertebrates.

RANGE: The island of Nihoa (northwestern Hawaiian Islands). **WINTER:** Resident. **IN PERIL:** Throughout its limited habitat. As of 1986, about 2,200 birds remained.

NOTES: In 1967 the Nihoa Finch was introduced to Tern Island and French Frigate Shoals as a safeguard against catastrophic weather on Nihoa, but the introductions failed. This bird closely resembles the Laysan Finch.

JEOPARDIZED: By such natural disasters as hurricanes and tidal waves, and by introduced plants, rats, and various insects that transmit avian diseases.

LISTING: Listed as **Endangered** in March 1967.

RECOVERY PLANS: Nihoa has been protected since 1909, when President Theodore Roosevelt created the Hawaiian Islands Reservation. By 1940 the island was designated as a wildlife refuge, and it is now qualified as a Research Natural Area, with access permitted only to scientific researchers. Habitat monitoring to detect the invasion of exotic species is essential.

'O'U
Psittirostra psittacea

NESTING: Now restricted to ohia forests at elevations between 2,500 and 5,000 feet. The 'O'u's nest has not been described.

FOOD: Mostly fruits (lobelia, mountain apple, guava, and, formerly, banana and peach) and flowers, but its main food is probably the fruits of ieie and possibly 'olapa (the 'O'u generally occurred where 'olapa was common). The 'O'u also takes insects (feeding many caterpillars to its young) and nectar, foraging mainly in the forest canopy.

RANGE: Originally the six largest Hawaiian Islands, now restricted to windward slopes and the 'Ola'a region on the island of Hawaii and in Kauai's Alakai Swamp.

WINTER: Resident. **IN PERIL:** Throughout its shrinking range. In the 1980's the population was estimated at 400 birds, with 300 on Hawaii and 100 on Kauai. Since then, there have been very few sightings, and what had been most favorable habitat on Hawaii was covered by a lava flow in 1984.

NOTES: This honeycreeper is one of the largest of its family, and often perches motionless in tall trees above the canopy. It is known to travel in family groups. The 'O'u's habit of moving to lower elevations in search of fruit may have increased its vulnerability to disease-bearing mosquitoes.

JEOPARDIZED: By habitat loss and fragmentation, deforestation (logging and conversion for agriculture and pasture), habitat degradation (by browsing and grazing animals and damage left behind by pigs), the dying off of ohia trees, introduced insects that transmit avian diseases and eliminate native insects that had been food, competition with black rats for food (especially fruit), and volcanic activity.

LISTING: Listed as **Endangered** in March 1967.

RECOVERY PLANS: Habitat protection and restoration, as well as the establishment of a successful captive breeding program, are central to the survival of this bird.

PALILA

Loxioides bailleui

NESTING: Now restricted to the mamane–naio forest ecosystem on the slopes of Mauna Kea above 6,000 feet. The Palila's lichen-lined nest is constructed primarily from twigs and placed on horizontal branches in the crowns of larger trees.

FOOD: Primarily mamane seeds taken from green pods; also insects (especially caterpillars), naio berries, mamane buds, flowers, and young leaves. While foraging on pods, the Palila pins them with its feet, then rips them open with its bill.

RANGE: The island of Hawaii. **WINTER:** Resident. **IN PERIL:** Throughout its shrinking habitat. In 1991 an estimated 3,200 birds remained, although the numbers fluctuate annually.

NOTES: The Palila is the largest member of the Hawaiian honeycreeper family and is one of the most intensively studied. It is most often found where there are higher trees, more crown cover, and an understory rich in native vegetation. Nesting success is greater in years when there is a good mamane pod crop.

JEOPARDIZED: Primarily by forest fragmentation and disturbance. Foraging feral goats, feral sheep, and mouflon sheep take young mamane trees, thus degrading the habitat and inducing a change in the composition of forest species. Weather (aseasonal rains), predation, woodland fires, and disturbance by people are further problems. Good nesting areas are extremely restricted, and a local fire in the wrong place could spell disaster for this species.

LISTING: Listed as **Endangered** in March 1967.

RECOVERY PLANS: In 1988, an intensive study (including radiotelemetry monitoring) was initiated to broaden understanding of the Palila's daily activities, and the U.S. Fish and Wildlife Service is also conducting an intensive study. An effective fire-control program would improve habitat quality. Efforts to control goats, mouflon, and other sheep on Mauna Kea are needed if the mamane trees are to regenerate. In a landmark decision, the U.S. courts determined that mouflon sheep constituted harm to Palila habitat, as defined by the Endangered Species Act. The impact of this lawsuit may be widespread.

MAUI PARROTBILL

Pseudonestor xanthophrys

NESTING: Now restricted to montane ohia and ohia-koa forests between 5,000 and 7,000 feet elevation.

FOOD: Insect larvae and pupae, which the Parrotbill gleans by using its parrotlike bill to rip open dead branches. It prefers foraging on the dead branches of live trees, and hangs upside down, usually remaining in subcanopy trees and bushes in the undergrowth. It also occasionally probes flowers and leaf axils.

RANGE: Maui, now only in Kipahulu Valley and on the northeast slopes of Haleakala outside of the main crater (and largely outside of Haleakala National Park). **WINTER:** Resident. **IN PERIL:** Throughout its shrinking habitat. As of a 1980 estimate, 500 birds remained; the population size is thought not to have changed significantly since then.

NOTES: This chunky, short-tailed honeycreeper is also sometimes referred to by its generic name *Pseudonestor*; the Hawaiians had no name for it that we know of. It is likely to be seen in flocks with the Maui Creeper, and had formerly flocked with the Nukupu'u. Cut by sheer gorges and crossed by ravines, parrotbill habitat is trackless and remote, making censusing both hazardous and difficult.

JEOPARDIZED: Primarily by habitat degradation through the rooting and trampling of feral pigs, which causes persistent erosion and encourages the invasion of introduced plants, and by the loss of native koa forest to logging and pastureland. Losses to introduced cats and introduced insects that transmit avian diseases pose additional potential problems.

LISTING: Listed as **Endangered** in March 1967.

RECOVERY PLANS: Areas above 1,500 feet elevation must be protected from further damage by feral pigs. In 1903 the State Forest Reserve system was established to protect the watershed. It created fenced areas, encouraged the hunting of feral animals, and set up reforestation programs. The system now manages one-third of Hawaii's forests. Efforts to control exotic plants include the fencing of part of the Haleakala Crater district, which has been undertaken by the Nature Conservancy (as manager of the Waikamoi Kamakou preserves) and Haleakala National Park.

NUKUPU'U

Hemignathus lucidus

NESTING: Restricted (on Kauai) to the dense wet forest of the eastern Alakai Swamp (at an elevation of 4,000 feet) and (on Maui) to forest and woodlands of the Kipahulu Valley and the northwestern slope of Haleakala. The Nukupu'u's nest not been described.

FOOD: Wood-boring insects, weevils, insect larvae (especially caterpillars), and spiders gleaned from tree trunks and branches. The Nukupu'u does less excavating than does the 'Akiapola'au. It also feeds (on Kauai) on or among ohia flowers, and (on Maui) takes some nectar from understory flowers.

RANGE: Kauai and Maui, formerly Oahu.

WINTER: Resident. **IN PERIL:** Although not uncommon 100 years ago, the Nukupu'u is now extremely rare and on the verge of extinction. Perhaps a very few individuals of the Kauai subspecies (*H. l. hanapepe*) still exist, but none was seen during surveys in the 1980's. Fewer than 30 individuals of the Maui subspecies (*H. l. affinis*) remain. The subspecies on Oahu (*H. l. lucidus*) is extinct.

NOTES: The Nukupu'u's sickle-shaped upper mandible is twice the length of the lower, and the bird can roll its tongue into a tube to facilitate the sucking of nectar. On Kauai the Nukupu'u may join flocks of creepers; on Maui it joins mixed flocks of Po'o-ulis, creepers, and perhaps Maui Parrotbills. On Maui the Nukupu'u apparently tolerated a narrower range of conditions than does the Maui Parrotbill, possibly explaining why it is so much rarer.

JEOPARDIZED: By deforestation (conversion for agriculture), habitat degradation (trampling, browsing, and rooting by goats and feral pigs, which encourages introduced plants), predation, and probably insect-borne diseases. Managers on Kauai anticipate that the Nukupu'u will be jeopardized by the introduction of the mongoose, which seems increasingly probable.

LISTING: Listed as **Endangered** in March 1967.

RECOVERY PLANS: The Alakai Wilderness Preserve on Kauai protects almost 10,000 acres, including prime Nukupu'u habitat. Another 19,500 acres of forest, most of it now administered by the Hawaii Division of Forestry and Wildlife, has been identified in the Recovery Plan for forest bird populations as crucial habitat. Habitat protection, however, may well be irrelevant to this bird, whose recovery (or indeed existence) on Kauai is very doubtful. The State Forest Reserve system, which protects the watersheds on Maui, created fenced areas, encouraged the hunting of feral animals, and set up reforestation programs. The system now manages one-third of Hawaii's forests. Efforts to control exotic ungulates include the fencing of a portion of the Haleakala Crater district and adjacent lands by the Nature Conservancy (as manager of the Waikamoi Kamakou preserves) and Haleakala National Park. Steep

'AKIAPOLA'AU
Hemignathus munroi

terrain above 1,500 feet must be protected from further erosion of the sort caused by feral pigs, goats, and other ungulates.

NESTING: Now restricted to koa–ohia and mamane–naio forests between about 3,500 and 9,000 feet elevation. The cup nest is made of sticks and surrounded by a sort of "picket fence" of wood fragments and fibers of tree ferns. The 'Akiapola'au usually uses older trees for foraging and nesting.

FOOD: Beetle larvae and other insects gleaned while the bird creeps along branches. It has a distinctive bill: the short, straight woodpecker-like lower mandible chisels bark to expose insects, while the sickle-shaped upper mandible extracts them once exposed. The 'Akiapola'au prefers foraging on koa and other trees that are richer in wood-boring prey.

RANGE: The island of Hawaii. **WINTER:** Resident. **IN PERIL:** Throughout its shrinking habitat. Though the species was relatively abundant 100 years ago, only an estimated 1,500 birds now remain, in four separate populations: Hamakua, with about 900 birds; Kau, with about 500; Mauna Kea, with 50; and Kona, with about 20.

NOTES: This chunky-bodied honeycreeper is little studied but commonly joins mixed-species flocks and is thought to travel in family groups. It can sometimes be located by the tapping noise that it makes on trees. The 'Akiapola'au was sometimes referred to in the early literature as the Hawaii Nukupu'u.

HAWAII CREEPER
Oreomystis mana

JEOPARDIZED: Primarily by the fragmentation and degradation of koa–ohia forest, but the pressures affecting other Hawaiian forest birds, such as habitat degradation by domestic cattle and pigs, logging, fires, and insect-borne diseases, may have affected this one as well.

LISTING: Listed as **Endangered** in March 1967.

RECOVERY PLANS: Management of habitat on the windward sides of Mauna Loa and Mauna Kea (at about 4,500 feet) is central to the 'Akiapola'au's long-term survival. Habitat protection and restoration are the goal, with efforts centered on containing the dying off of koa trees, controlling and preferably freeing the forest of certain introduced animals (mouflon sheep and other grazing animals, introduced predators, and competitors), reestablishing the native plants, and reforesting so as to link populations. In 1985 the Nature Conservancy, the state of Hawaii, and the U.S. Fish and Wildlife Service joined forces to purchase more than 8,000 acres of native forest on the island of Hawaii as the first portion of the proposed Hakalau Forest National Wildlife Refuge on the northwestern slope of Mauna Kea. This refuge now totals 33,000 acres.

NESTING: Now restricted to wet montane mixed koa–ohia forests, usually above 3,500 feet elevation, that support more koa trees and fewer tree ferns than is usual. Most nesting apparently occurs within ungrazed, unlogged, closed-canopy koa–ohia forest. The first complete nest, located in 1983, was a cup of mosses, liverworts, tree ferns, fiber, and hair, and had been placed beneath sheltering foliage in the fork of an ohia tree. The bird also uses cavities.

FOOD: Adult insects and larvae, especially those of beetles, which the Hawaii Creeper usually gleans from well-developed tree bark while foraging like a nuthatch, but the bird may also hunt in foliage. It takes spiders, worms, snails, and other invertebrates and may also take nectar.

RANGE: The island of Hawaii. **WINTER:** Resident. **IN PERIL:** Throughout its shrinking habitat. The Hawaii Creeper was common in the vicinity of Kilauea Crater 100 years ago, but not any more. As of a 1986 estimate, some 12,500 birds remain, in four separate populations. About 2,100 birds are found in Kau, 10,000 are estimated in Hamakua, and two populations, one with 300 birds and one with 75, persist in Kona.

NOTES: This honeycreeper may join flocks, and mixed-species post-breeding flocks may be large. It is thought to travel in family groups. Very little is known of its breeding biology, but courtship feeding has been recorded.

JEOPARDIZED: By deforestation (logging

of prime koa–ohia forest and conversion for agriculture, pasture, and urban uses), habitat degradation by feral pigs, mouflon sheep, and domestic stock (including cattle), which leads to the encroachment of non-native plants (such as the banana poka), the death of ohia trees, introduced insects that transmit avian pox and avian malaria, and, possibly, competition with the insectivorous Japanese White-eye. Alteration of the native forest habitat will likely have a significant effect on this bark-foraging specialist.

LISTING: Listed as **Endangered** in September 1975.

RECOVERY PLANS: The goal is the preservation and protection of forest habitat, with efforts centered on the recovery of the understory, freeing the forest of rooting pigs and other introduced herbivores, introduced competitors, and carriers of avian diseases, and reestablishing native plants.

OAHU CREEPER, or 'ALAUAHIO

Paroreomyza maculata

NESTING: In ohia forest in the mountains north of Honolulu.

FOOD: Insects gleaned from leaves and branches. Although the Oahu Creeper's habits are poorly understood, the species is known sometimes to hunt prey by creeping over tree bark. There are some reports of individuals foraging on koa sap.

RANGE: Oahu. **WINTER:** Resident. **IN PERIL:** The Oahu Creeper, if still extant, is limited to one habitat; the last sighting was in 1985.

NOTES: Some ornithologists think the Oahu Creeper is conspecific with the Maui Creeper. The last sighting was of a female and a juvenile, suggesting that, like other members of the genus *Paroreomyza*, the Oahu Creeper may travel in family groups.

JEOPARDIZED: Apparently by deforestation, habitat degradation, and introduced insects that transmit avian diseases.

LISTING: Listed as **Endangered** in October 1970.

RECOVERY PLANS: This little-understood creeper is so rare that its survival is very much in doubt.

MOLOKAI CREEPER, or KAKAWAHIE

Paroreomyza flammea

'AKOHEKOHE, or CRESTED HONEYCREEPER

Palmeria dolei

NESTING: Now restricted to ohia forests with a dense understory of mosses, vines, and tree ferns, above 4,000 feet elevation.

FOOD: Insects and other invertebrates; the Molokai Creeper typically hangs upside down like a nuthatch to extract prey from trunks and large branches.

RANGE: Molokai. **WINTER:** Resident.

IN PERIL: Though the species was common and widely distributed 100 years ago, the bird was last seen in 1963, on the Ohialele Plateau.

NOTES: This little-studied bird is larger than the other Hawaiian creepers and the only one that is dichromic: males are scarlet and females are mostly brown. Its Hawaiian name, Kakawahie, means "woodchopping."

JEOPARDIZED: By deforestation (large tracts were cleared for agriculture) and by habitat degradation (by the rooting of pigs and the spread of non-native plants).

LISTING: Listed as **Endangered** in October 1970. The Molokai Creeper remains listed, even though researchers doubt its continued existence.

RECOVERY PLANS: Habitat preservation is central. In 1903 the State Forest Reserve system was established to protect watersheds. It also created fenced areas, encouraged the hunting of feral animals, and set up reforestation programs. The system now manages one-third of Hawaii's forests, including those on Molokai, although the Nature Conservancy is managing a major part of the habitat critical to this bird.

NESTING: Now restricted mostly to wet ohia forests on the windward slope of Haleakala at elevations between about 4,500 and 7,000 feet. No nests have been described.

FOOD: Mostly nectar, primarily of the ohia flower; also nectar from other flowers, as well as some insects found in foliage and, when nectar supplies are low, fruit.

RANGE: Maui; formerly also Molokai.

WINTER: Resident. **IN PERIL:** Throughout its shrinking habitat, although the population appears to be more secure than previously assumed. Locally abundant 100 years ago, but as of 1984 an estimated 3,800 birds remained. The Molokai population is almost certainly extinct.

NOTES: When foraging in the crown of flowering trees, the 'Akohekohe tends to dominate other species, including the Iiwi and Apapane.

JEOPARDIZED: By habitat loss to ranching, habitat degradation (from the browsing and rooting of feral goats, pigs, and axis deer, which leads to the encroachment of non-native plants), and possibly introduced insects that transmit diseases, especially avian pox and avian malaria.

LISTING: Listed as **Endangered** in March 1967.

RECOVERY PLANS: In 1903 the State Forest Reserve system was established to protect watersheds. It also created fenced areas, encouraged the hunting of feral animals, and set up reforestation programs. The system now manages one-third of Hawaii's forests. Efforts to control exotic plants include the fencing of a portion of the Haleakala Crater district by the Nature Conservancy (as manager of the Waikamoi Kamakou preserves) and Haleakala National Park. 'Akohekohes, however, occur outside the fence on state land in the Upper Hanaui and Kipaula areas; the latter is part of Haleakala National Park. Although the population is relatively large and widely distributed, forest habitat must be protected from pigs (especially) and goats. The 'Akohekohe's distribution is similar to that of the Maui Parrotbill, but lies more to the west.

PO'O-ULI

Melamprosops phaeosoma

NESTING: In closed-canopy, wet ohia forests on the northeast slope of Haleakala between 5,000 and 7,000 feet elevation. The birds are found concentrated in areas providing a dense shrub understory. The Po'o-uli places its bowl-shaped nest, constructed from sticks, lichen, moss, and grass, in ohia trees.

FOOD: Mostly snails and beetles; also a variety of adult insects and larvae gleaned mostly from ohia, olapa, ohelo, and kana-woa while probing under moss, lichens, and bark. Foraging behavior also includes tearing apart bark, epiphytes, mosses, and lichens.

RANGE: Maui. **WINTER:** Resident. **IN PERIL:** The Po'o-uli is on the verge of extinction. The population (where studied) declined by 90 percent from 1975 to 1985 (as pig activity increased by some 475 percent). Its single population is estimated at only 140 birds.

NOTES: This little-studied, chunky, short-tailed honeycreeper was discovered only in 1973. It is thought to travel in small family groups and form mixed-species flocks with Maui Creepers. The Po'o-uli has also been referred to as the Black-faced Honeycreeper.

JEOPARDIZED: By damage to forest understory (especially of prime old-growth ohia forest); by the browsing and rooting of feral goats, axis deer, and especially pigs, which encourages the spread of introduced plants and leads to changes in the mix of forest species; by predation by black and Polynesian rats, cats, and Indian mongooses; and, possibly, by the effects of a reduced gene pool. Feral pigs may reduce the availability of the snails eaten by the Po'o-uli by destroying habitat critical to the life cycle of the invertebrate.

LISTING: Listed as **Endangered** in September 1975.

RECOVERY PLANS: In 1903 the State Forest Reserve system was established to protect habitat, control feral animals, and eliminate introduced plant species. The system now manages one-third of Hawaii's forests. Critical habitat requires fencing (now being undertaken) and protection from pigs, but even with these safeguards, a captive breeding program may be required. Restoration of the native ecosystem will minimize competition with introduced birds.

THREATENED AND ENDANGERED HAWAIIAN SUBSPECIES

All that has been said about Threatened and Endangered Hawaiian species (see p. 62) is true also of Hawaii's six Endangered subspecies—except of course that a subspecies heading toward extinction (or already extinct) does not carry the same biological significance as does the loss of an entire species.

All six of the subspecies that follow are listed by the U.S. Fish and Wildlife Service as Endangered, none as Threatened.

DARK-RUMPED PETREL, or 'UA'U

Pterodroma phaeopygia sandwichensis

NESTING: In colonies on high barren mountain slopes with large rock outcrops, talus slopes, or lava flows. The bird enters or exits its burrow under the cover of night, and uses it year after year. Eggs may also be laid in rock crevices.

FOOD: Fish, squid, crustaceans, and plankton. The species feeds its young by regurgitation.

RANGE: Breeds primarily on Maui, but also on Kauai, Lanai, the island of Hawaii, perhaps on Molokai, and formerly on Oahu. **WINTER:** Disperses widely over the central and eastern tropical Pacific Ocean. **IN PERIL:** Throughout its range. As of a 1988 estimate, about 860 breeding adults remained. The Oahu population is already extinct.

NOTES: This subspecies may also be referred to as the Hawaiian Petrel. Another subspecies of the Dark-rumped Petrel nests on the Galapagos Islands, where it, too, is in grave trouble.

JEOPARDIZED: Primarily by predation from mongooses, black rats, and, especially at elevations above 3,000 feet, cats. Historically, the Hawaiians hunted the Dark-rumped Petrel for food.

LISTING: Listed as **Endangered** in March 1967.

RECOVERY PLANS: Predator-control measures, including traps and poison, were established in 1966. More recently, efforts have been restricted to the use of traps, though research has now found a poison that is effective in controlling mongooses.

HAWAIIAN GALLINULE (MOORHEN), or 'ALAE 'ULA

Gallinula chloropus sandvicensis

HAWAIIAN COOT,
or 'ALAE KE'OKE'O

Fulica americana alai

NESTING: In shallow freshwater wetlands in areas of dense emergent vegetation. The Hawaiian Gallinule often builds its nest over matted reeds.

FOOD: Mollusks, aquatic insects, seeds, algae, and other plant matter.

RANGE: Kauai, Oahu, and Molokai; formerly also Maui and Hawaii. **WINTER:** Resident. **IN PERIL:** Throughout its shrinking range. More than 750 birds remain.

NOTES: This is a reclusive, nonmigratory subspecies of the Common Moorhen of North America and Eurasia. Because of its secretive habits, it is difficult to census, though not as difficult as are Hawaiian forest birds.

JEOPARDIZED: By the loss of wetland habitat (both the draining of natural coastal plains for development and the conversion of flooded taro fields to dry sugar cane), habitat degradation (by the encroachment of introduced plants), and predation by introduced mongooses and cats.

LISTING: Listed as **Endangered** in March 1967.

RECOVERY PLANS: In 1972 a portion of Kauai's Hanalei Valley became the first national waterbird refuge in Hawaii. Four more wetlands have since been set aside, allowing gallinule populations to expand to their present sizes.

NESTING: In freshwater or brackish wetlands, including ponds, reservoirs, and irrigation ditches, below 700 feet. The bird nests in openings among marsh vegetation, where it anchors its nest to emergent plants.

FOOD: Seeds and leaves of aquatic plants, tadpoles, small fish, snails, crustaceans, and insects.

RANGE: Breeds on all the main Hawaiian Islands except Lanai. **WINTER:** Resident, except for occasional individuals that wander to the northwestern islands. **IN PERIL:** Throughout its range. A 1986 estimate put the total population at about 1,800 birds, but estimates vary, and some suggest a range from 2,000 to 4,500 individuals.

NOTES: This loud, fiercely territorial wetland bird is a subspecies of the American Coot, not of the widely distributed Eurasian species. Although capable of long flight, Hawaiian Coots rarely fly.

JEOPARDIZED: By habitat loss (including natural and cultivated wetlands, especially by conversion to dry sugar cane acreage) and habitat degradation (by encroachment of introduced plants).

LISTING: **Endangered**, October 1970.

RECOVERY PLANS: In the late 1800's, endemic wetland birds were protected so as to control the army worm, an agricultural pest. But the first statewide sanctuary to protect these species was not established until 1952. In 1972, part of Kauai's Hanalei Valley became a national waterbird refuge. Four more wetlands have since been set aside, and the coots have stabilized.

HAWAIIAN STILT, or AE'O

Himantopus mexicanus knudseni

MAUI 'AKEPA, or 'AKEPEU'IE

Loxops coccineus ochraeceus

NESTING: In loosely defined colonies around fresh or brackish ponds, marshlands, or mudflats. The Hawaiian Stilt prefers small, sparsely vegetated islets in shallow ponds but will settle for dry, barren areas near shallow water, or areas with artificial floating structures, for its stone-, twig-, and debris-lined scrape.

FOOD: A variety of freshwater or tidal aquatic organisms, including small fish, crabs, insects, and worms.

RANGE: All main Hawaiian Islands, except Lanai. **WINTER:** Resident. **IN PERIL:** Everywhere, although stable, with an estimated 1,800 birds remaining (1988).

NOTES: This opportunistic long-legged wader probably originated from Black-necked Stilts that colonized Hawaii from North America many centuries ago.

JEOPARDIZED: By the loss of wetlands (draining for dry agriculture and especially for development associated with tourism), wetland degradation (encroachment by introduced plants), and predation.

LISTING: Endangered, October 1970.

RECOVERY PLANS: Center on habitat restoration and preservation. Maui's first state sanctuaries were established at Kanaha Pond and Kealia Pond. In 1972 a portion of Kauai's Hanalei Valley became a national waterbird refuge. Four additional refuges have allowed stilt populations to reach their present sizes. When the total population stabilizes at 2,000 for three years, the USFWS will consider reclassifying the Hawaiian Stilt as **Threatened.**

NESTING: Now restricted to upland closed-canopy mixed ohia–koa forests, primarily on the windward slopes of Haleakala. Like the Hawaii 'Akepa, the Maui 'Akepa apparently places its woven cup nest in natural cavities of ohia or koa trees.

FOOD: Insects (especially caterpillars), spiders (primarily gleaned from ohia leaves or koa foliage), and occasional nectar from ohia and other flowers of the forest canopy. The 'Akepa's jaw musculature and unusual bill allow the bird to capture insects by first twisting apart buds, galls, small green seed pods, and leaf clusters, then probing for the insects.

RANGE: Maui. **WINTER:** Resident. **IN PERIL:** Throughout its limited habitat. Locally abundant on eastern Maui 100 years ago, the Maui 'Akepa has been considered very rare and local ever since, and as of 1984 an estimated 230 birds remained.

NOTES: The 'akepa found on Kauai differs markedly from the other three island populations of 'akepa in its morphology, behavior, and ecology, and it is now viewed as a distinct species (*Loxops caeruleirostris*, the Akekee). The 'akepas of Maui, Hawaii, and Oahu are each regarded currently as distinct subspecies of one species (*Loxops coccineus*) that may eventually warrant status as three separate species. The Oahu population appears to be extinct. The small, finchlike Maui 'Akepa often forms small flocks that dwell within the canopy. It is considered among the three most threatened forest birds on Maui.

JEOPARDIZED: Probably by the same general pressures faced by other native forest birds on Maui: deforestation (from logging and conversion to pasture); forest degradation (from grazing and browsing and rooting by feral pigs, which encourages the spread of introduced exotic plants); the death of ohia trees; predation; introduced insects that transmit disease (including avian pox and avian malaria); and depletion of the native insects previously taken as food by the birds. But the precise factors responsible for the Maui 'Akepa's rarity are unknown.

LISTING: Listed as **Endangered** in October 1970.

RECOVERY PLANS: The goal is to preserve and protect forest habitat (especially from pigs, goats, and ungulates), with efforts centered on preserving the koa–ohia forest. If protected, the current habitat of the Maui 'Akepa is sufficiently large to sustain its population, but if it degrades, captive breeding may become necessary.

HAWAII 'AKEPA, or 'AKEPEU'IE

Loxops coccineus coccineus

NESTING: Most often in upper-elevation mixed ohia–koa forests on windward slopes above 4,500 feet elevation. The bird places its woven cup nest in a cavity high in an ohia or koa tree. Mature trees and snags may be essential. The moss nest is lined with strips of bark and fine grass.

FOOD: Insects (especially caterpillars), spiders, and occasional nectar from ohia and other flowers of the forest canopy. The 'Akepa's jaw musculature and asymmetric bill allow the bird to capture insects by first twisting apart buds, galls, small green seed pods, and leaf clusters, then probing for the insects.

RANGE: On the windward slopes of Mauna Loa and Mauna Kea, on the island of Hawaii. **WINTER:** Resident. **IN PERIL:** Throughout its limited habitat. As of 1984, an estimated 14,000 birds remained, in three widely separated populations, of which one is found in the Hakalau Forest National Wildlife Refuge's koa and ohia rainforest on the northwestern slope of Mauna Kea.

NOTES: The 'akepa found on Kauai differs markedly from the other three island populations of 'akepa in its morphology, behavior, and ecology, and it is now viewed as a distinct species (*Loxops caeruleirostris*, the Akekee). The 'akepas of Maui, Hawaii, and Oahu are each regarded currently as distinct subspecies of one species (*Loxops coccineus*) that may eventually warrant status as three separate species. The Oahu population appears to be extinct. The small, finchlike Hawaii 'Akepa often moves in small flocks, usually remaining in the canopy.

JEOPARDIZED: By deforestation (from logging and conversion to pasture), forest degradation (from grazing and browsing by mouflon sheep and especially domestic stock and from rooting by feral pigs, which encourages the spread of introduced plants), the death of ohia trees, predation, and introduced insects that transmit disease (including avian pox and avian malaria) and deplete the native insects previously eaten by the birds.

LISTING: Listed as **Endangered** in October 1970.

RECOVERY PLANS: The goal is to preserve and protect forest habitat, with efforts centered on preserving the koa–ohia forest, especially above 4,500 feet elevation, where degradation is severe, and to reestablish the native ecosystem, which will also minimize competition with introduced birds.

Of the four Endangered birds that breed only in Puerto Rico (one of the four is a subspecies), two require forest and two are habitat generalists. The two forest birds became jeopardized primarily by past deforestation and collection. The habitat generalists are subject to habitat loss, nest parasitism by Shiny Cowbirds (see p. 220), predation by animals imported into Puerto Rico, nest-hole competitors, human encroachment, nesting disturbance, and unregulated hunting. Of the four birds, one has a wild population in excess of 1,000, two have populations between 100 and 1,000 individuals, and one has fewer than 100 individuals. One of the four, the Puerto Rican Plain Pigeon, is an endemic subspecies of a more widely distributed bird.

Puerto Rico is also home to the Least Tern (which is Endangered) and the Roseate Tern. Both species inhabit inshore areas, bays, and flats, but neither bird is endemic to the island.

An additional seven birds that breed in Puerto Rico are candidates for federal listing. All seven are Category 2 candidates (see p. 102). They include the West Indian Whistling-duck, Lesser White-cheeked Pintail, West Indian Ruddy Duck, Puerto Rican Broad-winged Hawk, Virgin Islands Screech-owl, Caribbean Coot, and the Elfin Woods Warbler. (The Southeastern Snowy Plover, which breeds on the U.S. mainland, also breeds in Puerto Rico.) According to the U.S. Fish and Wildlife Service's listing priority system, Category 2 candidates are those for which the Service has information indicating the possible appropriateness of listing, but for which further information is still needed. The Puerto Rican Sharp-shinned Hawk was formerly listed, but as of 1990 it is classified in Category 3C (candidates found to be more abundant or widespread than previously believed, or not subject to the threats that place the continued existence of the bird at risk).

PUERTO RICAN PARROT, or COTORRA DE PUERTO RICO

Amazona vittata

NESTING: Now restricted to deep, largely undisturbed, mature forests in which there are trees (such as the palo colorado, tabonuco, larel sabino, and nuez moscada) sufficiently large in diameter to accommodate the parrots' nesting cavities.

FOOD: Fruit, seeds, and leaves.

RANGE: Puerto Rico. **WINTER:** Resident. **IN PERIL:** Abundant when Columbus landed in 1493, this parrot has been on the verge of extinction for 20 years. It once also inhabited the neighboring islands of Culebra, Vieques, and Mona, but by 1940 it was limited to the Luquillo Mountains of eastern Puerto Rico. By 1954 about 200 individuals remained, by 1966 there were about 70, and in 1975 the wild population bottomed out at 13. By 1989 there had been modest improvement: some 100 birds remained (about 47, including four breeding pairs, in the wild; and 53 in captivity). A census taken after Hurricane Hugo initially showed losses of 50 percent in the wild population; subsequent counts revealed that all breeding pairs in the wild had survived and a new pair had been established; the captive flock was also spared.

JEOPARDIZED: By deforestation (the parrot's current habitat is wetter than its originally preferred one, and wet cavities reduced nesting success), high mortality, low reproduction rate, collectors (stealing birds from their nests, and felling nest trees in the process), shooting (for sport and in viewing the bird as an agricultural pest), and severe weather. Pearly-eyed Thrashers compete for nest sites and prey on the eggs and young of the parrots. Red-tailed Hawks and black rats also rob nests. The Puerto Rican Parrot's decline began with the arrival of the Europeans in the 1500's and the loss of fruit-bearing trees and cavity-rich habitat. Palo colorado trees, the preferred nesting sites, were selectively harvested (especially between 1945 and 1950) for charcoal and to improve growth in stands of other timber species.

LISTING: Listed as **Endangered** in March 1967.

RECOVERY PLANS: By 1912, 80 percent of Puerto Rico had been deforested, and less than 1 percent of the original virgin forest remained. In 1946, about 28,000 acres (the Caribbean National Forest) in the Luquillo Mountains was declared a wildlife refuge, and today, 40 percent of the island is wooded, including 40,000 acres in the Luquillo Mountains, the current home of the parrot. A captive breeding population of more than 50 birds produced six chicks in 1989, and researchers removed eggs from two of the four active wild nests to be reared in incubators. Plans to establish a new population in the Rio Abajo forest (on the island's western end) are under way, but concern over the small number of new breeders and the security of the research facilities continues. Monitoring, funding, and volunteers are critical to protecting the populations from human interference, facilitating breeding (by freeing natural cavities of water, providing artificial cavities, reducing competition with Pearly-eyed Thrashers and bees, treating warble-fly infestations, and providing protection from predators), building up the captive breeding stock and reintroducing captives into the wild, and establishing multiple populations so as to guard against catastrophic loss from hurricane, fire, or disease.

PUERTO RICAN NIGHTJAR, or GUABAIRO PEQUEÑO DE PUERTO RICO

Caprimulgus noctitherus

NESTING: Now restricted to coastal plains and lowland serpentine and limestone slopes supporting dry, mixed, deciduous–evergreen forests with a closed canopy, where the nightjar lays its eggs on leaf litter sheltered by bushes.

FOOD: Flying insects.

RANGE: Puerto Rico. **WINTER:** Resident. **IN PERIL:** Throughout its shrinking habitat. It had been thought extinct after no birds were sighted for over 70 years. The Guanica population was discovered in 1961, and by 1973 its population was estimated at 450 to 500 pairs. Today an estimated 1,100 birds, restricted to the southwestern portion of the island, remain in three areas: in the Guanica State Forest, 800; in the Susa State Forest, 200; and in the Guayanilla Hills, 100. Formerly probably found throughout Puerto Rico's limestone forests, and now limited to 3 percent of its original range.

NOTES: This robin-sized nocturnal bird is thought by some to be a race of the mainland Whip-poor-will, although its vocalizations are quite different.

JEOPARDIZED: By introduced predators (especially mongooses, which were introduced in 1877), deforestation, and other disturbances by humans. The Guayanilla population is downwind from a petrochemical refinery, and concern over the effects of its effluents on insect populations continues. Dry-forest irrigation has been introduced, bringing with it the threat of mammalian predators. Critical habitat has not been protected, and urban sprawl continues to consume nightjar habitat.

LISTING: Listed as **Endangered** in June 1973.

RECOVERY PLANS: The Guanica State Forest is one of UNESCO's Biosphere Reserves, the international network of areas protected because of their ecological importance. Nightjar populations located within the state forests are provided protection, and private landowners should be urged to protect habitat under their control. When the Guanica population reaches 1,200, the Susa population 400, and the Guayanilla Hills population 800, and when long-term habitat protection has been provided, the U.S. Fish and Wildlife Service will consider the species for a change in status.

YELLOW-SHOULDERED BLACKBIRD, or MARIQUITA

Agelaius xanthomus

NESTING: In various wooded and wetland habitats, including mangroves, tree-bordered lowland pastures, coconut and royal palm plantations, suburbs, cactus scrub, and coastal cliffs. The Yellow-shouldered Blackbird usually builds an open nest, but may place its nest in a cavity.

FOOD: Primarily insects; also some plant material, including cactus fruit.

RANGE: Puerto Rico. **WINTER:** Resident. **IN PERIL:** Throughout its limited range. In 1975 the population in Boqueron Forest was estimated at 250 pairs, and that at Roosevelt Roads Naval Station, about 200 birds; by 1982 the former declined by about 80 percent, to no more than 50 pairs, and in 1983 the latter had declined by more than 60 percent, to about 75 birds. In contrast, 200 birds were found on Mona Island in 1975; and 220 in 1982. The main population (about 250 individuals) was not in the path of Hurricane Hugo. All in all, an estimated 720 birds remain, restricted to the southwestern and northeastern extremities of Puerto Rico, including Mona Island.

NOTES: This blackbird, also called Capitán, is something of a habitat generalist. Shiny Cowbirds, although on Mona Island in small numbers, are not yet impacting that population, and may not, because of the "reluctance" of female cowbirds to enter the cliff-side cavities where the blackbirds nest.

JEOPARDIZED: By habitat destruction (especially the loss of flooded fields to dry sugar cane), housing developments, and nest parasitism by Shiny Cowbirds (see p. 220), but especially by nest predation by introduced rats and mongooses, disease, and nest-site competition from Pearly-eyed Thrashers.

LISTING: Listed as **Endangered** in November 1976.

RECOVERY PLANS: The Department of Natural Resources administers the Mona Island Refuge, whose blackbird population is offered complete protection. The Roosevelt Roads Naval Station has been zoned to reduce disturbance to the blackbirds. The Cabo Rojo National Wildlife Refuge Youth Conservation Corps has built nest boxes and cowbird traps; since 1977, almost 100 nest boxes have been placed in the Boqueron State Forest. Provision of young mangroves, the blackbird's preferred nesting habitat, should be included in management plans, and studies of winter ecology are needed. Initiation of a captive breeding program has been recommended.

Just one Puerto Rican bird, an Endangered pigeon, is federally listed at the subspecies level. The Plain Pigeon as a whole is widespread but rare throughout much of the Greater Antilles. The Endangered subspecies is endemic to Puerto Rico, and although recovery efforts are having some success, it may be headed for extinction.

PUERTO RICAN PLAIN PIGEON, or PALOMA SABANERA

Columba inornata wetmorei

NESTING: Formerly, the Puerto Rican Plain Pigeon used a wide variety of habitats; today it is found most often in second-growth woodlots of native and introduced trees, but it is not restricted to any particular habitat.

FOOD: A wide variety of plant seeds and fruits, including those of the royal palm, mountain immortelle, West Indies trema, and white pickle.

RANGE: Puerto Rico. **WINTER:** Resident. **IN PERIL:** Throughout its limited range. By the mid-1930's this pigeon was on the verge of extinction. In 1963 it was discovered at Cidra in east-central Puerto Rico, and that remains its largest population. As of a 1988 estimate, 150 birds remained in the wild. A census taken after Hurricane Hugo indicated a total of 200 birds, but their main breeding habitat had been damaged. The captive flock, numbering 125 individuals, was not harmed in the storm, but an epizootic disease, infecting 90 birds, struck a few weeks after the hurricane.

NOTES: The species as a whole is now rare but surviving everywhere, in reduced numbers, except on Hispaniola, where it is locally common. (Whether or not the Puerto Rican Plain Pigeon deserves subspecific status is controversial.)

JEOPARDIZED: By deforestation, nesting disturbance, introduced rats, and unregulated hunting.

LISTING: Listed as **Endangered** in October 1970.

RECOVERY PLANS: Because its nesting sites are so frequently disturbed, a captive breeding program for the Puerto Rican Plain Pigeon was established in 1983, and by 1988 almost 50 young had been fledged. The release of these captive-bred pigeons at the Rio Abajo Commonwealth Forest in the island's interior will establish a second population. Nonetheless, with a low reproductive rate, an aging population, and inexorable human encroachment into the Cidra habitat, it may be too late to save this subspecies. Successful reintroductions into safer sites are clearly critical to its survival. By 1985, critical habitat had not been designated, although the Cidra habitat had been closed to hunting since 1978. This does not necessarily solve the problem: the bird is so easy to take that it is known as Paloma boba (fool pigeon).

CANDIDATES FOR FEDERAL LISTING AS OF 1990

The U.S. Fish and Wildlife Service has 3,650 "candidate" plant and animal species awaiting disposition and possible placement on its official list of Threatened and Endangered species. Candidates include about 2,180 plants and 1,470 animals (52 of them birds). Among the animals, 75 (two of them birds) merit Category 1.

There is a paucity of readily accessible information on the threats placing candidate species at risk. One of the few well-known exceptions is the Southwestern Willow Flycatcher, which has been extirpated from many areas and now is rarer than some birds already awarded federal protection. Its plight has been repeatedly reported in the scientific literature, but damage to its riparian habitat continues and its populations are declining. Similarly, reports on the plight of Belding's Savannah Sparrow have been published as developers in southern California work to gain access to its highly valued upper-marsh habitat. In contrast, it is difficult to find any information on the Cactus Ferruginous Pygmy-owl or the Northern Gray Hawk, which are also candidates from the Southwest.

Clearly, a concise overview of candidates, their populations and distribution, their habitat constraints, the factors affecting their declines, and their relationships to similar or related birds would be of great value. But sufficient information does not exist. In the interim, we include the following table of the current candidates for federal listing in the U.S. (the Canadian Wildlife Service does not maintain a formal list of candidates). (Note that a page number following a bird's name refers either to the text account for that bird or to the account of a related bird.)

CATEGORY 1 BIRDS ON THE CONTINENT
(those with substantial information to support the biological appropriateness of listing, topping the list of candidates)

California Black Rail *Laterallus jamaicensis coturniculus*	Arizona, California, and Mexico	111
Appalachian Bewick's Wren *Thryomanes bewickii altus*	from Maryland south through Georgia; from western Pennsylvania and Ohio south through Alabama; and Canada	114

CATEGORY 2 BIRDS ON THE CONTINENT
(those that are possibly appropriate additions to the list, but require further examination)

Reddish Egret *Egretta rufescens*	Florida, Texas, Mexico, and West Indies; and a visitor along the Gulf states from Alabama through Louisiana and in California	143
White-faced Ibis *Plegadis chihi*	from Colorado, Oklahoma, and Texas west to the Pacific, and in Oregon; and a visitor in Idaho, Wyoming, and Mexico	
Fulvous Whistling-duck (sw U.S. population) *Dendrocygna bicolor*	Arizona and California, and a visitor in Mexico	145
Ferruginous Hawk *Buteo regalis*	from the Dakotas south to Texas and west to the Pacific (except Arizona and California); Canada; and a visitor in Arizona, California, and Mexico	151
Apache Northern Goshawk *Accipiter gentilis apache*	New Mexico, Arizona, and Mexico	
Northern Gray Hawk *Buteo nitidus maximus*	from Texas west through Arizona, and Mexico	
Southeastern American Kestrel *Falco sparverius paulus*	from Georgia and Florida west along the Gulf states through Louisiana	
Western Sage Grouse *Centrocercus urophasianus phaios*	Washington, Oregon, and Canada	155
Columbian Sharp-tailed Grouse *Tympanuchus phasianellus columbianus*	from Montana south through Colorado and west to the Pacific, and Canada	154
Mangrove Clapper Rail *Rallus longirostris insularum*	Florida	38
Western Snowy Plover *Charadrius alexandrinus nivosus*	from Kansas south through Texas, and west to the Pacific (except Arizona); Washington and Oregon; and a visitor in Arizona and Mexico	148
Southeastern Snowy Plover *Charadrius alexandrinus tenuirostris*	from Florida west across the Gulf states through Louisiana; Puerto Rico and the Greater Antilles	148
Mountain Plover *Charadrius montanus*	from the Dakotas south through Texas, and from Montana south through New Mexico; a visitor in Utah and Arizona west to the Pacific; Mexico	117
Long-billed Curlew *Numenius americanus*	Wisconsin and Iowa, and from the Dakotas south through Texas and west to the Pacific (except in Arizona); Canada; and a visitor in Louisiana, Minnesota, Arizona, and Mexico	149
Bristle-thighed Curlew *Numenius tahitiensis*	Alaska, and a visitor in Hawaii and several central Pacific islands	112
Elegant Tern *Sterna elegans*	California and Mexico	

SPECIES OR SUBSPECIES	HISTORIC RANGE	PAGE
Marbled Murrelet *Brachyramphus marmoratus*	Alaska and Canada and across north Pacific rim to Japan; and from Washington south through California	113
White-crowned Pigeon *Columba leucocephala*	Florida, West Indies, and Central America	
Cactus Ferruginous Pygmy-owl *Glaucidium brasiliarum cactorum*	Texas, Arizona, and Mexico	
Spotted Owl *Strix occidentalis*	Texas, Colorado, and from New Mexico west to the Pacific (except Nevada); Washington and Oregon; and Mexico (Note: the Northern Spotted Owl, found in Washington, Oregon, and California, was listed as Threatened in 1990.)	53
Southwestern Willow Flycatcher *Empidonax traillii extimus*	New Mexico, Arizona, California, and Mexico	162
California Gnatcatcher *Polioptila californica* (formerly Coastal Black-tailed Gnatcatcher, *P. melanura californica*)	California and Mexico	191
Migrant Loggerhead Shrike *Lanius ludovicianus migrans*	south from Maine through North Carolina and west to the Mississippi; from Minnesota south through Arkansas; and from Nebraska south through Texas; Canada; and a visitor from South Carolina south through Florida and west across the Gulf States through Louisiana	136
Tropical Parula (Olive-backed Warbler) *Parula pitiayumi nigrilora*	Texas and Mexico	
Stoddard's Yellow-throated Warbler *Dendroica dominica stoddardi*	Florida and Alabama	
Brownsville Common Yellowthroat *Geothlypis trichas insperata*	Texas and Mexico	
Saltmarsh Common Yellowthroat *Geothlypis trichas sinuosa*	California	
Texas (Sennett's) Olive Sparrow *Arremonops rufivirgatus rufivirgatus*	Texas and Mexico	
Bachman's Sparrow *Aimophila aestivalis*	Pennsylvania and Maryland south through Florida and west to the Mississippi (south of Iowa); Oklahoma and Texas	139
Texas Botteri's Sparrow *Aimophila botterii texana*	Texas and Mexico	
Belding's Savannah Sparrow *Passerculus sandwichensis beldingi*	California and Mexico	
Wakulla Seaside Sparrow *Ammodramus maritimus junicola*	Florida	60
Smyrna Seaside Sparrow *Ammodramus maritimus pelonota*	Florida	60
Amak Song Sparrow *Melospiza melodia amaka*	Alaska	200
Suisun Song Sparrow *Melospiza melodia maxillaris*	California	200

SPECIES OR SUBSPECIES	HISTORIC RANGE	PAGE
San Pablo Song Sparrow *Melospiza melodia samuelis*	California	200
Alameda (South Bay) Song Sparrow *Melospiza melodia pusillula*	California	200
Tricolored Blackbird *Agelaius tricolor*	Oregon, California, and Mexico	
Audubon's Oriole *Icterus graduacauda audubonii*	Texas and Mexico	
Mexican Hooded Oriole *Icterus cucullatus cucullatus*	Texas and Mexico	
Sennett's Hooded Oriole *Icterus cucullatus sennettii*	Texas and Mexico	

CATEGORY 2 BIRDS IN HAWAII

Bishop's O'o *Moho bishopi*	Hawaii	115

CATEGORY 2 BIRDS IN PUERTO RICO

West Indian Whistling-duck *Dendrocygna arborea*	Puerto Rico, Virgin Islands, West Indies	
Lesser White-cheeked Pintail *Anas bahamensis bahamensis*	Puerto Rico, Virgin Islands, West Indies, and South America	
West Indian Ruddy Duck *Oxyura jamaicensis jamaicensis*	Puerto Rico, Virgin Islands, and West Indies	
Puerto Rican Broad-winged Hawk *Buteo platypterus brunnescens*	Puerto Rico	
Virgin Islands Screech-owl *Otus nudipes newtoni*	Puerto Rico and Virgin Islands	
Southeastern Snowy Plover (see above)		
Caribbean Coot *Fulica caribaea*	Puerto Rico, Virgin Islands, and West Indies; and a vagrant in southern Florida	
Elfin Woods Warbler *Dendroica angelae*	Puerto Rico	

CATEGORY 3 BIRDS

(those removed from the active list either because they (A) are thought to be extinct, (B) were once thought to be distinct species or subspecies but have subsequently been reclassified, or (C) are found to be notably more abundant than previously thought)

CATEGORY 3A

Santa Barbara Song Sparrow *Melospiza melodia graminea*	California	200

CATEGORY 3B

Western Yellow-billed Cuckoo *Coccyzus americanus occidentalis*	from Texas, Colorado, and Idaho west to the Pacific; western Canada and Mexico; and a visitor in Central and South America	129

CATEGORY 3C

Tule White-fronted Goose *Anser albifrons elgasi*	Alaska, and a visitor in Oregon and California	
American Swallow-tailed Kite *Elanoides forficatus forficatus*	from the Carolinas and Tennessee south through Florida; from Wisconsin and Minnesota south through Louisiana; from Nebraska south through Texas; and a visitor in Central America	
Swainson's Hawk *Buteo swainsoni*	from Minnesota south through Missouri; from the Dakotas south through Texas and west to the Pacific; Alaska and Canada; and a visitor in Florida, Mexico, and Central and South America	150
Arizona Bell's Vireo *Vireo bellii arizonae*	Utah and Arizona west to the Pacific, and a visitor in Mexico	57
Colima Warbler *Vermivora crissalis*	Texas, and a visitor in Mexico	
Yuma Rufous-crowned Sparrow *Aimophila ruficeps rupicola*	Arizona	
Yuma Canyon Towhee *Pipilo fuscus relictus*	Arizona	58

CATEGORY 3C BIRD IN PUERTO RICO

Puerto Rican Sharp-shinned Hawk *Accipiter striatus venator*	Puerto Rico	126

THREATENED OR ENDANGERED: Candidates

BIRDS REFLECTING THE SPECTRUM OF PROTECTION

This group includes eleven birds that exemplify the spectrum of vulnerability of North American birds and the recognition that each has received (or has not received). The eleven we have selected by no means exhaust the examples of vulnerable but unlisted birds. The Golden Eagle *is* accorded federal protection, even though it is not on the federal list of Endangered and Threatened Wildlife and Plants. A rail and a wren, both Category 1 candidates, head the list of 52 birds from the 50 states and Puerto Rico waiting to be added to the federal list. Three more species—a curlew, a murrelet, and an 'o'o (the only Hawaiian candidate for listing, and quite likely extinct)—have been subjects of petitions for inclusion, but still await decisions by the U.S. Fish and Wildlife Service, which seeks further information on the status of their populations. The next two birds in this group, a kite and a Hawaiian honeycreeper, are both very rare, but neither is on the waiting list for federal listing, although two subspecies of the kite *are* listed and researchers are very concerned about the unacknowledged rapid decline of the honeycreeper. The last three birds in this group, a duck, a plover, and a sparrow, are included because their status is unique: their Canadian populations are Threatened or Endangered, but their U.S. populations are not.

The **Golden Eagle** is protected in the United States under the Migratory Bird Treaty Act and the Bald Eagle Act (which was extended to include the Golden, because the juveniles look alike, and renamed the Eagle Protection Act). Today's U.S. Golden Eagle population is estimated at 100,000 to 200,000 birds, and is not in decline except in areas of urban and suburban encroachment into its range.

The Eagle Protection Act prohibited the taking of eagles or their nests, but it was amended in 1978 to allow taking certain nests if they were interfering with the development or recovery of a resource. At issue were Golden Eagle nests in the coal-rich areas of Montana, Wyoming, Colorado, and Utah that interfered with mining practices, but conflicts over nests could also arise in association with oil and gas exploration, timber harvesting, and dam, pipeline, road, and powerline construction. Eagles typically produce young in only one nest a year, but many pairs have alternative, inactive nests. A final ruling, in 1983, decreed that an inactive nest (one that had not sheltered adults, eggs, or dependent young in the previous 10 days) could be removed with the proper permit.

Few people have seen one of the 3,500 or so remaining **California Black Rails.** This subspecies, which has been petitioned for inclusion on the federal list but remains a Category 1 candidate, is not only rare, it is very secretive and seldom comes into view.

Like the California Black Rail, the **Appalachian Bewick's Wren** has been nominated for inclusion on the federal list, but as of 1991 it remains a Category 1 candidate. Another Bewick's Wren subspecies, on San Clemente Island, is already extinct, as a result of human modification of the habitat (albeit on a different scale; see p. 198).

There are not many **Bristle-thighed Curlews,** perhaps only 7,000 birds. One might assume that breeding in remote tundra would be safer than breeding in most other habitats, but because predators—even there—are attracted to nearby development, there is rising concern for these birds. More critical, however, are changes on its wintering territory; its vulnerability on these grounds—some of the most coveted shoreline on Earth—is increasing, while its protection in most areas is not.

The biology of the **Marbled Murrelet** is exceptional. This diving seabird may fly inland 20 miles, or considerably farther, to nest in old-growth forest. This practice, undertaken by at least the species' southern populations, places the Marbled Murrelet at significant risk from the logging of coastal old-growth forests. The ongoing debate over its possible listing as Threatened in Washington, Oregon, and California, a debate similar in many ways to that surrounding the listing of the Northern Spotted Owl, will keep discussion of this small seabird in the media for some time to come.

The **Bishop's 'O'o,** also called the Molokai 'O'o, is a little-known forest bird of Hawaii. Its nest has never been found, and there is little hope that any survive. The last confirmed sighting on Molokai was in 1904. If it still exists, it may be hanging on in Maui, where a decade ago an individual was reportedly sighted on the northeastern slopes of Haleakala.

The **Hook-billed Kite** is included here because it is an extremely rare newcomer to the United States and its habitat requirements are virtually unstudied. Some 15 years ago the Hook-billed Kite was first found nesting north of the Rio Grande. The nest, in the Santa Ana National Wildlife Refuge in Texas, marks the northern range extremity of this tropical species. We need to know much more about the biology of the Hook-billed Kite, a rare bird even in Mexico and beyond.

The **Kauai Creeper,** or Akikiki, is of special interest because of the precipitous drop in its numbers over the last 20 years. In 1981 the International Council for Bird Preservation (ICBP) listed the bird as Rare, and in 1988 as Threatened. Today, ornithologists are in full agreement that it requires protection, even though it is not recognized by the U.S. Fish and Wildlife Service as a bird in jeopardy. This 5-inch native of Hawaii is found only on the island of Kauai, and is now restricted to the higher-elevation forest in the Alakai Swamp and Koke'e State Park. Because the Alakai shelters a number of other birds formally designated as Endangered, an umbrella of protection is indirectly provided. Indirect protection, however, is not enough. The habitat to which the 6,000 remaining birds are restricted is quite likely marginal, and the research urgently needed to identify other factors limiting the species' survival may well have to await federal listing.

Despite its name, the **Mountain Plover** is a denizen of the prairie, a habitat that is fast disappearing from North America. The range of this plover is contracting in Canada (where the bird is listed as Endangered) and in the U.S. as well. In the U.S., however, the bird is not yet accorded federal protection; it remains a Category 2 candidate for listing.

Baird's Sparrow is listed as Threatened in Canada because its prairie habitat is being converted to agricultural and grazing land. The range of this sparrow in the U.S., although shrinking, has yet to put the bird at risk there.

Although eastern populations of the **Harlequin Duck** are Endangered in Canada, the reasons behind the decline are unclear, and significant losses have not been reported in the U.S. Declines in Dipper populations (which are dependent on similar river and stream habitat) *have* been recorded, however, especially in Europe, where the effects of acid precipitation have been implicated.

Accounts for each of these eleven birds follow. To be consistent with the other treatments in this book, we present them basically in taxonomic order. (The three imperiled Canadians are kept in a group at the end. Of the three, the listing of the Harlequin Duck is the most surprising, and that it warrants concern is controversial even among Canadians; hence, we place it last.)

REFERENCES: Dunstan, 1989; Ehrlich, Dobkin, and Wheye, 1988; Federal Register, 1983; Graham, 1991; Marshall, 1989; Russakoff and Barringer, 1984; Scott et al., 1986; Wilcove, 1990.

HOOK-BILLED KITE

Chondrohierax uncinatus uncinatus

NESTING: Usually requires trees in open swampy areas or lowland forest ranging from marsh to woodland, where it builds a flimsy platform of dead twigs and branches with a shallow depression.

FOOD: Mostly tree and land snails, rarely frogs, salamanders, and insects. The Hook-billed Kite forages by swooping down on prey from an elevated perch or by snatching snails from tree trunks or branches with its bill. After capturing a snail, it flies to a tree branch, braces the snail against the branch with its left foot, inserts its bill into the opening of the shell, and breaks the shell apart. Bill size accurately predicts relative prey size.

RANGE: Southern Texas to northern Argentina; also Grenada, Trinidad, and Cuba.

WINTER: Resident. **IN PERIL:** In at least the northern extreme of its range and in Grenada, Trinidad, and Cuba.

NOTES: Hook-billed Kites soar, occasionally in flocks of up to 25 individuals. Although the Everglade Snail Kite is also a snail eater (see p. 46), the two species are not closely related.

JEOPARDIZED: By its limited range in the U.S. and by our limited understanding of its biology. This is a tropical species whose northern extreme has only recently reached southern Texas, but the bird is not recognized as threatened in Texas (as it is in the Caribbean).

LISTING: Two West Indian populations, the Grenada Hook-billed Kite and the Cuban Hook-billed Kite, are included on the federal list of Threatened and Endangered Wildlife and Plants. The first U.S. nesting record of the Hook-Billed Kite was in 1976 at the Santa Ana National Wildlife Refuge, in Texas. It has nested intermittently there as well as elsewhere in Texas: at the Rio Grande National Wildlife Refuge, Bentsen Rio Grande State Park, and Rancho Santa Margarita in Starr County. Because its presence in Texas had been considered accidental, it has never been Blue-Listed.

GOLDEN EAGLE

Aquila chrysaetos

NESTING: Usually on a cliff ledge, on which it builds a platform of sticks interwoven with brush and leaves. The Golden Eagle will also nest in trees, especially in mountainous or open, hilly habitat.

FOOD: Mostly small mammals, especially jackrabbits and ground squirrels, but the Golden Eagle opportunistically takes large birds, reptiles, insects, and carrion. While hunting, it usually soars at high altitude, or swoops down from a perch to snatch prey from the ground in its talons.

RANGE: Breeds throughout much of western North America south through the Mexican highlands, and in eastern Canada; also Eurasia and North Africa. **WINTERS:** Over most of its breeding range, some birds reaching the Gulf of Mexico. **IN PERIL:** Individual Golden Eagles are protected by the Bald Eagle Act throughout the two species' ranges, but the Golden's favored foraging habitats are often converted into agricultural or suburban land uses. At present, its populations in the West and southwest are relatively stable, with severe declines occurring only near urban areas.

NOTES: In most of the West, territories are occupied year-round. Occasionally in winter, Golden Eagles roost communally, usually when prey densities are high. Mated pairs occasionally hunt together.

JEOPARDIZED: By the killing of tens of thousands of birds under the guise of livestock protection, mostly by sheep ranchers, in spite of little evidence of livestock depredation. The Golden Eagle also continues to be subject to powerline electrocution, poison intended for coyotes, occasional shootings, and habitat loss to urban sprawl.

LISTING: Because the plumages of juvenile Bald Eagles and juvenile Golden Eagles are so similar, the Bald Eagle Protection Act led to a similarity-of-appearance protection for the Golden Eagle in 1962 (see pp. 107, 229); thus the Goldens are automatically protected under the Act.

CALIFORNIA BLACK RAIL

Laterallus jamaicensis coturniculus

NESTING: The California Black Rail requires marshes, either salt or fresh, where it can conceal its deep, coiled, canopy-covered grass cup in vegetation from 1.5 to 2 feet high.

FOOD: Mostly insects but also crustaceans and the seeds of aquatic vegetation. The Black Rail hunts by either probing the substrate or picking food from the surface.

RANGE: The Pacific coast of California from the San Francisco Bay Area south, at least formerly, to San Quintín, Baja California; also in Imperial Valley and the lower Colorado River Valley, in southeastern California and southwestern Arizona. **WINTERS:** Apparently throughout its breeding range; the extent of its dispersal is still obscure. **IN PERIL:** Throughout its range. An estimated 3,300 birds remain in northern San Francisco Bay, and perhaps about 100 at the Salton Sea and along the Colorado River in California. Small numbers hang on in other scattered San Francisco Bay Area marshes and in Tomales Bay, Bolinas Lagoon, and Morro Bay. The species has already been extirpated from San Diego County.

NOTES: Little of the biology of this shy bird, the size of a sparrow, is known. Other Black Rail subspecies occur in widely scattered, disjunct populations in Kansas and along the Atlantic and Gulf of Mexico coasts.

JEOPARDIZED: By habitat degradation and destruction and by predation, and perhaps by pesticides used in rice cultivation in California. See comments for the California Clapper Rail (p. 38).

LISTING: Nominated for inclusion on the federal list of Endangered and Threatened Wildlife and Plants. As of early 1991, the California Black Rail continues to be recognized as a Category 1 candidate, according to the U.S. Fish and Wildlife Service's listing priority system. Category 1 candidates are those for which the Service has substantial data to support the proposal to list.

NOT OFFICIALLY LISTED IN THE U.S.: The Spectrum

BRISTLE-THIGHED CURLEW

Numenius tahitiensis

NESTING: Requires montane tundra, where the bird makes a scrape in lichen on dry, flat, exposed ridges. Its primary breeding grounds include the Nulato Hills in the northern Yukon Delta and the Kougarok Mountains in the western Seward Peninsula.

FOOD: Crowberries, blueberries, eggs, and probably insects. Bristle-thighed Curlews usually forage by picking up food from the ground.

RANGE: Breeds in western Alaska. **WINTERS:** In Hawaii and on the central Pacific islands from the Marshall Islands south and east to Fiji, Tonga, Samoa, and the Marquesas and Tuamotu islands. During migration, accidental in British Columbia, and casual on the Pribilof and Aleutian Islands. **IN PERIL:** On both breeding and wintering grounds, with perhaps 7,000 individuals remaining.

NOTES: Information on migration is scarce, and only two staging areas are known to be visited before the transoceanic flight from Alaska to Hawaii. The primary site, used for up to one month, is the Yukon-Kuskokwim Delta on the southwest coast of Alaska, and a smaller number of birds use the coastal lowlands of the Seward Peninsula.

JEOPARDIZED: On the breeding grounds by ravens, which may prey on curlew nests and are attracted to the general vicinity by the garbage generated in nearby villages; on the Pacific wintering grounds by tourism and predation by introduced dogs, cats, and rats.

LISTING: Nominated for inclusion on the federal list of Endangered and Threatened Wildlife and Plants. As of early 1991, the Bristle-thighed Curlew remains a Category 2 candidate, according to the U.S. Fish and Wildlife Service's listing priority system; thus, the Service has information indicating the possible appropriateness of listing, but feels that further information is still needed. The Service appears to be undertaking a program to protect the Bristle-thighed Curlew on its wintering grounds in the Marshall Islands.

MARBLED MURRELET

Brachyramphus marmoratus

NESTING: In the north of the species' range, where trees are sparse or absent, on north-facing open ground or in rock crevices on islands or sites well inland, where it makes its partly guano-encircled scrape. From southeastern Alaska southward, nesting is high in old-growth trees of conifer forests near the coast or inland lakes. About 15 nests have been found, including some in Siberia and Japan. Tree nests consist of a depression in the moss covering a limb, although one cup nest has been found. The lush moss required is found only in northwestern forests that are 150 or more years old.

FOOD: Mostly fish, but also aquatic invertebrates, especially crustaceans. While foraging, the Marbled Murrelet usually floats and then dives to depths of up to 100 feet, swimming underwater using its feet and wings, hunting often within 500 feet of shore. Adults usually return to their nest with a single fish per trip.

RANGE: Breeds along North Pacific coasts from Korea, Japan, Siberia, and Alaska south to central California. **WINTERS:** Offshore near the breeding range, but it tends to depart the northern portions of its range and occurs as far south as San Diego.

IN PERIL: In foraging areas where gill-net fishing is common, and throughout the southern part of the range where nesting habitat in old-growth coniferous forest is being logged. Its coastal population was tentatively estimated at 2,500 breeding pairs.

NOTES: The first North American nest was discovered in 1974 near Santa Cruz, California, by a tree surgeon. Detailed information on the species' breeding biology is needed. The National Audubon Society has recently purchased habitat in Oregon along Tenmile Creek that supports the largest concentration of Marbled Murrelets in that state. Only one young is produced per year. The Asiatic subspecies (*B. m. perdix*) occurs from the sea of Okhotsk, Kamchatka, and the Commander Islands to the Kurile Islands, Japan, and Korea.

JEOPARDIZED: By the logging of old-growth forests and by gill-net fishing. The very behaviors that make this seabird unique make it difficult to study and monitor.

LISTING: In 1988, the National Audubon Society (and 37 local chapters), Oregon's Natural Resources Council, and the Point Reyes Bird Observatory (California) petitioned for listing this species as **Threatened** in Washington, Oregon, and California. As of mid-1991, it continues to be recognized as a Category 2 candidate, according to the U.S. Fish and Wildlife Service's listing priority system, and is being studied for possible listing. It was listed as **Threatened** in Canada in 1990.

APPALACHIAN BEWICK'S WREN

Thryomanes bewickii altus

NESTING: In open shrubland, woodland, suburban areas, or farms with trees, snags, overturned trees, and brush piles, where it can find a cavity in which to place its twig-and-grass nest.

FOOD: Insects and spiders.

RANGE: Extreme southern Ontario and Pennsylvania south through the Appalachian region to central Alabama and Georgia. **WINTERS:** Throughout its breeding range. **IN PERIL:** Throughout its range.

JEOPARDIZED: Perhaps by the decline in small farms and their woodlots, leading to declines and the isolation of populations, but ornithologists are not sure why the bird is disappearing. Some point to competition with the House Wren (which has extended its range into part of Appalachia), but the Bewick's disappeared from some areas prior to the House Wrens' invasion, and the two species occur together in other parts of their ranges. Similarly, competition with the European Starling, House Sparrow, and Song Sparrow has been suggested, but the evidence is weak. Pesticides in agricultural areas also have been suggested as factors in the decline of this species.

LISTING: Nominated for inclusion on the federal list of Endangered and Threatened Wildlife and Plants. As of early 1991, the Appalachian Bewick's Wren continues to be recognized as a Category 1 candidate, according to the U.S. Fish and Wildlife Service's listing priority system. Category 1 candidates are those for which the Service has substantial data to support the proposal to list. No particular population centers remain to be protected, however, even though suitable habitat remains plentiful, and the Appalachian Bewick's Wren's range remains extensive. Listing requires that it be "distinct" from other Bewick's (without gene flow from adjacent populations), and its distinctness has not been established.

BISHOP'S 'O'O, or MOLOKAI 'O'O

Moho bishopi

NESTING: Apparently in the canopy of dense, higher-elevation rainforest, but no nests have ever been described.

FOOD: Apparently nectar, preferring flowers of lobeliads. The species has also been recorded as visiting ohia and banana flowers and taking some fruit and insects.

RANGE: Maui; formerly also Molokai.

WINTER: Resident. **IN PERIL:** Throughout its shrinking range, if indeed it is still extant. Last seen on Molokai in 1904; a survey in 1936 failed to produce any sightings. In 1981, however, in the ohia rainforest on Haleakala, Maui, an 'O'o, identified as a Bishop's, was reported to have been seen. Surviving individuals, if any exist, are most likely to be found on the northeastern slope of Haleakala.

NOTES: Discovered in 1892, the species was named after Charles R. Bishop, founder of the Bishop Museum in Honolulu. Bishop's 'O'o was characterized as active, timid, and alert.

JEOPARDIZED: In the past by Hawaiian plume-hunters, who valued its yellow feathers. Today, its preferred habitat, where lobelias are abundant, suffers damage from feral pigs.

LISTING: As of 1991, Bishop's 'O'o continues to be recognized as a Category 2 candidate, according to the U.S. Fish and Wildlife Service's listing priority system; thus, the Service has information indicating the possible appropriateness of listing, but feels that further information—on whether the bird still exists—is still needed.

KAUAI CREEPER, or AKIKIKI

Oreomystis bairdi

NESTING: Restricted to trees in remote upper-elevation forested slopes of the Alakai Swamp, especially in areas that support a tree-fern understory, where it places its cup nest built largely of rootlets and moss.
FOOD: Insects and other invertebrates; the Kauai Creeper forages in the manner of a nuthatch, slowly gleaning its prey from trunks, branches, or foliage or prying them from cracks in or beneath bark.
RANGE: Kauai. **WINTER:** Resident.
IN PERIL: Throughout its remaining range, now confined within the Alakai Swamp. Common and widespread 100 years ago, the Kauai Creeper has suffered severe losses since 1964. A 1984 estimate indicated that only 6,800 birds remain.
NOTES: The species forms loose, mixed flocks, and family members often travel together.
JEOPARDIZED: Apparently by the same threats that have reduced other Kauai passerines, especially insect-borne diseases. According to some reports, competition with the introduced Japanese White-eye has also been significant.
LISTING: Listed as **Rare** by the ICBP in 1981 and **Threatened** in 1988. The Kauai Creeper has not been officially listed by the U.S. Fish and Wildlife Service, despite urging from the scientific community.

MOUNTAIN PLOVER

Charadrius montanus

BAIRD'S SPARROW
Ammodramus bairdii

NESTING: Usually requires a flat area between hummocks on open plains, especially shortgrass prairie at moderate elevations. The Mountain Plover is also found on lightly grazed pastures, moist meadows, and drier rangeland, where it lines a simple scrape with cow chips, rootlets, and grass.

FOOD: Insects, especially grasshoppers, beetles, crickets, and flies. The Mountain Plover takes its prey from the gound.

RANGE: From extreme southern Alberta, Montana, and North Dakota (formerly) south through eastern Wyoming, western Nebraska (probably accidental), Colorado, and western Kansas (also probably accidental) to central and southeastern New Mexico, western Texas, western Oklahoma, and western Missouri. **WINTERS:** From central California, southern Arizona, and central and coastal Texas south to southern Baja California and northern mainland Mexico. **IN PERIL:** In Canada and, to a lesser degree, in the U.S., where prairie habitat is also in decline.

NOTES: This plover usually forages in small flocks, but in winter the flocks may be quite large.

JEOPARDIZED: Until 1900, this plover was an important gamebird for market hunters. Today its range continues to contract with the continuing conversion of shortgrass prairie to agriculture.

LISTING: The Mountain Plover was listed as **Endangered** in Canada in 1987. As of 1990, it remains a Category 2 candidate for federal listing in the U.S. (see p. 99).

NESTING: Requires shortgrass prairie, where the bird can place its cup of dried grass and forbs in a scraped or natural depression that often is concealed in vegetation.

FOOD: Mostly insects, but also spiders and the seeds of grass and forbs. Baird's Sparrow forages on the ground. It feeds its young entirely insects.

RANGE: From southeastern Alberta, southern Saskatchewan, and southern Manitoba south to central and eastern Montana, west-central Minnesota, and southeastern North Dakota. **WINTERS:** From southeastern Arizona, southern New Mexico, and north-central Texas south to southern Texas and northern Mexico. **IN PERIL:** At least in Canada.

NOTES: Baird's Sparrow is not a common cowbird host. Males are strongly territorial, but during breeding the birds form semicolonial groups of a few pairs. This sparrow does not form winter flocks.

JEOPARDIZED: By its confinement to native prairie. The range of this bird has contracted with the loss of its shortgrass prairie habitat to agriculture and grazing.

LISTING: Baird's Sparrow was listed as **Threatened** in Canada in 1989.

HARLEQUIN DUCK

Histrionicus histrionicus

NESTING: Usually uses coastal rocky islets, or vegetated riverside or streamside sites where fast-flowing water cuts through forested slopes. The Harlequin Duck usually nests in a hollow sheltered by a shrub, within 60 to 90 feet of water, but will also nest in a rock crevice among boulders, within a tree cavity, or in a puffin burrow. Nesting occasionally occurs on open tundra.

FOOD: Mostly aquatic invertebrates, including crustaceans, mollusks, and aquatic insects, but the bird also takes a few fish. This duck forages by diving into fast-flowing streams, searching for prey among rocks. It can dive into torrents from the air and emerge directly into flight. Like the Dipper, it seldom flies over land.

RANGE: In the west, from western Alaska, northern Yukon, northern British Columbia, and southern Alberta south to Alaska, Vancouver Island, eastern Oregon, the Sierra Nevada of California, and central Idaho to western Wyoming; in the east, from southern Baffin Island south to central and eastern Quebec and eastern Labrador, (perhaps to) northern New Brunswick and Newfoundland; also in Greenland and Iceland and from eastern Siberia and Kamchatka south to northern Mongolia and the Kurile Islands. **WINTERS:** Along the Pacific coast from Alaska south to central (and rarely southern) California; along the Atlantic coast from southern Labrador, Newfoundland, and Nova Scotia south to New York, sometimes to the Great Lakes, casually inland, and south along the coast to Florida and on the Gulf coast; in eastern Eurasia from Manchuria and Kamchatka south to Korea and southern Japan. **IN PERIL:** Only the eastern populations in Canada are noted to be in decline.

NOTES: The Harlequin Duck depends on food-rich turbulent streams, usually those draining lakes. Eastern and western populations are isolated from one another, but are not thought to be different subspecies.

JEOPARDIZED: The reasons behind the eastern Canadian declines are unclear, but acid rain may be a culprit.

LISTING: The eastern populations of the Harlequin Duck were listed as **Endangered** in Canada in 1991.

BIRDS ON THE BLUE LIST:
WARNING OF IMPENDING LOSSES

American Birds, the National Audubon Society's ornithological field journal, began publishing the "Blue List" in 1971 to provide early warning of reductions in the range or population size of North American species. The list was designed to augment the U.S. Fish and Wildlife Service's Threatened and Endangered Species List (see p. 12) by identifying cases of imminent endangerment or continuing patterns of serious losses in regional bird populations. Providing advance warning was considered important, for by the time a species is officially listed as Endangered, it tends to be already on the verge of extinction, especially vulnerable to changes in its habitat, and reduced to a restricted distribution. Many species on the Blue List remain common in local areas, but the declines they appear to be undergoing elsewhere raise significant concern for each of these species as a whole. (Unlike the Service's Threatened and Endangered list, the Blue List deals only with species, not subspecies or populations.)

American Birds requested reports and recommendations from its readership to incorporate into updates of the Blue List. Regional editors forwarded the readers' views to the publication, where a final judgment was made on birds to be added or dropped from the list. Wherever possible, reports included findings from Christmas Bird Counts, Winter Bird Population Studies, Breeding Bird Censuses, the U.S. Fish and Wildlife Service's Breeding Bird Surveys, nesting season reports, spring and autumn migration reports, and winter season reports.

Then, in 1981, *American Birds* published a "decade list" covering the 1970's. It included the 69 birds nominated for listing that year as well as all species that had previously been listed. This review made it easier to confirm the changing status of species meriting "Blue-Listing," those warranting "Special Concern" (see p. 140), those of only "Local Concern" (see p. 173), and those that had recovered. Updates of the Blue List continued, and as of 1986 (the last list), 19 species were Blue-Listed and another 51 warranted "Special" or "Local" Concern. A map delineating regional reporting areas is given on p. 234. It is accompanied by a list of the imperiled birds in each area.

As in the case of birds listed as Threatened or Endangered, the goal is the recovery of each species to an extent that allows it to be placed in a category reflecting a less serious threat, and ultimately to be removed from *all* lists. Submission of data to the editors of the Blue List allowed field observers to stimulate policy changes in state and federal agencies concerned with avian research and species protection. Since 1986, there has been a temporary hiatus in compiling the Blue List (and its inventory of birds warranting Special or Local Concern), but according to the National Audubon Society's *American Birds* it has not been discontinued. More information is available from American Birds Blue List, c/o *American Birds,* National Audubon Society, 950 Third Avenue, New York, NY 10022.

An approach to birds facing special difficulties in the tropics (where birders and field guides are less common and information on rarities is scanty) has been suggested by Christoph Imboden, director of the International Council for Bird Preservation (ICBP). Imboden proposes compilation of "Green Lists" containing those species definitely known to be *secure.* Shifting the burden of proof to those who maintain that "all is well" may yield a more realistic indication of the extinction crisis.

REFERENCES: Arbib, 1971; Diamond, 1988; Ehrlich, Dobkin, and Wheye, 1988; Tate, 1981, 1986; Tate and Tate, 1982.

HORNED GREBE
Podiceps auritus

NESTING: Requires the shallow water of marshes, lakes, and ponds, or sometimes slow-moving streams, where it anchors a floating platform (of underwater plants, decaying vegetation, debris, and mud) to emergent vegetation. The highest densities of breeding Horned Grebes are found in the pothole marshes of aspen woodland in southwestern Manitoba.

FOOD: In summer, mostly aquatic insects; also mollusks and crustaceans. In winter, mostly crustaceans and fish. The Horned Grebe usually floats and then dives, pursuing prey under water. Its stomach often contains a ball of feathers (occupying as much as half the space) that is thought to provide protection against the bones of the bird's fish prey.

RANGE: Breeds inland across northern North America and Eurasia. **WINTERS:** In North America, mostly along the coasts, south to northern Baja California and the Gulf of Mexico. **IN PERIL:** In the Northeast and evidently in the West. See under Listing.

NOTES: Horned Grebes are often solitary, but occasionally fish in flocks. Dives may last three minutes and take the birds some 500 feet under water.

JEOPARDIZED: Threats have not been described, but for reasons that are not clear, there has been a decline in the number of wintering birds.

LISTING: Blue-Listed in 1986, when reports from parts of the northeast section of the Horned Grebe's wintering range (Atlan-

LEAST BITTERN

Ixobrychus exilis

tic coastal areas) indicated that migrant and wintering birds were declining greatly in numbers, even though in Quebec, where most eastern birds breed, there are no clear signs of a decline.

NESTING: The Least Bittern usually requires a site that is near or over fresh water with emergent vegetation, where it builds a platform of emergent vegetation and sticks. It also occasionally places its platform on the ground or in a low shrub, sometimes in coastal brackish marshes or mangroves.

FOOD: Mostly fish, also some aquatic invertebrates, insects, amphibians, small mammals, and possibly the eggs and young of marsh-nesting blackbirds. It usually stalks prey and then spears it while standing motionless on a bank or in the water. It feeds its young by regurgitation.

RANGE: Wide but patchy distribution from southern Oregon and southeastern Canada south to northern Argentina.

WINTERS: North as far as the southeastern U.S. and, rarely, southern California; south to Costa Rica, and from the Greater Antilles to northern Colombia. **IN PERIL:** In parts of the East and Midwest and in California. See under Listing.

NOTES: The Least Bittern is solitary or loosely colonial. Its clutches are larger in the northern portion of its range.

JEOPARDIZED: By the draining and filling of marshes. Commonly reported as being in decline or absent from areas formerly occupied. Marsh Wrens occasionally destroy bitterns' eggs.

LISTING: Blue-Listed since 1979 (some nominated it as early as 1976). By 1982 the Least Bittern was stable, at reduced numbers, in parts of the Northeast (Niagara–Champlain Region), with low numbers

AMERICAN BITTERN
Botaurus lentiginosus

from Ontario south through the Western Great Lakes to the Middle and Southern Atlantic Coast regions, and nearly extirpated in the Western Great Lakes Region, except for a single local area where it was stable. According to reports, there was no evidence of nesting or birds for a number of years in the Appalachian Region. By 1986 it was gone from some areas and in severe decline through a wide portion of its range. The Least Bittern was listed as **Vulnerable** in Canada in 1988.

NESTING: Usually in the tall emergent vegetation of freshwater and brackish marshes. The American Bittern builds a minimal platform of sticks, grass, and sedges. It may also select drier areas beneath arching grass or build over deep water.

FOOD: Mostly fish, but the diet is varied and includes essentially any animal an American Bittern can seize, including aquatic invertebrates, insects, and small vertebrates. The bird usually stalks prey and then spears it while standing motionless on a bank or in the water. It feeds its young by regurgitation.

RANGE: Breeds from central Canada south very patchily to southern California, central Mexico, and the southeastern U.S.

WINTERS: From southwestern British Columbia and the central U.S. south to southern Mexico and the Greater Antilles.

IN PERIL: Across the continent.

NOTES: The American Bittern is solitary, cryptic, and deliberate in its movements. Territorial males have a distinctive booming call.

JEOPARDIZED: Presumably from the destruction of wetland habitat in general. This is most evident in the central and eastern portions of the species' range.

LISTING: Blue-Listed since 1976. The American Bittern was only tentatively added in 1976, but by 1977 two-thirds of the reports recommended listing, with the mid-continental area showing evidence of the decline first. By 1980 populations were also shrinking in coastal areas, and by 1982 it was reported in severe decline in the Appalachian, Western Great Lakes, and Northern Great Plains regions, probably undergoing less severe losses in the Ontario, Niagara–Champlain, and Northeastern Maritime regions (although it was declining in the Atlantic coast regions), and was stable or undergoing a slight increase farther south and west. The Breeding Bird Survey detected no significant trend, but by 1986 the American Bittern was reported to be undergoing a continent-wide decline, along with most other wetland species.

UPLAND SANDPIPER
Bartramia longicauda

NESTING: In drier grasslands, particularly short-grass prairies, dry meadows, fields, forest openings, and, in Alaska, scattered timberline woodlands. The Upland Sandpiper conceals its nest in overarching grass. Today's breeding habitat resembles historic short-grass prairie habitat.

FOOD: Mostly insects, but also seeds, grain, and other terrestrial invertebrates. The Upland Sandpiper seizes prey and gleans seeds from the ground.

RANGE: Breeds from Alaska and central Canada south to northeastern Oregon, northern Texas, and Virginia. **WINTERS:** In South America south to central Argentina and Uruguay. **IN PERIL:** Throughout its range.

NOTES: The Upland Sandpiper nests in loosely defined colonies and is seldom found near water.

JEOPARDIZED: In the 1880's, when populations of the Passenger Pigeon plummeted, market hunters switched to this species as their prime target, causing precipitous declines. When hunting of the Upland Sandpiper ceased, with the signing of the Migratory Bird Treaty of 1918, its numbers increased, and its range expanded eastward as it adapted to open cropland, but today's eastern populations are declining as old fields mature to woodland or are replaced by housing developments, and western populations are declining as suitable habitat is overgrazed. The species' wintering habitat has been usurped by agriculture.

BLACK TERN

Chlidonias niger

LISTING: Blue-Listed since 1975. By 1982 populations of the Upland Sandpiper were slowly shrinking, constant at low levels, or missing from much of the species' earlier eastern range. The decline of a small breeding colony in northern Lancaster County, Pennsylvania, pointed to the destruction or maturation of habitats as a reason behind the eastern losses. The Breeding Bird Survey, however, showed stability in the east and an increase in the Northern Great Plains Region. But by 1986, as more habitats were maturing or being replaced, losses in the east continued.

NESTING: In dense vegetation in freshwater marshes, sloughs, and wet meadows, where it builds a sometimes elaborate but more often flimsy floating cushion of damp vegetation that elevates its eggs (which are often wet) barely above the water. Black Terns also may nest on muskrat houses or in the used nests of grebes, or occasionally build no nest at all.

FOOD: In summer, mostly insects, also aquatic invertebrates, including crayfish and mollusks, and fish caught from the surface. The Black Tern usually hawks insects over meadows and marshes, or flies low over water picking insects from the surface, but also follows farming equipment to capture the prey the machines stir up. It feeds its young mostly insects.

RANGE: Breeds inland from northern Canada south to central California, Nebraska, and Pennsylvania; also in Eurasia.

WINTERS: Largely offshore in the tropics, in the New World near the coast from Panama south to Peru and Surinam. **IN PERIL:** Throughout its North American range. See under Listing.

NOTES: The Black Tern is gregarious throughout the year, forming loosely defined colonies, and frequently returns to breed in the colony where it was born.

JEOPARDIZED: Mostly by wetland loss and degradation. Populations in many areas are in decline. Nest success is often exceptionally low, but the Black Tern is especially diminished in the upper Midwest,

NORTHERN HARRIER

Circus cyaneus

possibly as the result of exposure to agricultural chemicals.

LISTING: Blue-Listed since 1978. By 1982, the species was stable or perhaps in slight decline in most reporting regions. Problems were evident, however, in the Northern Great Plains Region, where the Saskatchewan populations were in severe decline, possibly in response to drought. The Breeding Bird Survey showed an ongoing decline in all areas east of the Rockies, and by 1986 the Black Tern was reported in decline or in serious decline throughout its North American range.

NESTING: In prairies, savannas, sloughs, wet meadows, or marshes. There the Northern Harrier builds a loose platform of sticks and grass on somewhat elevated ground or in thick vegetation.

FOOD: Mostly small mammals (especially voles), but also small birds, snakes, frogs, and large insects (particularly grasshoppers), and carrion. The Northern Harrier usually hunts in a low, searching flight over open vegetation and, like owls, uses its curved, sound-directing facial ruff to help locate prey. Flight may be slow, and may follow a zigzag path; hovering is common. In the nonbreeding season, females fiercely defend preferred feeding areas from males.

RANGE: Breeds widely across Canada and the United States; also Eurasia. **WINTERS:** In the New World, from southern Canada south to Barbados, northern Colombia, and northern Venezuela. **IN PERIL:** Almost everywhere in North America. See under Listing.

NOTES: In a 25-year study in Wisconsin, polygyny (one male mating with more than one female) occurred among 25 percent of the nests, and often involved subadult females; the incidence was found to increase with high populations of voles. The Northern Harrier was formerly known as the Marsh Hawk.

JEOPARDIZED: By habitat destruction and exposure to pesticides. In 1970, one in five eggs showed evidence of shell thinning. The great majority of the species' habitat in

SHARP-SHINNED HAWK

Accipiter striatus

southern California has been lost to urbanization.

LISTING: Blue-Listed since 1972. In 1982 a small increase was evident in the Southwest Region, where mesquite invasion of the Northern Harrier's habitat was being controlled. Migrant and winter populations were reported as stable or increasing, but concern continued in the Northeast (mostly due to urbanization), and the Breeding Bird Survey data showed losses in Texas, Oklahoma, Kansas, and Minnesota. By 1986, populations were reported in decline almost everywhere.

NESTING: In conifers or deciduous trees in northern woodlands or mountain forests where it builds a wide, level platform of twigs and sticks. Sharp-shinned Hawks also occasionally refurbish abandoned nests of crows and squirrels.

FOOD: Mostly birds. The Sharp-shinned Hawk takes more birds as prey than do its other close relatives in the genus *Accipiter,* only rarely eating small mammals, frogs, lizards, and insects. It hunts by making a quick flight from a perch or a longer, searching flight. It chases birds and catches them in midair, or takes them by surprise, snatching them from their perch or flushing and then seizing them.

RANGE: Breeds from Alaska and northern Canada south to central California, the high mountains of southern Mexico, and South Carolina; also in the Greater Antilles. Other populations, possibly separate species, range over Central and South America. **WINTERS:** From southern Alaska and southern Canada south to the Greater Antilles and central Panama.

IN PERIL: In the eastern half of the continent. See under Listing.

NOTES: Large numbers often flock together in migration.

JEOPARDIZED: In the early 1970's the species showed severe losses in the eastern U.S. Shell thinning was apparent in 8 to 13 percent of the eggs examined.

LISTING: Blue-Listed since 1972. By 1982 the Sharp-shinned Hawk was, by consensus, greatly declining or failing to breed

COOPER'S HAWK
Accipiter cooperii

over a large portion of the eastern half of the continent. The stable or increased numbers reported from migration sightings were assumed to reflect merely a larger number of hawk-watchers. By 1986, increasing numbers in migration were still being reported, but the number of known breeders continued to be very low. As of 1991, the Puerto Rican Sharp-shinned Hawk, a subspecies, continues to be recognized as a Category 3C candidate, according to the U.S. Fish and Wildlife Service's listing priority system. Category 3C candidates have been found to be more abundant or widespread than previously believed, or at least not subject to the threats that place the continued existence of the bird at risk.

NESTING: In forests or woodlands, and particularly in broad-leafed trees in riparian areas. Cooper's Hawk typically builds a wide and shallow or narrow and thick platform of sticks and twigs in a tree, but sometimes adopts the used nests of crows or, very rarely, nests on the ground.
FOOD: Mostly birds; also small mammals, some reptiles, and amphibians. Like the Sharp-shinned, the Cooper's hunts by making a quick flight from a perch or a longer, searching flight. It chases birds and catches them in midair, or takes them by surprise, snatching them from their perch or flushing them into the air.
RANGE: Breeds across North America from southern Canada south to northern Mexico and central Florida. **WINTERS:** Largely from the northern U.S. south to Guatemala and Honduras. **IN PERIL:** Perhaps throughout its range, although general improvements have been reported in some areas. By 1988, numbers in southeastern New Mexico and Arizona were declining. See under Listing.
JEOPARDIZED: Between 1941 and 1945, populations were declining by more than 13 percent yearly. In 1948 the rate rose to as much as 25 percent as DDT use became widespread. But the precipitous decline in populations was followed by an upturn in 1968, and especially after DDT was banned in 1972.
LISTING: Blue-Listed 1972–81 but warranted only **Special Concern** in 1982. In 1982, populations remained below those

of 30 years earlier, but there was some evidence of increases in the Southwest, Mountain West, Niagara–Champlain, Hudson–Delaware, Middlewestern Prairie, and Ontario regions, and more birds were seen on migration and during the winter in the eastern half of the continent. Pending confirmation of those observations, the Cooper's Hawk was transferred in 1982 to the Special Concern category, but by 1986 it was again Blue-Listed, despite many reports of improvement in the eastern part of the continent. Cooper's Hawk was listed as **Vulnerable** in Canada in 1983.

RED-SHOULDERED HAWK
Buteo lineatus

NESTING: In riparian forests or wooded swamps with deciduous trees, sometimes in conifers in the western part of its range. The Red-shouldered Hawk builds a platform of sticks, twigs, and finer plant parts that is used year after year. In California, it is expanding into a wider variety of woodlands, including even stands of eucalyptus trees amid urban sprawl.

FOOD: Small mammals, also snakes, lizards, amphibians, birds, insects, and a few snails. The Red-shouldered Hawk usually hunts in a low, searching flight, in open woodland and along the forest edge, but also takes prey by swooping down on it after spotting it from an elevated perch.

RANGE: Two disjunct populations: one in California, the other from southeastern Canada through the eastern U.S. to eastern Mexico. **WINTERS:** Most birds in the northeastern range extremity migrate south. **IN PERIL:** In eastern North America.

NOTES: A pair or kin may use the same territory for many years.

JEOPARDIZED: Red-shouldered Hawks are known to concentrate organochlorine pesticides and PCBs, but habitat loss is probably the cause of most problems. The species can persist in the face of human disturbance if large trees with a high canopy are preserved.

LISTING: Blue-Listed since 1972. In 1982 there were no reports of increasing numbers anywhere in the East, and by 1986, populations were down or, at best, stable at low numbers. The Red-shouldered Hawk was listed as **Vulnerable** in Canada in 1983.

YELLOW-BILLED CUCKOO
Coccyzus americanus

NESTING: Requires trees or shrubs in open woodlands (particularly where undergrowth is most dense), extensive riparian woodlands, thickets, or parks, where it can build a scraggly platform of twigs. In the West, nesting is limited to tall cottonwood and willow riparian woodland.

FOOD: Mostly insects (particularly caterpillars); also tree frogs, a few bird eggs, berries, and other fruit. The Yellow-billed Cuckoo usually gleans items from foliage or branches, sometimes while hovering, or sallies from a perch to capture prey on the wing. It feeds its young by regurgitation the first day after hatching, then progressively offers larger whole-prey items.

RANGE: Includes most of North America, from Canada to the West Indies and Mexico. **WINTERS:** From northern South America south to eastern Peru, Bolivia, and northern Argentina. **IN PERIL:** Especially in western riparian habitat, where it is nearly extinct, but it is also declining in the East.

NOTES: Breeding often coincides with the appearance of massive numbers of cicadas, tent caterpillars, and other large insects. When prey is plentiful, extra cuckoo eggs may be laid. This excess may lead to brood parasitism (see p. 219), the Yellow-billed occasionally parasitizing the Black-billed Cuckoo and (rarely) other birds. Ecologically, the eastern and western populations differ significantly.

JEOPARDIZED: Primarily by habitat loss in the West, particularly where mature riparian woods have been severely disturbed and reduced. Drought and prey scarcity (especially the loss of sphinx-moth caterpillars to pesticides in the West) appear to play a role in cuckoo declines even where suitable nesting habitat remains. Direct pesticide stresses and habitat loss on the wintering grounds and along the migration route may also be involved. The western subspecies, *C. americanus occidentalis*, ceased breeding in British Columbia in the 1920's, in Washington in the 1930's, and in Oregon in the 1940's; and by 1987, fewer than 85 pairs remained in California and western Arizona. The figures for California reflected a 65- to 80-percent decrease in just ten years. Populations in most other areas have been declining, too.

LISTING: Blue-Listed from 1972 to 1981, and in 1986; but warranted only **Special Concern** in 1982. The history of the Yellow-billed's decline (and one-time apparent improvement, in 1982) is complex, and the failure to have it included on the U.S. Fish and Wildlife Service's List of Threatened and Endangered Species has been discouraging. By 1986, the eastern population appeared to be declining in the Appalachian Region and in parts of the Middlewestern Prairie and Southern Great Plains regions, and the western population was so threatened that the Service qualified it as a Category 2 candidate for listing. By 1990, however, even though it had been decades since the Yellow-billed had been seen in areas where it was once common, and

even though the California Department of Fish and Game had listed it as endangered in the state, the Yellow-billed moved farther from federal listing: the Service switched it to Category 3B "candidate" status (see p. 103), indicating that it failed to meet the legal definition for listing. This appears to have been a political rather than a scientific decision.

SHORT-EARED OWL

Asio flammeus

NESTING: Requires low, concealing vegetation in prairies, savanna, meadows, marshes, or tundra, where it makes a depression that is sometimes used year after year. The Short-eared Owl also, rarely, nests in burrows.

FOOD: Mostly small mammals, particularly rodents, also birds and insects. The Short-eared Owl usually hunts in twilight, seeking prey in a low, searching flight, or swooping down in a spread-wing gliding descent from a perch to snatch prey from the ground in its talons. When prey is plentiful, the owls occasionally hunt in groups.

RANGE: Breeds from Alaska and northern Canada south to central (formerly southern) California, Kansas, and Virginia; also in the Greater Antilles (including Puerto Rico), Hawaii, and across northern Eurasia. **WINTERS:** In North America, mostly from southern Canada south to southern Mexico. **IN PERIL:** In most of its range, most clearly in the prairie provinces, along the Pacific coast, in portions of the Southeast, and recently in the southern portion of the Northeast Region.

NOTES: The Short-eared Owl is an irruptive, nomadic species, moving into areas with high rodent populations to settle and breed. Clutch sizes increase when prey is abundant. Where prey is sufficient, Short-eared Owls maintain winter territories.

JEOPARDIZED: By destruction and degradation of marshes and grasslands.

LISTING: Blue-Listed since 1976. By 1982, populations were declining at the boundary of the species' breeding range in southern Ontario and in the Niagara–Champlain Region, and reports of declines stretched westward into the Middlewestern Prairie Region and the Northern and Southern Great Plains regions. By 1986 the Short-eared Owl was widely reported in trouble in the Hudson–Delaware, Ontario, Middlewestern Prairie, and Southern Great Plains regions, in severe decline in the Central Southern, Prairie Province, and Middle Pacific Coast regions, and long since extirpated from southern California.

WHIP-POOR-WILL
Caprimulgus vociferus

NESTING: In lowland moist deciduous forests, mixed deciduous/coniferous woodlands, or montane pine–oak woodlands. The bird builds no nest but lays its eggs directly on well-drained ground near the edge of a wood or in open woodland. The depression found around eggs is merely a consequence of the sitting adult.

FOOD: Insects, particularly moths, which the bird hunts while in prolonged, continuous flight.

RANGE: Disjunct: one subspecies breeds in the deciduous and mixed deciduous/coniferous forests of southeastern Canada and the eastern U.S.; others breed in mountains mostly from Arizona south through Mexico to Central America. **WINTERS:** From southeastern U.S. and northern Mexico south to western Panama. **IN PERIL:** Throughout its range. See under Listing.

NOTES: The Whip-poor-will's reproductive cycle coincides with the lunar cycle, so that moonlit nights are available when the birds are foraging for their brood. Over the years, local populations increase and decrease dramatically as forested habitat is cut and regrows.

JEOPARDIZED: Reasons for the Whip-poor-will's decline are not entirely clear, but habitat fragmentation and loss, combined with the susceptibility of ground-nesting birds to increased predation, are likely causes.

LISTING: Blue-Listed 1980–81 and in 1986 but relegated to only **Special Concern** in 1982, when the Breeding Bird Survey indicated that populations on the whole were stable, even though declines were reported throughout the breeding range and the birds had deserted some areas. By 1986, reports of widespread declines brought about a return to the Blue List.

COMMON NIGHTHAWK
Chordeiles minor

NESTING: Usually on the ground in open or partially open habitats, particularly savanna, grasslands, and fields (preferring sandy soil in the South); also nests in cities and towns, especially on gravel rooftops. The Common Nighthawk usually needs no nest, but occasionally lays its eggs on stumps or in an abandoned Robin's nest. If a depression is apparent, it is merely a consequence of the sitting adult. Reports of preferred roosting or nesting on rooftops may be misleading; Nighthawks may accept (rather than prefer) roofs to take advantage of prey attracted to artificial lights.
FOOD: Insects, captured day or night while in prolonged, continuous flight. It regurgitates insects to feed its young.
RANGE: Breeds over much of North America, except the Southwestern deserts, south to Panama. **WINTERS:** In South America south to northern Argentina. **IN PERIL:** Over much of the continent.
NOTES: In most desert regions the Common Nighthawk is replaced by the Lesser Nighthawk; in the Florida Keys, it is interspecifically territorial toward the Antillean Nighthawk.
JEOPARDIZED: Though the reasons are unclear, the widespread decline is likely due in part to the loss of breeding habitat and increased predation on nests.
LISTING: Blue-Listed 1975–81 but granted only **Special Concern** in 1982, although there were no significant increases anywhere, and in the Niagara–Champlain, Northeastern Maritime, and possibly Hudson–Delaware regions, as well as the Northern and Southern Great Plains and Mountain West regions, the species appeared to be undergoing declines. By 1986 it was returned to the Blue List because of reported widespread losses.

RUBY-THROATED HUMMINGBIRD

Archilochus colubris

BEWICK'S WREN

Thryomanes bewickii

NESTING: In deciduous or mixed woodlands, open areas with a few trees, parks, and gardens. The Ruby-throated Hummingbird places its lichen-covered cup nest of bud scales on a small, sloping branch of a deciduous or sometimes coniferous tree, often selecting sites near or over streams. It sometimes occupies the same nests over several seasons; if so, they are refurbished yearly.

FOOD: Mostly nectar, also insects, spiders, and tree sap from holes drilled by sapsuckers. The birds forage while hovering.

RANGE: Breeds from central and southeastern Canada south through the eastern U.S. **WINTERS:** Mostly from southern Texas south through Mexico to Panama.

IN PERIL: Declines are widespread.

NOTES: Males appear to migrate separately from females, and are the first to arrive and depart. Northern populations may depend at times on tree sap from the holes that sapsuckers drill.

JEOPARDIZED: Reasons for decline are unknown, but the destruction of tropical wintering habitat may be a primary contributor to the species' steady disappearance.

LISTING: Blue-Listed since 1978. By 1982 the center of the decline lay within the Hudson–Delaware Region, where sightings were drastically reduced. There were favorable reports from the Breeding Bird Survey elsewhere, but by 1986, reports of declines were widespread.

NESTING: In open woodlands, shrublands, farmlands, or suburbs, Bewick's Wren builds a nest of twigs and grass in natural cavities in trees and snags, in various other cavities, amid roots of overturned trees, or in brush-piles.

FOOD: Insects and other terrestrial invertebrates, especially spiders. While foraging, Bewick's Wren usually picks items from the substrate or gleans foliage and branches.

RANGE: Breeds from southwestern British Columbia, Wyoming, and extreme southern Ontario south to southern Mexico.

WINTERS: Mostly in place, but retreats from the northeastern extremity of its range and enters parts of the desert Southwest and southeastern U.S., where it does not breed. **IN PERIL:** See under Listing.

NOTES: Bewick's Wrens occasionally attack eggs in nests of other species and of other Bewick's Wrens. Competition with the House Wren is well documented. One subspecies (San Clemente Island) is already extinct and populations of another (Appalachian) are greatly reduced.

JEOPARDIZED: Possibly because of the disappearance of small farms, with their woodlots and outbuildings (see p. 114).

LISTING: Blue-Listed since 1972. By 1982 a number of populations in the Mountain West and Southern Great Plains regions and the Northern and Southern Pacific Coast regions seemed to be stable or increasing somewhat, although Bewick's Wrens remained scarce or absent where formerly common in the Appalachian, South-ern Atlantic Coast, and Central Southern regions. Reports from the Middlewestern Prairie Region were mixed. The Breeding Bird Survey showed continued losses except in the West. By 1986 Bewick's Wren was in decline in the Middlewestern Prairie Region and in severe decline in the Central Southern, Appalachian, and Southern Atlantic Coast regions. Elsewhere, the responses were mixed. The southeastern population, while down considerably, did not qualify as a candidate for listing by the U.S. Fish and Wildlife Service (see pp. 99 and 114). As of 1991, one of the subspecies, the Appalachian Bewick's Wren, continues to qualify as a Category 1 candidate, which places it high on the list of nominations for Endangered status.

LOGGERHEAD SHRIKE

Lanius ludovicianus

NESTING: Often in open fields with a few trees, or in open woodlands or scrub. The birds place their bulky, well-constructed cup of twigs, herbaceous plants, and bark strips in a shrub or a vine tangle.

FOOD: Mostly large insects (particularly in the West) and other land invertebrates, but also mice, birds, lizards, and carrion. It usually captures prey by sallying from a perch on a short flight, chasing (birds) in flight, or snatching prey from their perches. Lacking the talons of raptors, it stuns or kills flying birds with a blow from its powerful beak. It often stores prey by impaling it on barbed wire or a plant spine, hence its common name "butcher bird."

RANGE: Breeds over most of North America from central Canada south to southern Mexico. **WINTERS:** Throughout most of its breeding range, but retreats somewhat from Canada. **IN PERIL:** Possibly throughout its range, but especially in the Midwestern, New England, and Middle Atlantic states. It is one of the few birds showing significant declines in all continental regions included in the Breeding Bird Survey. Christmas Count records indicate that populations in the southeastern Atlantic coast states declined more than 20 percent between 1961 and 1978, and declines in the upper Midwest have been around 6 percent per year for more than two decades.

NOTES: The Loggerhead Shrike nests earlier than most other passerines. Males and females defend separate territories during the nonbreeding season.

JEOPARDIZED: By habitat destruction and exposure to pesticides (particularly in the middle of its range) and possibly from impact with cars speeding on roads within nesting and hunting territories, but there is little agreement among biologists on the causes of the decline.

LISTING: Blue-Listed 1972–86, and the subspecies found on San Clemente Island, California, was listed as **Endangered** in 1977 (see p. 55). By 1982 there were a few reports of migration and winter increases—a change in the pattern of very major breeding losses nearly everywhere else, and a report noting that more Peregrine Falcons than Loggerhead Shrikes were seen in 1981. The Breeding Bird Survey uncovered evidence of losses in all parts of the shrike's breeding range. By 1986 it was reported in decline or serious decline everywhere east of the Mississippi River and was qualified for Category 2 candidacy by the U.S. Fish and Wildlife Service, targeting it for prompt study and evaluation for future listing. As of 1991, the subspecies of the Loggerhead Shrike occurring over most of the eastern U.S. continues to be recognized as a Category 2 candidate, according to the Service's listing priority system; thus the Service has information indicating the possible appropriateness of listing, but feels that further information is still needed. The Loggerhead Shrike was listed as **Threatened** in Canada in 1986, and eastern populations were listed as **Endangered** in Canada in 1991.

BELL'S VIREO
Vireo bellii

NESTING: Requires bushes in dense thickets along stream courses, in stands of mesquite or scrub oaks (typically near water in semi-arid areas), or within the hedgerows dividing fields. The bird suspends its usually deep nest cup of leaves, bark, other plant fibers, and spider silk from a horizontal fork of a shrub. The types of habitat used vary widely among the Bell's Vireo's four subspecies.

FOOD: Mostly insects; after July, some fruit. Bell's Vireo gleans foliage and branches.

RANGE: Breeds from southern (formerly northern) California and northern Baja California east and south to Indiana, Louisiana, and central Mexico. **WINTERS:** From northwestern Mexico south to Honduras. **IN PERIL:** See under Listing.

JEOPARDIZED: By destruction of the birds' riparian habitat in combination with cowbird parasitism (see p. 219). Bell's Vireo sometimes responds to cowbird eggs by building a second floor in its nest to bury them.

LISTING: Blue-Listed 1972–82, then placed in the **Special Concern** category in 1986 when the California subspecies (Least Bell's Vireo) was listed by the U.S. Fish and Wildlife Service as **Endangered** (see p. 56). By 1982 a few small populations were stable or barely increasing in the Middlewestern Prairie and Southern Great Plains regions. The Breeding Bird Survey indicated losses on the Osage Plains of Kansas, Oklahoma, and Texas. The compounding of riparian habitat loss with cowbird parasitism is clearly responsible for declines in California, but the reasons behind declines in mesquite habitat are less apparent. By 1986 Bell's Vireo was reported in decline or serious decline in parts of the Southern Great Plains Region, and declining in the South Texas Region. Southwestern populations remained of Special Concern, and the U.S. Fish and Wildlife Service qualified them for Category 3 notice of review (see p. 103). Populations elsewhere were of **Local Concern.** As of 1991, the Arizona Bell's Vireo continues to be recognized as a Category 3C candidate according to the Service's listing priority system. Category 3C candidates have been found to be more abundant or widespread than previously believed, or not subject to the threats that place the continued existence of the bird at risk.

GRASSHOPPER SPARROW

Ammodramus savannarum

NESTING: Usually in native grasslands or prairies, sometimes in cultivated or old fields or open savannas. The Grasshopper Sparrow places its nest in a shallow depression (so that the nest rim rests flush with the ground) and conceals the cup of dried grass with overhanging grass and herbaceous plants that form an arch or dome at the rear.

FOOD: Mostly insects (primarily grasshoppers) and other terrestrial invertebrates; also seeds of grass and other herbaceous plants. While foraging, the Grasshopper Sparrow usually picks items from the substrate.

RANGE: Breeds locally from southern Canada south to southern California, northern Sonora, and Florida. Other subspecies extend from central Mexico and the Greater Antilles south to northern South America. **WINTERS:** From the southern U.S. south through the rest of the breeding range. **IN PERIL:** See under Listing.

NOTES: The Grasshopper Sparrow nests in semicolonial breeding groups of 3 to 12 pairs. Local populations are subject to wide yearly variation in numbers.

JEOPARDIZED: By the habitual loss of nests to mowing machines in cultivated grassland. Even after the cover is mowed, the birds stay and suffer further losses to predators. The primary threats are urban sprawl and the conversion of native prairie to cultivated fields.

LISTING: Blue-Listed since 1974; the Florida subspecies (the Florida Grasshopper Sparrow) was federally listed as **Endangered** in 1986. By 1982 there was confirmation of declines, although reports from a number of areas conflicted. Losses in important breeding states from the Dakotas and Nebraska east to New York, New Jersey, and Maryland were evident from Breeding Bird Survey data. By 1986 the Grasshopper Sparrow was reported as declining in parts of the Northeastern Maritime Region, in Ontario, in parts of the Middlewestern Prairie Region, and in the Central Southern and Southern Great Plains regions. It was seriously declining in the Florida and Appalachian regions.

BACHMAN'S SPARROW
Aimophila aestivalis

NESTING: On the ground in old-growth pine stands over 80 years old, or in clearings during the first five years after clearcutting. Both habitats have a similar grass-herb layer in which Bachman's Sparrow conceals its open or domed cup of coarse grass and herbaceous plants.

FOOD: Mostly seeds, particularly those of grasses, sedges, and other herbaceous plants. Also some insects and other terrestrial invertebrates, including a few spiders, snails, and millipedes. While foraging, it picks items from the substrate.

RANGE: Restricted to the southeastern U.S., from the Ohio Valley and Maryland south to eastern Texas and Florida. **WINTERS:** From the states around the Gulf of Mexico east to North Carolina. **IN PERIL:** Throughout its range.

NOTES: Bachman's Sparrow is an uncommon host of the Brown-headed Cowbird.

JEOPARDIZED: By the loss of old-growth stands. Originally a "fugitive species" that bred wherever fires had created the necessary conditions in the understory, or had removed the forest canopy, the bird suffers where pines are grown commercially and cut every 30–40 years. The birds then cannot find enough young stands and require old-growth areas as habitat "reservoirs." The species benefits from management for Red-cockaded Woodpeckers (p. 29), which encourages development of old-growth stands.

LISTING: Blue-Listed since 1972. By 1982 there was nearly complete agreement favoring Blue Listing, because the species was declining or seriously declining in the Middlewestern Prairie, Appalachian, Central Southern, and Southern Atlantic Coast regions. There was some suggestion in the Piedmont that competition from Field Sparrows prompted losses. In addition, the Breeding Bird Survey reported losses in the Lower Coastal Plain. By 1986, Bachman's Sparrow was reported in severe decline in the Southern Atlantic Coast and Middlewestern Prairie regions. As of 1991, it continues to be recognized as a Category 2 candidate according to the U.S. Fish and Wildlife Service's listing priority system; thus the Service has information indicating the possible appropriateness of listing, but feels that further information is still needed.

NOT OFFICIALLY LISTED IN THE U.S.: The Blue List

BIRDS OF
SPECIAL CONCERN

Many of the avian species that are not federally listed as Threatened or Endangered are nonetheless moving rapidly one way or the other along the continuum between relative vulnerability and relative safety. But the movement, sadly, trends heavily toward vulnerability: although some small reversals toward safety, such as that of the Osprey, are apparent, more than one in nine of the 650-odd species breeding in North America are included in this book; for them, the National Audubon Society has reported losses in all or parts of their ranges and placed them on its Blue List or auxiliary lists of birds of Special or Local concern. Preferring to err on the conservative side, we see as much reason to keep an eye on previously vulnerable birds (like the Osprey) that appear to be recovering as to keep watch on those that are generally regarded as safe but whose jeopardy in local areas may have begun to spread.

When it has been confirmed that a Blue-Listed bird (see p. 119) appears to be recovering from a past decline (when it no longer shows clear, recent signs of population reductions in all or major parts of its range), the species may be removed from the Blue List but still be considered of Special Concern. Should its recovery continue, the species may be listed as of only Local Concern (see p. 173), or eliminated from listing altogether. To remain of Special Concern, the bird must be recommended for listing over a reasonably large area and still be in need of systematic information on changes in its condition.

Note that it was not until 1982 that the National Audubon Society partitioned the Blue List by moving some of its species into the new categories of Special Concern and Local Concern, and movement from the Blue List to either of these two new categories in 1982 would therefore be erroneous, because of the absence of such finer geographic distinctions prior to 1982. (We report the changes in vulnerability between 1982 and 1986, which is the most current version of the list, in the Listing portion of each species treatment.) In the case of birds previously thought to be safe, reports of regional declines are often the first sign of significant, impending, long-term losses. Thus, becoming listed may carry with it the benefit of gaining for a bird the attention of birders and ornithologists, possibly attracting funds to aid in its conservation, and sometimes enlisting the clout of political activists at a point when intervention may be most timely (see p. 225). By assigning priority to these species over those not seeming to need special protection, we hope to encourage ornithologists to expand our knowledge of these species' biology and thus provide the background necessary for steps that will aid their conservation.

Assigning relative vulnerability and relative safety is clearly more difficult and much more controversial among ornithologists than determining whether or not a bird is in imminent danger of extinction. The Willow Flycatcher, for example, is warranted only Special Concern even though the western subspecies is moving rapidly toward extinction and is a candidate for federal listing. It is probably in worse shape than many species on the Blue List, but when considered at the entire-species level, the picture for this flycatcher looks significantly, and misleadingly, brighter.

On the basis of reports from the National Audubon Society, then, 32 birds warranted Special Concern by 1986.

REFERENCE: Tate and Tate, 1982.

WESTERN GREBE

Aechmophorus occidentalis

NESTING: In the shallow water of marshes and lakes, where it builds a tight floating platform of fresh and rotting vegetation typically anchored to, or built up over, living vegetation. The nest may be in the open or hidden.

FOOD: Mostly fish, but also aquatic invertebrates, some amphibians, and feathers—the latter presumably to pad sharp fish bones during digestion; the young, in fact, consume the feathers of adults. While foraging, a Western Grebe floats and then dives, pursuing its prey under water.

RANGE: Breeds in western North America from southeastern Alaska and central Saskatchewan south to central Mexico.

WINTERS: North to southwestern British Columbia and Utah, with much of the population moving to the Pacific coast, south to central Mexico. **IN PERIL:** In no recognized portion of its range in particular, but confirmation of stable populations is needed.

NOTES: The Western Grebe forms groups throughout the year and joins breeding colonies that vary from tens to hundreds of nests. Ornithologists recently split the Western Grebe into two species (Western and Clark's) after finding that a difference in one of their vocalizations prevents the two species from hybridizing. The Western Grebe habitually feeds nearer to shore than does the Clark's, but the two are often found together, often with other grebes.

JEOPARDIZED: Formerly by plume hunters, who decimated populations, and now by disturbance of its breeding colonies and oil pollution of its coastal winter range.

LISTING: Blue-Listed 1973–82, and listed as of only **Special Concern** in 1986. By 1982 the winter and migrating populations were smaller in the Mountain West Region but seemed to be stabilizing at a low level in general. By 1986 no sources from any region indicated declines, but further information is needed.

CLARK'S GREBE

Aechmophorus clarkii

NESTING: Requires the shallow water of marshes and lakes, where it builds the same type of floating platform built by the Western Grebe (see p. 141).

FOOD: Same as the Western Grebe's, so far as is known.

RANGE: Similar to that of the Western Grebe, though perhaps in relatively greater numbers toward the south. Differences between the two remain to be fully elucidated. **WINTERS:** In a pattern much like that of the Western Grebe. **IN PERIL:** As with the Western Grebe, in no recognized portion of its range in particular, but confirmation of stable populations is needed.

NOTES: Clark's Grebe forms groups throughout the year and joins breeding colonies that vary from tens to hundreds of nests. Ornithologists recently split Clark's from the far more numerous Western Grebe, after finding that a difference in one of their vocalizations prevents the two species from hybridizing. Clark's Grebe habitually feeds farther from shore than does the Western. Its range broadly overlaps with that of the Western, but it is rare within the northern portion of the Western's range. Clark's may perform more "springing" dives (leaping from the water before submerging) than does the Western. That may allow steeper dives into deeper foraging habitat, and lead to partitioning of food resources with Westerns, which may forage nearer the surface.

JEOPARDIZED: Formerly by plume hunters, who decimated its populations, and now by disturbance of its breeding colonies and oil pollution of its coastal winter range.

LISTING: Blue-Listed (as the Western Grebe) 1973–82, and listed as of only **Special Concern** in 1986. Until the Western and Clark's Grebes were discovered to be distinct species, few observers distinguished between the two, including both in surveys as Western Grebes.

REDDISH EGRET

Egretta rufescens

NESTING: In brackish marshes and shallow coastal habitats, particularly mangroves, in which the Reddish Egret selects small trees or shrubs (or sometimes sites on the ground) on which to place its level platform of sticks, or sometimes of twigs, rootlets, and grass.

FOOD: Mostly fish, also aquatic invertebrates and small vertebrates, taken usually in salt water. The Reddish Egret hunts very actively, often pursuing schools of fish in shallow water, but occasionally raking the bottom with its foot to stir up prey. It feeds its young by regurgitation.

RANGE: Breeds locally around the Gulf of Mexico, in Mexico, and through the Caribbean. **WINTERS:** North to San Diego and south to Costa Rica and Venezuela.

IN PERIL: In Florida, Texas, Louisiana, Alabama, California, Mississippi, Mexico, and the West Indies, but see under Listing.

NOTES: The Reddish Egret nests in colonies. White-phase individuals, found in the Gulf of Mexico and the Caribbean, can be the offspring of red-phase parents.

JEOPARDIZED: By plume hunters, who virtually exterminated most populations (although they may have overlooked one Texas colony). From 1927 to 1937, the numbers in Florida colonies plummeted but later reestablished themselves. Now perhaps 2,000 pairs nest in the U.S., and the species remains vulnerable to coastal development.

LISTING: **Blue-Listed** in 1972 and from 1975 to 1980, but listed as of only **Special** **Concern** since 1981. By 1982, surveys in Texas and Florida indicated that the Reddish Egret remained rare but was stable or increasing. By 1986 the U.S. Fish and Wildlife Service had qualified it for Category 2 candidacy where it nests in Florida, Texas, Mexico, and the West Indies, and where it regularly appears in Alabama, California, Louisiana, and Mississippi. As of 1991 the Reddish Egret continued to be recognized as a Category 2 candidate according to the Service's listing priority system; thus the Service has information indicating the possible appropriateness of listing, but feels that further information is still needed.

AMERICAN BLACK DUCK

Anas rubripes

NESTING: The American Black Duck nests in brackish or freshwater wetlands with emergent vegetation or in wooded swamps. It conceals its nest in clumps of grass or thickets, and methodically fills a depression with dry grass and leaves. It also, although very rarely, uses abandoned nests of other birds found in trees.

FOOD: Mostly aquatic invertebrates, including insects, worms, and snails, also seeds, tubers, other aquatic vegetation, grass, herbaceous plants, berries, and grain. The Black Duck feeds by dabbling—floating in shallow water and ducking its head to reach submerged food on or near the bottom while raising its hindquarters above the surface.

RANGE: Breeds mostly in northeastern North America, but throughout the region from northern Saskatchewan and Labrador south to Illinois and North Carolina. **WINTERS:** From southeastern Canada south to the Gulf of Mexico. **IN PERIL:** In the Northeast and Middle Atlantic regions, but see under Listing.

NOTES: The Black Duck is genetically very similar to the Mallard, and the two species hybridize. Geographic barriers to hybridization were removed as native forests were cut and prairie pothole-breeding Mallards came into contact with woodland pond-breeding Black Ducks. Hybridization has been accelerated by the large numbers of Mallards that are reared on game farms and released into the heart of the Black Duck's range.

JEOPARDIZED: By aerial spraying for spruce budworm, and by habitat loss, acid precipitation, and hybridization and competition with Mallards. The Black Duck was formerly the most abundant duck breeding in the U.S.

LISTING: Blue-Listed 1980–81, but listed as of only **Special Concern** since 1982. By 1982 the Black Duck was declining in the Middlewestern Prairie Region, and there were mixed reports of stable or decreasing numbers from the Hudson–Delaware, Niagara–Champlain, and Northeastern Maritime regions. Because no field data on the number of Black Ducks carrying Mallard genes were available, the degree of hybridization remained unclear, and the Black Duck therefore remained of Special Concern. By 1986 hybridization was known to be blurring the species' distinctness and shrinking its eastern populations.

FULVOUS WHISTLING-DUCK
Dendrocygna bicolor

NESTING: On a levee above flooded rice-fields, hummocks in shallow freshwater and brackish marshes and lagoons, or areas between ponds or swamps, where the female builds a neatly woven bowl, sometimes building it up 6 inches above the ground, then snips the surrounding reeds and sedges within 4 to 5 feet of the nest.

FOOD: Mostly greens—which may include the leafy parts of both aquatic and terrestrial plants—and also seeds, particularly rice, but also alfalfa and corn. The Fulvous Whistling-duck usually feeds by dabbling—floating in shallow water and ducking its head to reach submerged food on or near the bottom while raising its hindquarters above the surface—but also picks food from the substrate. It feeds mostly at night.

RANGE: Breeds from southeastern (formerly central) California, Texas, and southern Florida south patchily to central Argentina; also East Africa and India.

WINTERS: Over most of the breeding range, but now rarely in California or Arizona. **IN PERIL:** In the Southern Atlantic Coast and Southern Pacific Coast regions, but see under Listing. Already extirpated from northern California.

NOTES: This bird is closely associated with rice cultivation. Females habitually lay eggs in the nests of other Fulvous Whistling-ducks (see p. 219).

JEOPARDIZED: By destruction of marshes and by other, as yet unidentified, factors. Pesticides, such as Aldrin, used in Louisiana ricefields led to declines in the 1960's. When Aldrin use was discontinued, populations recovered.

LISTING: Blue-Listed 1972–79, but listed as of only **Special Concern** since 1982. By 1982 the species was considered stable in the Central Southern Region but in severe decline in the Southern Atlantic Coast Region and therefore of Special Concern in that area. By 1986 it warranted Special Concern from reported declines in parts of the Southern Atlantic Coast Region and severe declines in the Southern Pacific Coast Region. The U.S. Fish and Wildlife Service qualified the southwestern population (Arizona and California) for Category 2 candidacy. As of 1991 the Fulvous Whistling-duck continues to be recognized as such, according to the U.S. Fish and Wildlife Service's listing priority system; thus the Service has information indicating the possible appropriateness of listing, but feels that further information is still needed.

CANVASBACK
Aythya valisineria

KING RAIL
Rallus elegans

NESTING: Usually requires ample emergent vegetation over water less than 2 feet deep bordering on open stretches of freshwater marshes, lakes, ponds, rivers, or bays. The Canvasback builds a well-concealed basket, sometimes selecting a muskrat house or, rarely, dry ground for a site.

FOOD: Mostly aquatic vegetation, also aquatic invertebrates, particularly small clams. While foraging, it usually floats and then dives, feeding underwater.

RANGE: Breeds in northwestern North America, from Alaska south and east to northeastern California, Kansas, and western Ontario. **WINTERS:** From Alaska, the Great Lakes, and New England south to Florida and southern Mexico. **IN PERIL:** Throughout its breeding range.

NOTES: Females habitually fly back to breed in the area where they were born; males almost never do. Nests are often parasitized by Redheads (see p. 219).

JEOPARDIZED: By the loss of breeding habitat as prairie potholes and freshwater marshes are drained and cultivated.

LISTING: Blue-Listed 1975–81, but listed as of only **Special Concern** since 1982. By 1982, the migrating and wintering populations were still in a 30-year decline, although there were some reports that the numbers had improved. By 1986, the continuing downward trend seen in many species of waterfowl had not eased. The controversy over hunting continued, but was seen by many as a distraction from the more basic issue of wetland preservation.

NESTING: Requires hummocks 6 to 8 inches above water within the emergent vegetation of freshwater swamps and marshes, ricefields, coastal brackish marshes, or, occasionally, grassy areas. The King Rail arches dry grass over its neat, deeply hollowed platform of dry aquatic vegetation.

FOOD: Mostly aquatic invertebrates, particularly crustaceans, also insects, fish, frogs, a few seeds, and grain in winter. While foraging, the King Rail usually probes in the mud or sand (in or near shallow water) or picks items from the substrate.

RANGE: Breeds in eastern North America from eastern Nebraska and Massachusetts south to southern Mexico and Cuba. **WINTERS:** Mostly from southern Texas and southern Georgia south through the remainder of the breeding range. **IN PERIL:** Throughout its range, as populations appear to be universally low, but persisting.

NOTES: King and Clapper Rails occasionally hybridize where brackish and freshwater habitat meet along tidal creeks and rivers of the Atlantic coast and Gulf of Mexico.

JEOPARDIZED: By habitat loss and agricultural pesticides.

LISTING: Blue-Listed 1976–82, but listed as of only **Special Concern** in 1986. By 1982 there was a steady decline in the Middlewestern Prairie Region. Throughout its range, the King Rail either had held stable at low levels or was entirely absent, with reports of increases only in the Central Southern Region, where the population was low but building in the ricefields of southwestern Louisiana. By 1986 the species was relegated to Special Concern, as its populations were stable or increasing (where reports were available). The King Rail was listed as **Vulnerable** in Canada in 1985.

SNOWY PLOVER
Charadrius alexandrinus

NESTING: On beaches, dry mud or salt flats, or the sandy edges of rivers, lakes, or ponds. The nest is only a scrape, though the birds often place it within grass tufts or among bits of debris and twigs that conceal the eggs.

FOOD: Mostly insects, also aquatic invertebrates and small fish. While foraging, the Snowy Plover usually hunts visually, sometimes quivering its leg to stir up prey, running and picking items from the substrate, and probing beneath the surface of mud or sand (in or near shallow water).

RANGE: Widespread, reaching all but northern Asia, New Zealand, and Oceania.

WINTERS (North American populations): mostly from northwestern Mexico and the Bahamas south to Venezuela (in the east) and Chile (in the west). Part of the California population does not migrate.

IN PERIL: The species faces extirpation as a breeder on the U.S. west coast, and a recent survey of Gulf of Mexico beaches from Mississippi to Florida found fewer than 200 pairs.

NOTES: The Snowy Plover sometimes forms poorly defined colonies. Populations in the East produce one brood per year, but many pairs in the West produce two.

JEOPARDIZED: By the loss of suitable breeding habitat and by disturbance and destruction of nests on the remaining beach habitats.

LISTING: Blue-Listed 1972–82 and listed as of **Special Concern** in 1986. By 1982 there was confirmation that the Southern Pacific Coast and Middle Pacific Coast regions were undergoing serious losses. Losses on the Pacific Coast were verified by the Christmas Bird Count, which showed a 93-percent decline in central California and a 68-percent decline in southern California. It was suggested that the condition of inland nesting habitat might account for local problems. By 1986, Special Concern was warranted, as declines were reported only from the Middle Pacific Coast Region, owing, perhaps, to insufficient coverage by observers in other parts of the species' range. Reports did not indicate major regional population declines in the Southeast, although declines were reported in parts of Florida and Ontario, and moderate to severe declines were reported in the Southern Great Plains Region. The U.S. Fish and Wildlife Service qualified the western subspecies, *Charadrius alexandrinus nivosus,* and the southeastern subspecies, *C. a. tenuirostris,* as Category 2 (see p. 99) candidates. As of 1991, both the western and the southeastern subspecies continue to be recognized as Category 2 candidates, according to the U.S. Fish and Wildlife Service's listing priority system; thus the Service has information indicating the possible appropriateness of listing, but feels that further information is still needed.

LONG-BILLED CURLEW
Numenius americanus

NESTING: In grassy meadows or prairies, where the bird scrapes a hollow that sometimes forms a substantial platform.

FOOD: Mostly insects, also marine invertebrates, including worms, burrowing crustaceans, and mollusks, the eggs and nestlings of other birds, toads, and a few berries. While foraging, the Long-billed Curlew uses its bill to probe beneath the surface of mud or sand (in or near shallow water) but also takes prey from within the water column, plucks berries, or picks items from the substrate.

RANGE: Breeds inland from central Canada south to northeastern California, New Mexico, and Kansas. **WINTERS:** From central California and the Gulf of Mexico south to Costa Rica along beaches and mud flats. **IN PERIL:** See under Listing.

NOTES: Our largest shorebird. Males are more likely than females to return to breed in the area where they were born.

JEOPARDIZED: Mainly from the ongoing loss and degradation of the bird's breeding habitat, but also apparently as a result of organochlorine poisoning.

LISTING: **Blue-Listed** 1981 and 1982, but listed as of only **Special Concern** in 1986. By 1982 the Long-billed Curlew was stable at the previous year's low numbers in the Southwest and declining in the Northern Rocky Mountain–Intermountain and Southern Great Plains regions (although the Breeding Bird Survey reported a stable population). By 1986 it was reported declining in parts of the Southern Great Plains Region. The U.S. Fish and Wildlife Service qualified it for Category 2 candidacy (see p. 99) throughout its extensive western range. As of 1991 the Long-billed Curlew continues to be recognized as a Category 2 candidate, according to the U.S. Fish and Wildlife Service's listing priority system; thus the Service has information indicating the possible appropriateness of listing, but feels that further information is still needed.

NOT OFFICIALLY LISTED IN THE U.S.: Special Concern

SWAINSON'S HAWK

Buteo swainsoni

NESTING: In savanna, prairies, deserts, open pine–oak woodlands, cliffs, and cultivated lands with scattered trees in which it builds a platform of large sticks, twigs, brambles, and grass. The Swainson's Hawk sometimes uses the abandoned nests of other birds, particularly those of magpies.

FOOD: Mostly small mammals, including rabbits, also birds (usually fledglings), other smaller vertebrates, including lizards, snakes, frogs, and toads, as well as large insects, on which it sometimes gorges. Swainson's Hawk usually hunts by soaring at high altitude or by swooping down on prey from an elevated perch.

RANGE: Breeds in western North America from Alaska south and east to central (formerly southern) California, Missouri, and northern Mexico. **WINTERS:** Primarily on the pampas of southern South America.

IN PERIL: In California and probably other areas.

NOTES: Prior to World War II, on the northbound leg of its migration, flocks typically consisted of over 2,000 individuals.

JEOPARDIZED: Possibly by the loss of unbroken grasslands and by human disturbance of nest sites; it takes only minimal disturbance to induce Swainson's Hawks to desert their nests. Nests in agricultural shelter belts risk a one-in-three chance of destruction by wind and hail. Many individuals have been shot while perched along roads.

LISTING: Blue-Listed 1972–82, and listed as of only **Special Concern** in 1986. By 1982 it appeared that most populations were stable or growing, but in the Southern Great Plains Region the species' breeding numbers were clearly low, and a decline was recorded by the Kansas Breeding Bird Survey. In the Mountain West Region, Swainson's Hawk had declined or was missing entirely from its usual breeding habitat. By 1986 it warranted Special Concern because of a lack of reports, although the U.S. Fish and Wildlife Service qualified it for Category 2 (see p. 99) candidacy. As of 1991, Swainson's Hawk continues to be recognized as a Category 3C candidate, according to the Service's listing priority system. Category 3C candidates have been found to be more abundant or widespread than previously believed, or not subject to the threats that place the continued existence of the bird at risk.

FERRUGINOUS HAWK
Buteo regalis

NESTING: In sites offering a wide view, on prairies, plains, badlands, or similar open country. Nests are usually placed in conifers, but the Ferruginous Hawk will also use cliffs, banks, buttes, or slopes, where it builds a platform of heavy sticks, cow dung, bones, and debris.

FOOD: Almost entirely small mammals, particularly ground squirrels and jackrabbits, but also birds, reptiles—primarily snakes and lizards—and large insects. While hunting, the Ferruginous Hawk swoops down from a perch, striking prey on the ground, hovers and drops on prey, or scans in a low or high, searching flight.

RANGE: Breeds in western North America from eastern Washington and southern Saskatchewan south to eastern Oregon, southeastern Arizona, and northern Texas.

WINTERS: Through most of its breeding range and south to central Mexico.

IN PERIL: See under Listing.

NOTES: In some areas, how many pairs nest, how many eggs the pairs produce, and how many young are reared vary with the size of the jackrabbit or prairie dog population.

JEOPARDIZED: By the reduction of its populations by shooting (especially of birds perched along roads). Other factors contributing to the Ferruginous Hawk's decline are uncertain, but the species is now rare in many parts of its range.

LISTING: Blue-Listed 1972–81 and listed as of only **Special Concern** since 1982. By 1982 the Christmas Bird Count suggested that populations in the critical Southern Great Plains Region wintering areas were more or less stable, but winter populations in the Southwest Region were reported as severely declining, and in the Mountain West Region reports indicated that the Ferruginous Hawk had been absent from its usual breeding habitat since 1978. Overall, it appeared to be stable at a reduced level or locally declining, but its status was in need of confirmation. By 1986 it warranted Special Concern because of a lack of reports over the preceding four-year period. The U.S. Fish and Wildlife Service qualified it for Category 2 (see p. 99) candidacy. As of 1991 the Ferruginous Hawk continues to be recognized as a Category 2 candidate, according to the Service's listing priority system; thus the Service has information indicating the possible appropriateness of listing, but feels that further information is still needed. The Ferruginous Hawk was listed as **Threatened** in Canada in 1980.

CRESTED CARACARA

Polyborus plancus

NESTING: The Crested Caracara places its nest in trees, often palmettos, and occasionally pines, giant cacti, or shrubs. Any of these must provide a broad view of open country, particularly semiarid brushlands, but also pastureland, areas under cultivation, or semideserts. The nest is a bulky, loose, and deeply hollowed platform of sticks, vines, and twigs. The Caracara often prefers arid areas, but it also uses moist habitats. Its nests are used year after year, and may be shared with Great-tailed Grackles or other smaller birds.

FOOD: Mostly carrion, also small mammals and other small vertebrates, including reptiles, turtle eggs, and fish, as well as invertebrates. While foraging, the Crested Caracara gleans the ground, seeks prey in a low, searching flight, or soars at high altitude. Its long legs and flat claws facilitate chasing after prey that are quick, and raking the ground for those that are slow. Caracaras feed at carcasses with vultures, often harassing the vultures until they disgorge.

RANGE: Baja California, southern Arizona, Texas, and Florida south to southern South America. **WINTER:** Resident.

IN PERIL: Populations are apparently declining throughout the Crested Caracara's U.S. range (areas in southern Arizona, New Mexico, southern Texas, Florida, and, rarely, southwestern Louisiana).

NOTES: The Crested Caracara is the national bird of Mexico. Information on its breeding biology is needed.

JEOPARDIZED: Primarily by the conversion of habitat for agriculture.

LISTING: Blue-Listed 1972–79 and in 1981, and listed as of only **Special Concern** in 1982 and 1986. By 1982 the Crested Caracara's numbers were declining at the northern edge of its range (Florida and Texas), and the species continued to be of Special Concern because of its past listing. By 1986 Special Concern continued because of a lack of reports, and the U.S. Fish and Wildlife Service qualified the Florida population for Category 2 (see p. 99) candidacy.

MERLIN
Falco columbarius

NESTING: Usually in trees or cliffs with a wide view of the savanna or open woodlands, but the Merlin sometimes nests in cities, and often appropriates the abandoned nests of crows, magpies, or hawks. It may also use tree cavities or make a scrape on the ground in treeless country.

FOOD: Mostly birds, which commonly make up more than 90 percent of its diet. Small mammals and insects constitute the remaining prey items. Hunting typically involves low, searching flights to flush prey. Merlins also dive into bird flocks or attack prey after a quick flight from an elevated perch. They capture flying insects by sallying from a perch on short flights. Males, being much smaller, take lighter prey than do females.

RANGE: Breeds from Alaska and northern Canada south to Oregon, Minnesota, and Nova Scotia; also across northern Eurasia.

WINTERS (North American populations): From southern Canada south through Central America and the West Indies to northern South America. **IN PERIL:** Throughout the southern portions of the Canadian prairie provinces and the easternmost portions of the U.S. breeding range.

NOTES: The male arrives on its breeding grounds first, usually returning to the same area. Yearlings, particularly males, may assist as helpers, defending the territory and providing food for the female. Urban merlins may be only partially migratory.

JEOPARDIZED: By pesticides, loss of habitat, and shooting, but these birds are relatively uncommon and their status is unclear. Individuals in eastern Canada display the effects of pesticides, and some in western Canada show evidence of mercury accumulation.

LISTING: Blue-Listed 1972–81, and listed as of only **Special Concern** since 1982. By 1982 there were some recommendations from the periphery of the breeding range that the Merlin should be removed from listing. Data were based on reports of migrating and wintering populations, and there was no apparent regional decline. By 1986, however, the Merlin still warranted Special Concern because it had seldom been reported in the preceding four years, and accurate assessment based on the few reports on record was impossible.

SHARP-TAILED GROUSE

Tympanuchus phasianellus

NESTING: The Sharp-tailed Grouse inhabits grasslands, shrublands, savanna, or partly cleared boreal forests, where it conceals its shallow scrape under shrubs or in grass.

FOOD: Mostly greens, including leaves, buds, and flowers; also insects, nuts, fruit, and, in winter, waste grain. While foraging, the Sharp-tailed Grouse usually picks items from the substrate or browses on foliage. Its young take primarily insects.

RANGE: From Alaska and northern Canada south to northeastern Oregon, Colorado, and Michigan; formerly to northeastern California, Kansas, and Illinois.

WINTER: Resident. **IN PERIL:** In the southern portion of its range, from much of which the species has already been extirpated; recently reintroduced into northeastern Oregon.

NOTES: Male and females gather into winter flocks that typically contain 10 to 35 individuals but sometimes reach 100. The Sharp-tailed Grouse sometimes hybridizes with the Greater Prairie-chicken.

JEOPARDIZED: By overhunting, overgrazing, and conversion of native grasslands to agriculture.

LISTING: Blue-Listed in 1972 and from 1978 to 1982, and listed as of only **Special Concern** in 1986. By 1982 the Sharp-tailed Grouse was stable except in the Northern Great Plains Region, where attendance at leks (traditional sites used by the birds for mating) and hatching success were reportedly low. As of 1991 the Columbian Sharp-tailed Grouse (*T. p. columbianus*, whose historic range includes Canada south through Montana to Colorado and west to the Pacific) continues to be recognized as a Category 2 candidate, according to the U.S. Fish and Wildlife Service's listing priority system; thus the Service has information indicating the possible appropriateness of listing, but feels that further information is still needed.

SAGE GROUSE
Centrocercus urophasianus

NESTING: Requires communities dominated by sagebrush, where it can conceal its shallow scrape beneath shrubs.

FOOD: Mostly greens, including flowers and buds from herbaceous plants other than grass; also insects. While foraging, the Sage Grouse browses on foliage or picks items from the substrate. In the autumn and winter it relies virtually entirely on sagebrush leaves.

RANGE: Great Basin and Rocky Mountains from eastern Washington and southern Saskatchewan south to eastern California and northern New Mexico. **WINTER:** Remains within the breeding range.

IN PERIL: Declines have been particularly marked in the Northwest, and it has already been extirpated from British Columbia.

NOTES: Males and females gather into flocks in winter. The Sage Grouse is not equipped with the muscular gizzard of its relatives and must limit its diet to relatively soft foods.

JEOPARDIZED: By the loss of habitat to agriculture and grazing and the use of herbicides to destroy sagebrush, which have eliminated this bird from much of its historic range. Successful breeding within the sagebrush community depends upon the wet meadows or green areas that supply sufficient insects for broods to forage.

LISTING: Blue-Listed 1972–81, and listed as of only **Special Concern** since 1982. By 1982 two-thirds of reports indicated declines, but solid data were lacking. Consid-erable effort was being expended to keep populations stable, if at much lower levels than 30 years before. By 1986 the Sage Grouse still warranted Special Concern in Oregon, Washington, and the adjacent portion of Canada. The U.S. Fish and Wildlife Service qualified it for Category 2 candidacy (see p. 99) in that area, and it was of **Local Concern** elsewhere. As of 1991 the Western Sage Grouse continues to be recognized as a Category 2 candidate, according to the Service's listing priority system; thus the Service has information indicating the possible appropriateness of listing, but feels that further information is still needed.

COMMON BARN-OWL
Tyto alba

NESTING: The Barn-owl seeks open or partially open habitats, principally grasslands and farmlands (often in or near towns), where it can find a cavity in a snag, building, cave, or cliff crevice. It sometimes nests in arroyo walls, excavating a burrow. **FOOD:** Mostly rodents, particularly voles, also some birds, rarely amphibians, reptiles, and insects. The Barn-owl hunts in a low, searching flight or swoops down in a spread-wing gliding descent from a perch to capture prey on the ground. It may depend virtually entirely on mice and rats in some urban habitats.

RANGE: Almost worldwide, extending north in North America to southern Canada. **WINTERS:** Over most of the breeding range. **IN PERIL:** Apparently over much of North America.

NOTES: The number of eggs laid parallels the abundance of prey and the mildness of the preceding winter; similarly, low fledging success is seen following a severe winter. The Barn-owl roosts during the day, sometimes in groups, but individuals depart the roost one by one before sunset, circling as they leave.

JEOPARDIZED: Broad population declines are due mostly to the conversion of grassland and farmland by suburbanization.

LISTING: Blue-Listed 1972–81, and listed as of only **Special Concern** since 1982. By 1982 populations appeared low but stable over most of the Barn-owl's range, but very few observations were reported. Recommendations were made that nest boxes be made available in the owl's former nesting range. By 1986 the Barn-owl still warranted Special Concern and was widely reported as declining or severely declining. The Special Concern extended throughout the species' range, although the birds apparently responded positively to nest-box programs. The Common Barn-owl was listed as **Vulnerable** in Canada in 1984.

EASTERN SCREECH-OWL

Otus asio

NESTING: The Eastern Screech-owl occupies open deciduous forests, woodlands, scrub, riparian habitats, towns, and parks. It nests in cavities in snags, trees, or hollow stumps, and will use nest boxes and poles.

FOOD: Mostly insects and other terrestrial invertebrates, but there is significant regional variation, and the diet also includes a wide variety of small vertebrates. The Eastern Screech-owl hunts by swooping down in a spread-wing gliding descent from a perch to capture prey on the ground.

RANGE: Southeastern Canada, eastern U.S., and northeastern Mexico. **WINTER:** Resident. **IN PERIL:** See under Listing.

NOTES: The Eastern Screech-owl is active during the night and at dawn and dusk. Roosts may be located in hollow trees or in dense foliage close to a tree trunk. The species is abundant in suburban and urban areas that provide mature trees for nesting and roosting. The size of the owls' home range varies seasonally.

JEOPARDIZED: Populations have been reduced, in part, by the use of creosote on the telecommunication poles that the birds seek for nesting.

LISTING: Blue-Listed in 1981, and listed as of only **Special Concern** since 1982. By 1982 reports of scattered and localized areas of low populations continued. Because the Breeding Bird Survey showed populations shrinking in the west but stable in the east, the species was considered to warrant only Special Concern in some areas. By 1986, it again warranted Special Concern, for it was reported as down in the Hudson–Delaware, Southern Atlantic Coast, Appalachian, and Middlewestern Prairie regions.

BURROWING OWL

Athene cunicularia

NESTING: Requires mammal burrows found in grasslands, savannas, prairies, and other open areas. Burrows are used year after year, and the owls sometimes enlarge them by kicking dirt out, backward.

FOOD: Mostly insects and other terrestrial invertebrates; also rodents, lizards, and birds. The bird hunts night or day, swooping down in a spread-wing gliding descent from a perch and taking prey on the ground. It also hovers and drops onto prey, or catches insects in flight.

RANGE: Southwestern Canada south patchily to Tierra del Fuego. There is a disjunct resident Florida population. **WINTER:** Vacates the northern Great Basin and northern Great Plains; otherwise throughout the breeding range. **IN PERIL:** At least in California and Florida.

NOTES: The Burrowing Owl typically nests in small groups in burrows within colonies of ground squirrels or prairie dogs.

JEOPARDIZED: By the loss of its habitat to development and the destruction of nest sites as humans attempt to control and poison squirrels and prairie dogs.

LISTING: Blue-Listed 1972–81, and listed as of only **Special Concern** since 1982. By 1982, California populations remained low (displaced by suburbanization and agriculture) but stable. By 1986, the Burrowing Owl was reported in severe decline in parts of Florida and all of coastal southern California and declining in the Middle Pacific Coast Region. In a census of the San Francisco Bay Area and the central part of California's Central Valley in the spring of 1991, Burrowing Owls were found in only 62 percent of the census blocks that were known to have supported them in the previous five years, and very few new locations were found anywhere in the entire census area. The Burrowing Owl was listed as **Threatened** in Canada in 1979.

RED-HEADED WOODPECKER

Melanerpes erythrocephalus

NESTING: In deciduous woodlands (particularly those of beech or oak), open areas with a few trees, parks, old burned-over areas, or recent clearings. The Red-headed Woodpecker chisels a cavity (usually within 6 to 17 days) in a dead tree stripped of its bark or in a dead portion of a live tree. It will also use existing cavities, especially if nesting on treeless prairies where it must resort to poles, fences, or roofs.

FOOD: Largely insects, as well as a wide variety of plants and other animals, including bird eggs, nestlings, an occasional adult bird, mice, corn, various seeds and nuts, berries, and other fruit. The Red-headed Woodpecker captures flying insects by sallying from a perch in a short flight. It also forages by swooping down upon prey on the ground and by gleaning tree trunks, branches, and foliage. To cache insects, acorns, and beechnuts, it breaks them apart to fit them into natural crevices. It feeds its young insects, worms, spiders, and berries.

RANGE: Breeds in central and eastern North America from southern Canada south through the high plains to the Gulf of Mexico. **WINTER:** Most birds in the northern part of the breeding range retreat south. **IN PERIL:** In the Middle Atlantic states and southeastern U.S.

NOTES: Competes with European Starlings and other cavity-nesting species for nest sites.

JEOPARDIZED: By a variety of hazards, including the loss of nesting habitat to firewood cutting, clearcutting, and agricultural development. If nests are placed in creosote-coated utility poles, the eggs and young will die. European Starlings and Blue Jays raid the Red-headed Woodpecker's food caches.

LISTING: Blue-Listed in 1972, from 1976 to 1981, and listed as of only **Special Concern** since 1982. By 1982 the Red-headed Woodpecker was reported as seriously declining in the Southern Atlantic Coast Region, but there were mixed reports indicating that the problems might be local rather than regional. Regions that reported both stable and shrinking populations included the Hudson–Delaware, Appalachian, and Niagara–Champlain. The Breeding Bird Survey, however, reported the Southeast as the only region showing widespread declines. By 1986, the species still warranted Special Concern and was widely reported as declining or severely declining.

HAIRY WOODPECKER
Picoides villosus

NESTING: In deciduous or coniferous forests, woodlands, orchards, wooded swamps, and well-wooded towns and parks. The Hairy Woodpecker chisels a cavity into a tree or a snag that is typically used only once, although it often returns to the same nest tree. Excavation takes 7 to 25 days, the average being 20.

FOOD: Mostly insects gleaned from tree trunks and branches. The Hairy Woodpecker also feeds on sap taken from the wells drilled into trees by sapsuckers. During nesting, the female feeds at dawn and dusk, foraging within hearing distance of the young and making frequent trips; the male forages farther from the nest and returns infrequently, but provides larger prey. In the winter, the male often forages higher in the trees than does the female.

RANGE: Breeds throughout forested North America from Alaska and central Yukon across the northern prairie provinces into southern Quebec and Newfoundland and south through most of North America. **WINTER:** Resident, but some birds from high elevations or northern latitudes move downslope or migrate southward. **IN PERIL:** Over much of eastern North America and in the Pacific Northwest.

NOTES: Pair bonds are established in the winter.

JEOPARDIZED: The Hairy Woodpecker's nest cavities are commonly taken over by House Sparrows or European Starlings; these introduced birds may be a factor in the woodpecker's decline.

LISTING: Blue-Listed 1975–82, and listed as of only **Special Concern** in 1986. By 1982, populations in Ontario showed large increases, and the Hairy Woodpecker appeared stable throughout much of its range. It was, however, severely declining or declining in the Niagara–Champlain Region, through the Appalachian and Middle Atlantic Coast regions to the Central Southern Region, and declining in parts of the Northern Pacific Coast Region. Nonetheless, the Breeding Bird Survey indicated stable populations in general. By 1986 the species warranted Special Concern from reports that it was declining in the Northeastern Maritime, Southern Atlantic Coast, Appalachian, Middlewestern Prairie, and Central Southern regions, and in parts of the Southern Great Plains and Northern Pacific Coast regions.

EASTERN PHOEBE
Sayornis phoebe

NESTING: The Eastern Phoebe formerly placed its nest in crevices of cliffs, banks, or rocky ravines found in open and riparian woodlands or farmland with scattered trees. Now, however, it nests mainly on a variety of human-built structures such as culverts, wells, and particularly the underside of bridges. The nest is a cup of mud pellets, plant fibers, and moss. This phoebe often renovates used nests, sometimes those of Barn Swallows.

FOOD: Mostly insects, sometimes small fish and frogs, and, mostly in winter, berries and some seeds. To capture flying insects the Eastern Phoebe usually sallies from a perch on a short flight, often feeding just above the surface of ponds or streams.

RANGE: Breeds in central and eastern North America from northeastern British Columbia and southwestern Quebec to central New Mexico and northern Georgia.

WINTERS: Mostly from Texas east to Virginia and south to southern Mexico; in small numbers west to California.

IN PERIL: See under Listing.

NOTES: The metabolic expense of building a new nest is usually reflected in a smaller clutch size.

JEOPARDIZED: Although the reasons are not entirely clear, the loss of suitable wintering habitat is a likely contributor to the species' decline. The Eastern Phoebe is a common cowbird host (see p. 219), and if parasitized may build a second nest floor to cover the cowbird egg.

LISTING: Blue-Listed 1980 and listed as of only **Special Concern** in 1986. By 1982, there were reports of both local improvements and areas of decline in the Hudson–Delaware Region, stable to slightly declining populations in the Middlewestern Prairie and Appalachian regions, moderate declines in the Western Great Lakes and Southern Atlantic Coast regions, and a significant decrease in Alabama, on the basis of the 1980 Breeding Bird Survey and Christmas Bird Count data. By 1986 the Eastern Phoebe still warranted Special Concern and was reported as declining in the Hudson–Delaware, Southern Atlantic Coast, Ontario, Appalachian, Western Great Lakes, Central Southern, and Middlewestern Prairie regions, and seriously declining in parts of the Niagara–Champlain and Middlewestern Prairie regions, although many correspondents reported the species as stable or improving within the same regions.

WILLOW FLYCATCHER

Empidonax traillii

NESTING: Usually in thickets (especially willow) and swamps. The Willow Flycatcher builds a tight cup of grass, weed stems, and bark in a vertical or sloping fork of a shrub or deciduous tree.

FOOD: Insects and other arthropods, occasionally berries. While hunting for flying insects the bird sallies from a perch on short flights; it also hovers while foraging.

RANGE: Breeds from southern British Columbia, the southern Great Lakes Region, and New England south, at least formerly, to northern Baja California, western Texas, and Arkansas. **WINTERS:** From southern Mexico to Panama; range poorly known.

IN PERIL: In California, Baja California, Arizona, New Mexico, and many other parts of the West. Southwestern populations are approaching extinction; some northeastern populations are apparently expanding.

NOTES: The Willow Flycatcher defends its territory against the Alder Flycatcher where the ranges of the two species overlap in British Columbia and in the northeastern U.S.

JEOPARDIZED: By destruction and degradation (via cattle grazing) of riparian woodland in combination with heavy brood parasitism by cowbirds (see p. 219). Increases are possible if cattle grazing is restricted and riparian willows are protected. The Willow Flycatcher is a common cowbird host. It may be threatened by deforestation in its tropical wintering areas.

LISTING: Blue-Listed 1980–82, and listed as of only **Special Concern** in 1986. The Willow Flycatcher was listed in 1980 on the basis of declines in the Ontario, Southwest, Northern Pacific Coast, Middle Pacific Coast, and Southern Pacific Coast regions. By 1982 it was stable or improving in at least some parts of the eastern U.S. (Hudson–Delaware, Niagara–Champlain, and Southern Atlantic Coast regions). By 1986 the species warranted Special Concern as portions of the Northern Great Plains and Middle Pacific Coast regions reported declines, and the Southern Pacific Coast Region reported serious declines. As of 1991 the Southwestern Willow Flycatcher (*E. t. extimus*) continued to be recognized as a Category 2 candidate, according to the U.S. Fish and Wildlife Service's listing priority system.

PURPLE MARTIN

Progne subis

NESTING: In open country, including rural areas and savanna, particularly near water. The Purple Martin places its nest of grass, leaves, mud, and feathers in holes in snags, crevices in cliffs, other cavities, or, commonly, birdhouses (particularly in the eastern portion of its range).

FOOD: Insects, which the Purple Martin usually hunts while in prolonged, continuous flight. Occasionally it feeds on the ground, taking ants and other insects.

RANGE: Breeds widely but patchily over much of North America from southern Canada south to central Mexico and Florida. **WINTERS:** In South America, east of the Andes from Venezuela south to northern Bolivia and southeastern Brazil. **IN PERIL:** Over much of the species' range.

NOTES: The Purple Martin typically nests in colonies, and in some parts of its range readily uses colonial nest boxes. It is uncommon for a bird to return to breed in the colony where it was born. Before migrating at the end of the summer, Purple Martins gather into huge communal roosts. The species is currently the subject of a conservation program, co-sponsored by the Purple Martin Conservation Association and Pennsylvania's Edinboro University, to locate, register, and monitor all North American breeding colonies.

JEOPARDIZED: By forestry policies that eliminate standing dead trees, since that also eliminates many natural nest sites. House Sparrows and especially European Starlings, both introduced to North America, will take over the martin's nest cavities, and may be factors in its decline.

LISTING: **Blue-Listed** 1975–81, and listed as of only **Special Concern** since 1982. By 1982 no obvious pattern of regional losses had emerged from the U.S. Fish and Wildlife Service's Breeding Bird Survey data. In the eastern U.S., the Purple Martin responded well to efficient nest-box programs. In the hope that local populations would be managed even better and that published guidelines for more effective management programs would be implemented, it was retained in the Special Concern category. By 1986 it was reportedly declining in parts of the Appalachian and Middlewestern Prairie regions, and seriously declining in the Southern Pacific Coast, Hudson–Delaware, and Western Great Lakes regions. It was suggested, however, that with effective nest-box and nest-predator management programs in the East and Midwest, the species could soon be downlisted to **Local Concern**.

CAROLINA WREN

Thryothorus ludovicianus

SEDGE WREN

Cistothorus platensis

NESTING: Carolina Wrens breed in open deciduous woodlands, particularly those providing ample cover, and in farmlands and suburbs (although less commonly than House Wrens). Their nest of twigs, bark strips, leaves, and grass is placed in natural holes in trees or snags, niches among the roots of overturned trees, various other cavities, or brushpiles.

FOOD: Mostly insects, but also other invertebrates, small lower vertebrates, and some seeds. While foraging, the Carolina Wren usually picks items from the substrate or gleans foliage, tree trunks, and branches.

RANGE: Breeds in southernmost Ontario, the eastern U.S., and northeastern Mexico.

WINTER: Resident. **IN PERIL:** In the Northeast and portions of the Midwest.

NOTES: Pairs do not separate or leave their territories at the end of the breeding season.

JEOPARDIZED: By causes unknown.

LISTING: Blue-Listed 1980–81, and listed as of only **Special Concern** since 1982. By 1982 the general losses over large portions of the Carolina Wren's northern range reported previously seemed to be lessening; the species was reportedly stable in the central portion of its range. Losses were, however, reported in Alabama and northwest Florida. By 1986 the Carolina Wren still warranted Special Concern and was reported in severe decline in parts of the Ontario Region and declining in the Middlewestern Prairie Region and in parts of the Southern Great Plains Region.

NESTING: Requires grassy, wet meadows and drier marshes dominated by sedges rather than cattails. The Sedge Wren interweaves a ball of green and dry grass with growing grass that helps to camouflage the nest.

FOOD: Insects and other terrestrial invertebrates, including spiders. While foraging, the Sedge Wren picks items from the substrate and gleans foliage.

RANGE: Breeds from Alberta, southern Ontario, and New Brunswick south to Arkansas and Virginia; also from southern Mexico south patchily to southernmost South America. **WINTERS:** In North America, mostly from Tennessee and Maryland south to northeastern Mexico and Florida. In southern South America, the birds migrate north for the austral winter.

IN PERIL: In the Northeast and parts of the Midwest.

NOTES: The Sedge Wren is an opportunistic breeder, readily switching to new nesting areas in successive years and displaying no obvious preference for a particular site from year to year. It often destroys the eggs of other Sedge Wrens and those of other small neighboring species. The Sedge Wren was formerly known as the Short-billed Marsh Wren.

JEOPARDIZED: Presumably by degradation and loss of wetlands to development.

LISTING: Blue-Listed 1979 and 1981, and listed as of only **Special Concern** since 1982. By 1982 there was concern that the declines in the Middlewestern Prairie Region seen in 1981 might be accelerating. According to the Breeding Bird Survey, that decline was also apparent in the Northeast. By 1986 the Sedge Wren still warranted Special Concern and was reportedly declining in the Middlewestern Prairie Region and severely declining in the Northeastern Maritime, Hudson–Delaware, and Ontario regions.

EASTERN BLUEBIRD
Sialia sialis

NESTING: Requires snags along the forest edge, in burned or logged woodlands, or in open country with scattered trees. The Eastern Bluebird uses natural or woodpecker-chiseled cavities to house its flimsy cup of grass, weed stems, pine needles, twigs, and, sometimes, hair or feathers.

FOOD: Mostly insects and other terrestrial invertebrates, including earthworms and snails, but also fruit, particularly berries in winter. While foraging for flying insects the Eastern Bluebird sallies from a low perch on a short flight near the ground. It also gleans items from foliage.

RANGE: Breeds from southeastern Arizona, southern Saskatchewan, and Nova Scotia south to Nicaragua and Florida.

WINTERS: From the northeastern U.S. south through the remainder of the breeding range. **IN PERIL:** In the midwestern and northeastern U.S. and southeastern Canada.

NOTES: Young from earlier broods sometimes help at the nest.

JEOPARDIZED: By the removal of dead trees and the pruning of dead branches, which eliminate nest-hole sites and encourage competition with other cavity-nesting birds, particularly the House Sparrow and European Starling. Both of these were introduced into North America and may be factors in the Eastern Bluebird's decline. The species has been reduced by up to 90 percent in the last 90 years, and nest boxes are now critically important. Severe winters or spring storms may have been factors in declines during the 1970's.

LISTING: Blue-Listed in 1972 and from 1978 to 1982, and listed as of only **Special Concern** in 1986. By 1982, reports confirmed that efficient nest-box programs benefit bluebirds not only in those areas with stable low numbers, but also in areas where populations are declining or even severely declining. Those areas included parts of the Northeastern Maritime, Niagara–Champlain, Middlewestern Prairie, Hudson–Delaware, and Western Great Lakes regions (although some local populations in those regions appeared stable). The most chronically depressed populations were limited to the Northeastern Maritime, Niagara–Champlain, and Middlewestern Prairie Regions. By 1986, populations reportedly were seriously declining in the Northeastern Maritime, Ontario, and Western Great Lakes regions, and declining in the Hudson–Delaware Region. The Eastern Bluebird was listed as **Vulnerable** in Canada in 1984.

GOLDEN-WINGED WARBLER

Vermivora chrysoptera

NESTING: In a concealing clump of grass or in grass at the base of a tree in the early successional habitats of old fields. The nest is fashioned from long grass strips and grapevine bark into a scraggly cup.

FOOD: Mostly insects and other terrestrial invertebrates, especially spiders, which the bird gleans from foliage and dead leaves.

RANGE: Breeds mostly from Minnesota east through the northeastern U.S. and southern Ontario to New England, and south in the Appalachian Mountains to northern Georgia. **WINTERS:** From the Yucatan Peninsula and Guatemala south to northern South America, but mostly in the highlands of Costa Rica and Panama, on the eastern side of the mountains. **IN PERIL:** In the northeastern U.S. and the Appalachian Mountains.

NOTES: Expansion of its range northward and eastward during the past 175 years has brought the Golden-winged Warbler into contact and competition with the abundant Blue-winged Warbler. The two species hybridize to produce fertile offspring (known commonly as Brewster's and Lawrence's Warblers).

JEOPARDIZED: By competition with the Blue-winged Warbler, along with the decreasing availability of recently abandoned farmland and the increasing proportion of land in later successional stages (which the Golden-winged Warbler avoids). The species may also be threatened by deforestation in its tropical wintering areas. There have been suggestions about reclaiming surface mines and clearcutting sites by establishing habitats the Golden-winged Warbler will use. If current trends continue, the Golden-winged may well become extinct within the next few decades.

LISTING: Blue-Listed in 1981 and 1982, and listed as of only **Special Concern** in 1986. By 1982 the Golden-winged was still being overwhelmed by the Blue-winged in some areas, but was holding steady in the Hudson–Delaware Region north of the Wisconsin Moraine and in the Pocono Mountains. There were also reports suggesting that the Golden-winged was moving northward in Wisconsin and Minnesota beyond the range of the Blue-winged, but the Breeding Bird Survey indicated that, overall, Wisconsin showed losses. By 1986 the Golden-winged was reported in serious decline in the Northeastern Maritime and Middlewestern Prairie regions, and declining in parts of the Hudson–Delaware, Ontario, and Appalachian regions.

NOT OFFICIALLY LISTED IN THE U.S.: Special Concern

YELLOW WARBLER

Dendroica petechia

NESTING: In the East the Yellow Warbler prefers moist, second-growth woodlands, scrub, and gardens; in the West, it is restricted to riparian woodlands, especially of willows. The nest is a tight, uniform, sturdy cup of weed stalks, shredded bark, and grass.

FOOD: Mostly insects, also some berries. While foraging for flying insects, the Yellow Warbler may sally from a perch on short flights. It also hunts by gleaning foliage, branches, and bark, sometimes while hovering.

RANGE: Breeds widely from Alaska and northern Canada south to the Galapagos Islands, Peru, and Venezuela. **WINTERS:** From southern California and southern Florida south to the Brazilian Amazon, Bolivia, and Peru. **IN PERIL:** Over much of the U.S., but especially in the West, and most seriously in California and Arizona. The Yellow Warbler has already been extirpated from the lower Colorado River Valley, where it was once abundant.

JEOPARDIZED: By the loss of riparian woodland habitat in combination with heavy brood parasitism by cowbirds. Western populations can increase wherever grazing is restricted and herbicide use on willows is discontinued sufficiently to permit regrowth of riparian vegetation. The Yellow Warbler remains, however, one of the three most frequent hosts of the Brown-headed Cowbird (see p. 219).

LISTING: Blue-Listed 1973–82, and listed as of only **Special Concern** in 1986. By 1982, significant losses were found during the Breeding Bird Survey in Idaho and the Dakotas, although there were general gains in the East. Declines were also reported in the Middle Pacific Coast, Southern Pacific Coast, Mountain West, Central Southern, Hudson–Delaware, and Western Great Lakes regions, and some suggested that the cause may be the destruction of tropical forests. By 1986, reports of losses continued in the far West, in parts of the Ontario, Appalachian, Central Southern, and Southern Great Plains regions, and serious declines were reported in the Western Great Lakes and Central Southern regions.

HENSLOW'S SPARROW

Ammodramus henslowii

NESTING: Henslow's Sparrow prefers moist areas supporting grass, herbaceous plants, and a few shrubs for its cup of coarse grass and forbs. The nest is usually placed on the ground in fields or meadows with patches of concealing grass (typically providing the nest a partial roof) or vertical stems (to which the birds can attach and elevate an unroofed nest).

FOOD: Mostly insects and other terrestrial invertebrates, including spiders and snails; also some seeds of grass, other herbaceous plants, and sedges. While foraging, Henslow's Sparrow usually picks items from the substrate. It feeds its young only insects.

RANGE: Breeds from eastern South Dakota and central Kansas east to New England and North Carolina; formerly also near Houston, Texas. **WINTERS:** In the southeastern U.S. from Texas to South Carolina. **IN PERIL:** In much of the species' range, especially in the northwestern and eastern portions. One subspecies, the Texas Henslow's Sparrow, became extinct in the 1980's.

NOTES: Henslow's Sparrow often establishes loose breeding colonies, with males holding territories lacking well-defined boundaries. The validity of the extinct Texas subspecies of Henslow's Sparrow has been questioned recently. The characters supposedly distinguishing it do not differ from those of the subspecies west of the Appalachians.

JEOPARDIZED: Despite extensive deforestation that permitted the species' range to spread and its populations to expand. It is, rather, the drainage of lowlands and their replacement with cultivation that have diminished the Henslow's Sparrow's breeding habitat throughout this century. The birds will use unmowed hayfields, but then abandon the area as soon as it is cut.

LISTING: **Blue-Listed** 1974–81, and listed as of only **Special Concern** since 1982. By 1982 there were reports of continued losses in the diminished populations of the Central Southern, Southern and Middle Atlantic Coast, Hudson–Delaware, Niagara–Champlain, Ontario, and Western Great Lakes regions. By 1986, Henslow's Sparrow was reported in serious decline in parts of the Northeastern Maritime, Hudson–Delaware, and Appalachian regions, and declining in parts of the Southern Atlantic Coast and Central Southern regions. Henslow's Sparrow was listed as **Threatened** in Canada in 1984.

DICKCISSEL
Spiza americana

NESTING: In grasslands, meadows, savanna, and cultivated or abandoned fields. The Dickcissel weaves a bulky cup of grass, other coarse herbaceous plants, or cornstalks and a few leaves.

FOOD: Insects and seeds. While foraging, the Dickcissel usually picks items from the substrate. Adults take primarily insects (70 percent), otherwise grain and the seeds of grasses and other herbaceous plants. Younger birds take the reverse: 30 percent insects and the rest seeds.

RANGE: Breeds in central and east-central North America. **WINTERS:** From southwestern Mexico south, mostly on the Pacific slope, to northern South America, particularly in rice-growing areas. **IN PERIL:** See under Listing.

NOTES: The Dickcissel's breeding distribution from New England to the Carolinas has been inconsistent. The species nested there regularly in the 1800's, but by 1905 it was gone. Then, in the 1920's, it began to return, and it continues to breed there sporadically in low numbers. The Dickcissel's post-nesting roosts contain up to several hundred individuals; flocks formed in winter vary in size.

JEOPARDIZED: By mowing machines, which destroy nests and nestlings in clover and alfalfa fields. The Dickcissel is also a common cowbird host (see p. 219).

LISTING: **Blue-Listed** 1978–82, and listed as of only **Special Concern** in 1986. By 1982 the Middlewestern Prairie and the Northern and Southern Great Plains regions reported local improvement but overall losses. The previous year's losses continued. By 1986 the Dickcissel warranted Special Concern because of reported declines or serious declines in parts of the Middlewestern Prairie Region, and declines in the Central Southern and Southern Great Plains regions.

EASTERN MEADOWLARK
Sturnella magna

NESTING: In grasslands, savanna, or fields. The Eastern Meadowlark usually selects a natural (but sometimes scraped) depression in dense cover for its cup of coarse grass, which is domed with a canopy of grass interwoven into the surrounding vegetation.

FOOD: Mostly insects and a few spiders, seeds of grass and other herbaceous plants, and occasionally fruit. While foraging, the Eastern Meadowlark usually picks items from the substrate.

RANGE: Breeds from Arizona, Nebraska, and southeastern Canada south to Brazil.

WINTERS: Over most of the breeding range, withdrawing only from the far Northeast. **IN PERIL:** Northeastern populations are shrinking, and, as of 1991, populations continue to show drastic declines.

NOTES: Clutch sizes are larger in the north. The Eastern Meadowlark is territorial with the closely related Western Meadowlark where the ranges of the two species overlap; in some cases males sing the songs of both species. The range of the Western Meadowlark has expanded eastward beyond the Great Lakes following the clearing of eastern North American forests, and this has led to occasional interbreeding with the Eastern Meadowlark.

JEOPARDIZED: By the mowing of cultivated fields (where many nests are demolished) and by the conversion of grasslands into suburbs. The Eastern Meadowlark is a common cowbird host (see p. 219).

LISTING: Blue-Listed 1980–82, and listed as of only **Special Concern** in 1986. By 1982 the previous year's declines in the Western Great Lakes and Hudson–Delaware regions continued, and the Breeding Bird Survey showed far-ranging losses in the eastern states, which were partly attributed to the harsh winters of 1976–77 and 1977–78. By 1986 the Eastern Meadowlark warranted Special Concern because of widespread reports of declines in the Northeast.

ORCHARD ORIOLE

Icterus spurius

NESTING: In scrub, mesquite, open woodlands, and orchards, where the birds hang a pendant nest woven of long, green grass blades. The nest is usually placed in trees (mostly deciduous) or shrubs among camouflaging leaves on a forked terminal twig.

FOOD: Mostly insects, also fruit and some tree blossoms. While foraging, the Orchard Oriole usually gleans foliage. It also takes nectar in winter.

RANGE: Breeds from central and eastern North America south into Mexico. **WINTERS:** From central Mexico south to northern South America. **IN PERIL:** Populations are reportedly shrinking in many areas, particularly in the western portion of the species' range.

NOTES: The Orchard Oriole may sometimes form nesting colonies. Adults and their young remain together until they depart in the autumn. In some areas in the winter the species is solitary; in others it gathers into flocks.

JEOPARDIZED: Most likely by the destruction of tropical forests. The Orchard Oriole is also a common cowbird host (see p. 219).

LISTING: Listed as of **Special Concern** since 1982. By 1982, the Breeding Bird Survey showed losses across a section of its range from Kansas to Alabama. A decade-long 40-percent decline in the Central Southern Region was also revealed. By 1986, the species still warranted Special Concern and was reportedly declining in parts of the Hudson–Delaware, Appalachian, Middlewestern Prairie, and Southern Great Plains regions. It was also seriously declining in the Central Southern and Northern Great Plains regions.

BIRDS OF
LOCAL CONCERN

When populations inhabiting small, discrete areas or regions appear to be declining, but the downtrend has not been confirmed because documentation is sketchy or contradictory, the compilers of the National Audubon Society's Blue List have added the bird to their list of Species of Local Concern, thus alerting birders and ornithologists to look seriously for evidence of losses. Again, as seen with birds meriting Special Concern (see p. 140), this classification may constitute the earliest red flag of concern—the first notice of shifts from assumed stability.

Reducing the vulnerability of these birds may well depend upon action taken by local residents belonging to conservation groups, or to local chapters of national organizations. By encouraging local legislation, organizing volunteer workers, enlisting the help of students, and so forth (see pp. 223, 225), birders and ornithologists within the affected area may play a central role in drawing public attention to the situation and pressing for action. Some loons and herons, for example, are susceptible to local habitat decline even though it may take some time before their numbers reflect such changes. (And by the time their numbers are convincingly lower, the remedy may be far more difficult, far more costly, or even impossible to implement.) Monitoring changes in numbers or habitat use can be managed by any dedicated birder or group or ornithology class.

When local declines reflect manifestations of more widespread threats, however, the remedies become far more difficult. The impact of acid precipitation on Common Loons, for example, may be underestimated. A close watch of local populations (as is occurring in New Hampshire) will not necessarily improve the immediate situation, but it may help to provide early warning elsewhere. Some skeptics believe that the jury is still out on the issue of acid precipitation, and want more evidence. Experience, however, has taught us that as valuable as long-term observation and research has proved to be, if intervention is to be effective it often requires action taken on the basis of informed guesses, and taken early.

As of 1986, 19 birds warranted concern locally. Except for the California Gnatcatcher (a candidate for federal listing), these are widespread birds that have local populations in trouble. Although a complete accounting of birds that could be said to be of Local Concern in 1992 would no doubt differ from the 1986 list in the choices of some species, the 19 birds that follow serve as instructive examples of declines that in many cases stand a chance of remaining localized, especially if local conservation efforts prove successful.

REFERENCE: Tate and Tate, 1982.

NOT OFFICIALLY LISTED IN THE U.S.: Local Concern

COMMON LOON

Gavia immer

NESTING: In the shallow waters of northern vegetation-edged ponds and lakes. The Common Loon usually builds a platform of wet aquatic plants that is sometimes concealed and often used year after year. Sometimes, however, it makes only a simple scrape.

FOOD: Mostly fish, but also some aquatic invertebrates, particularly crustaceans. While foraging, the Common Loon floats and then dives, usually chasing and swallowing prey under water. It feeds its young small fish and aquatic invertebrates.

RANGE: Breeds from Alaska, northern Canada, and Greenland south to northeastern California (formerly), Iowa, and New England. **WINTERS:** Coastally from Alaska and Newfoundland to northwestern Mexico and the Gulf of Mexico; also along the Atlantic coast of Europe. **IN PERIL:** Throughout much of its breeding range, especially in areas with frequent human disturbance and throughout most of the 14 U.S. states where it continues to persist. In 1989, of those 14 states, half had only remnant populations: 314 breeding adults in New York, 302 in New Hampshire, 28 in Vermont, 20 in Massachusetts, 8 in Washington, and 2 in Idaho. Outside of Alaska, Minnesota has the only extensive U.S. population (about 10,000), and about 500,000 inhabit Alaska and Canada.

NOTES: Wintering birds defend feeding territories during the day but collect into rafts at night, suggesting that they have a vaguely cohesive social system.

JEOPARDIZED: By the destruction of nesting habitat, by acid precipitation, which threatens the supply of lake fish needed for food, by the continuing effects of boating, particularly powerboats, on the birds' nesting success, by increased numbers of predators such as raccoons, and by mercury poisoning. Against this array of forces, the promising use of artificial nesting platforms in quiet waters away from boats is largely unavailing.

LISTING: Blue-Listed in 1981 and 1982, when populations in the Northeast showed declines, but only of **Local Concern** in 1986 in parts of the Hudson–Delaware, Florida, Middlewestern Prairie, and Northern Great Plains regions, where declines were reported as slight.

RED-NECKED GREBE

Podiceps grisegena

NESTING: On the waters of shallow lakes and large ponds, or sometimes quiet rivers, edged with reeds or sedges. The nest is a floating platform of new and decayed reeds anchored to the vegetation.

FOOD: Mostly aquatic invertebrates and aquatic insects, also some amphibians and fish. While foraging, the Red-necked Grebe floats and then dives, pursuing prey underwater.

RANGE: Breeds from Alaska south and east to Oregon, Minnesota, and Ontario; also across northern Eurasia. **WINTERS** (North American populations): Along the coasts of North America. **IN PERIL:** See under Listing.

NOTES: The Red-necked Grebe is typically solitary, but sometimes nests in small colonies. Feather balls are contained in its stomach, probably as protection against the bones of vertebrate prey.

JEOPARDIZED: By recent losses from egg-shell thinning and egg inviability caused by pesticides and PCBs, and by egg predation by increasing numbers of raccoons.

LISTING: Blue-Listed 1974–81, but listed as of only **Local Concern** in 1986. This relatively scarce species never received strong support for listing, and by 1982 it was thought to be stable in central California and stable or declining locally elsewhere. By 1986 the Red-necked Grebe warranted Local Concern from reports of serious declines in parts of the Southern Atlantic Coast Region.

AMERICAN WHITE PELICAN

Pelecanus erythrorhynchos

NESTING: Requires islands in lakes and reservoirs isolated from mammalian predators. There the American White Pelican scrapes a depression, building up a rim of dirt, rubbish, stems, and wood bits.

FOOD: Mostly fish, also some salamanders and crayfish. While foraging, the White Pelican swims at the surface, submerging its head to catch prey, and consuming about 3 pounds of fish per day. White Pelicans sometimes fish cooperatively, forming a semicircle and herding fish into a feeding area. At first, they feed their young by regurgitation; later, they provide unswallowed fish.

RANGE: Breeds in scattered colonies from central Canada south to northeastern (formerly southeastern) California, Colorado, and Minnesota; also on the Gulf coast of Texas. **WINTERS:** Mostly from central California and the Gulf of Mexico south to Nicaragua. **IN PERIL:** In its western U.S. colonies, which shrank from 23 to fewer than ten, but are now generally stable.

NOTES: The White Pelican is colonial and is typically found nesting with Double-crested Cormorants. It appears more buoyant than the Brown Pelican, and not well-suited for diving. In the late 1980's, an American White Pelican collided with a B-1 bomber, with disastrous results for both aircraft and bird.

JEOPARDIZED: Anaho Island in Nevada's Pyramid Lake (now almost a peninsula because of drought) supports the largest U.S. White Pelican breeding colony. Because the lake does not provide adequate food (as a result of wetland losses to irrigation projects), the birds must now fly some 60 miles (one way) to forage on prey that is increasingly scarce and increasingly contaminated with arsenic, selenium, mercury, and boron. Nesting birds are easily disturbed.

LISTING: Blue-Listed 1972–81, but listed as of only **Special Concern** in 1982, and of **Local Concern** in 1986. By 1982 the American White Pelican was reported as stable (with indications in the Southwest of more than usual sightings). It was of concern more because its nesting habitat is vulnerable, than because there was evidence of significant regional losses. By 1986 the species warranted only Local Concern, and there were no nominations for listing at the regional level. Subsequently, however, several consecutive years of drought have once again jeopardized the security of several nesting colonies.

DOUBLE-CRESTED CORMORANT

Phalacrocorax auritus

NESTING: Along seacoasts, on coastal cliffs, and around lakes, rivers, and swamps, where the birds can build a platform of sticks, seaweed, and other drift material on the ground or in trees. Colonies are either terrestrial or arboreal, not both.

FOOD: Mostly schooling fish, also aquatic invertebrates, and rarely other small vertebrates. While foraging, the Double-crested Cormorant swims on the surface and then dives to capture fish. It feeds its young by regurgitation.

RANGE: Breeds in scattered colonies over much of North America, including the Caribbean. **WINTER:** Vacates the colder inland portions of its range. **IN PERIL:** See under Listing.

NOTES: The Double-crested Cormorant is typically colonial, with older, experienced birds usually breeding the earliest.

JEOPARDIZED: Many populations are now increasing. The Double-crested Cormorant strenuously and fiercely protects its eggs and young from avian predators, particularly Northwestern Crows and Glaucous-winged Gulls. The effect of ingesting PCBs is evident from the nestlings with crossed bills that appear with regularity on Lake Michigan in or near northern Green Bay, Wisconsin.

LISTING: Blue-Listed 1972–81, but listed as of only **Special Concern** in 1982, and of **Local Concern** in 1986. By 1982 the Double-crested Cormorant was reported as stable in seven areas, increasing in 14, and greatly increasing in three, with concern only in parts of the Western Great Lakes Region (this despite a large increase in nests on Lake Erie islands). It warranted Special Concern because of the uncertainty of the population-controlling factors of the Western Great Lakes and the potential effects of acid precipitation. By 1986 the species warranted Local Concern only, for it appeared to be increasing everywhere, and there were no nominations recommending listing at the regional level.

BLACK-CROWNED NIGHT HERON

Nycticorax nycticorax

NESTING: Generally near lakes, ponds, marshes, swamps, lagoons, or mangroves. The Black-crowned Night Heron usually selects trees or shrubs in which to place its usually flimsy (but sometimes substantial) platform of sticks, twigs, and reeds. Occasionally, however, it will conceal its nest in dense undergrowth.

FOOD: Mostly fish, typically from within its territory, but also the eggs and young of birds (especially terns, herons, and ibises), amphibians (especially in the spring), small mammals, other small vertebrates, aquatic invertebrates, and insects. While foraging, the Black-crowned Night Heron usually stalks prey and then spears it while standing motionless on a bank or in the water. It initially feeds its young by regurgitation, later with whole fish.

RANGE: Breeds widely in the Americas, eastern Asia, and Africa. **WINTERS** (North American populations): From southern Oregon across the Southwest and the Gulf Coast, north through the lower Ohio Valley and southern New England, and south throughout the breeding range.

IN PERIL: See under Listing.

NOTES: The species is colonial. Clutches in the north are larger than those laid in the south.

JEOPARDIZED: At one time, but populations are now stable or on the rise in most areas.

LISTING: Blue-Listed 1972–81, but listed as of only **Special Concern** in 1982, and **Local Concern** in 1986. By 1982 there were continued indications of recovery (although the species had yet to return to habitats from which it had been extirpated in the preceding ten years), and it was reported as stable or not at risk in most other areas. By 1986 it warranted Local Concern, for it was reportedly declining in parts of the Hudson–Delaware, Florida, Ontario, Mountain West, and Middle Pacific Coast regions, and seriously declining in parts of the Middlewestern Prairie and Central Southern regions. There were, however, more than 80 reports of stable or improving populations.

GREAT BLUE HERON
Ardea herodias

NESTING: Usually near brackish or freshwater marshes, mangroves, swamps, rivers, or lakes. To place its large, level, carefully woven stick platform, the Great Blue Heron selects trees, sometimes shrubs or, rarely, the ground, rock ledges, or coastal cliffs. If a repaired nest is used, it is usually lined with green needles.

FOOD: Mostly fish, also aquatic invertebrates, small mammals, other small vertebrates, nestlings, and scraps of human food. While foraging, the Great Blue Heron usually stalks prey, stands motionless on a bank or in the water, then spears it with a sudden, powerful stab. It feeds its young fish.

RANGE: Breeds over much of North America, including the Caribbean; also the Galapagos Islands. **WINTER:** Vacates most of Canada and the northernmost U.S.

IN PERIL: See under Listing.

NOTES: The Great Blue Heron's nesting colonies vary in size, and if this species nests in mixed colonies, it selects the highest sites. It is sometimes solitary. Clutches in the north are larger than those laid in the south. Birds with white plumage are limited to marine habitats in Florida and the Caribbean.

JEOPARDIZED: By the loss of wetlands (much of the species' former Atlantic coast habitat is now gone). Nonetheless, the bird's numbers are improving overall.

LISTING: Blue-Listed in 1980 and 1981, but listed as of only **Special Concern** in 1982, and **Local Concern** in 1986. By 1982 a possible decline that had been reported from southern Minnesota to Ohio seemed to be reversing. It was suggested that nesting-area disturbances could be controlling factors. With evidence of declines lacking, the Great Blue Heron was placed in the Special Concern category; by 1986 it warranted Local Concern from reports that numbers were only slightly down in parts of the Hudson–Delaware, Western Great Lakes, Middlewestern Prairie, and Mountain West regions.

TRUMPETER SWAN
Cygnus buccinator

NESTING: Along the vegetated edges of freshwater (or sometimes brackish) lakes and ponds, where the Trumpeter Swan builds a platform of aquatic and emergent vegetation, down, and feathers. It often builds on muskrat houses surrounded by water.

FOOD: Mostly leaves, seeds, and roots of aquatic vegetation; also aquatic invertebrates—including crustaceans and insects—and sometimes small vertebrates. The Trumpeter Swan feeds by floating on the surface and submerging its head, or by dabbling—floating in shallow water and ducking its head to reach submerged food on or near the bottom while raising its hindquarters above the surface. Its young feed on aquatic invertebrates for their first month.

RANGE: Breeds from Alaska south and east to Oregon and Wyoming; formerly to Nebraska, Indiana, and Manitoba. **WINTERS:** From Alaska and southwestern Canada south to California and New Mexico. **IN PERIL:** The range has contracted. Historically, it was widely distributed, breeding throughout north-central North America and wintering along the Mississippi River and coastal U.S. The year 1985 brought the first report of a wintering flock on the Atlantic in 180 years. See under Listing.

NOTES: Trumpeter Swans occupy relatively large, well-isolated nesting territories.

JEOPARDIZED: So thoroughly in its U.S. breeding grounds by development and agricultural expansion that the Trumpeter Swan was nearly extinct by the 1930's. Complete protection allowed populations to recover, and it has been reintroduced into parts of its former U.S. range. Ingestion of spent lead shot during feeding has been a significant threat.

LISTING: The Trumpeter Swan was removed from the federal list of Endangered and Threatened Wildlife and Plants in 1971 when the population reached 5,000. By 1982, the species' breeding habitat had seemed generally adequate, and there had been a significant increase in the 1980–81 midwinter Trumpeter Swan survey in Montana, Idaho, and Wyoming; and wintering numbers on the Pacific Coast had been increasing. **Blue-Listed** 1980; by 1986 the species warranted **Local Concern** because of constrictions of its existing wintering habitat. Concern about wintering habitat was more serious for the interior birds in Montana, Idaho, and Wyoming than for the Pacific Coast birds; since nearly all of the Canadian birds winter in that tri-state area, a single outbreak of disease could potentially wipe out the Canadian population. The Trumpeter Swan was listed as **Vulnerable** in Canada in 1978.

COMMON TERN
Sterna hirundo

NESTING: Amid sand, pebbles, shells, or beach wrack on islands or coastal beaches with sparse, matted vegetation and grassy areas. The tern shapes a depression by using its body or simply lays its eggs on the substrate.

FOOD: Mostly fish, which make up 90 percent of the Common Tern's diet. The species also takes aquatic invertebrates, including crustaceans and some insects. While foraging, it drops from height, diving into the water.

RANGE: Breeds from northern Alberta east across Canada and the northern U.S. and south along the coasts of the Atlantic Ocean and Gulf of Mexico to the West Indies; also in Eurasia. **WINTERS** (North American populations): Mostly from Mexico and South Carolina south to Peru and northern Argentina. **IN PERIL:** At least in Massachusetts and around the Great Lakes.

NOTES: The Common Tern nests in colonies consisting of from tens to thousands of individuals. Especially prior to incubation, pairs guard a separate feeding territory, which is located away from the breeding colony.

JEOPARDIZED: Formerly by the millinery trade (which decimated its populations), now by harassment (from gulls, pets, and people) at nesting colonies and habitat loss to beach erosion and development. Around the Great Lakes, the problems are rising water levels and nest-site competition from expanding Ring-billed Gull populations.

LISTING: Blue-Listed in 1978–81, **Special Concern** in 1982, and **Local Concern** in 1986. By 1982 the Common Tern was of Special Concern because of threats to its colonies, although there was no regional pattern to those threats. By 1986 it warranted Local Concern because of reports of declines or serious declines in parts of the Western Great Lakes Region.

TURKEY VULTURE
Cathartes aura

NESTING: For its nest site the Turkey Vulture usually prefers cliffs, but it also uses snags, caves (particularly in the West), and hollow stumps with minimal entrances. Generally, it lays its eggs directly on an unmodified surface; rarely, it first scrapes together a thin bed of stones, dry leaves, and wood chips.

FOOD: Essentially any dead animal, down to the size of a tadpole. The Turkey Vulture usually hunts while soaring at a high altitude. It feeds its young by regurgitation.

RANGE: Breeds from southern Canada south to the Straits of Magellan. **WINTER:** Most birds withdraw from Canada and the northern U.S. **IN PERIL:** See under Listing.

NOTES: The Turkey Vulture roosts communally throughout the year. Unlike the Black Vulture, if the Turkey Vulture loses its clutch, it will not renest.

JEOPARDIZED: By widespread eggshell thinning from pesticides ingested in contaminated food.

LISTING: Blue-Listed in 1972 and 1980, **Special Concern** in 1981 and 1982, and **Local Concern** in 1986. By 1982, although increasing in parts of the East, the Turkey Vulture continued to warrant Special Concern in other areas, including Oregon, where summer roost numbers had declined (at Malheur, from 100 in 1976 to 50 in 1981), and in the Southern Great Plains Region, where the average number of sightings was very low. By 1986 there were reports of only slight declines in the Central Southern and Southern Great Plains regions.

BLACK VULTURE

Coragyps atratus

NESTING: Usually on cliff ledges, but sometimes on a stump, in openings amid dense vegetation, or near garbage dumps.
FOOD: Mostly carrion; also some live vertebrates, including small mammals and young birds. The Black Vulture usually hunts by soaring at a high altitude, depending more on visual cues than does the Turkey Vulture. It feeds its young by regurgitation.
RANGE: Breeds from southern Arizona, Missouri, and the Middle Atlantic States, south to South America. **WINTER:** Resident. **IN PERIL:** In the southeastern U.S.
NOTES: The Black Vulture tends to nest and roost colonially. Parents and young stay together year-round, and communal roosts may comprise extended kin associations. The species has apparently expanded to the northeast.
JEOPARDIZED: By widespread eggshell thinning from pesticides ingested in contaminated food.
LISTING: Blue-Listed in 1972 and 1981, **Special Concern** in 1982, and **Local Concern** in 1986. By 1982, reports from parts of the Southern Atlantic Coast Region confirmed the serious declines reported the previous year. (The species had been undergoing a significant decline since 1930, following a smaller one over the preceding decade.) Elsewhere, populations were stable, and in the Hudson–Delaware Region, small increases due to a range expansion were apparent. By 1986 the Black Vulture was reported as slightly declining in the Florida, Central Southern, and Southern Great Plains regions, and seriously declining in the Southern Atlantic Coast Region.

HARRIS' HAWK

Parabuteo unicinctus

NESTING: In trees or large cacti in savanna, semi-arid woodlands, or semi-deserts (particularly if water is nearby). The nest is a platform of sticks, twigs, herbaceous plants, and roots.

FOOD: Mostly small mammals; also birds, snakes, and insects. Harris' Hawk hunts in a low, patrolling flight to flush prey, or swoops down on prey from an elevated perch, even darting into thickets in pursuit. This species sometimes hunts cooperatively in pairs or in groups of up to five birds.

RANGE: Breeds from Baja California (formerly southeastern California), southern Arizona, and Texas south to South America. **WINTER:** Resident. **IN PERIL:** Harris' Hawk has already been extirpated from the lower Colorado River Valley. Recent attempts at reintroduction there, however, are unlikely to be successful unless the valley is reforested.

NOTES: Harris' Hawk commonly lives in groups. One study found that nearly half of the nests were tended by polyandrous trios (one female mated with two males), with both males incubating the eggs and feeding and brooding the young. In many other cases, groups of up to seven birds nest cooperatively, and most often consist of the breeding pair and one or more auxiliary birds that help to defend the territory and gather food for the nestlings.

JEOPARDIZED: Possibly by destruction of riparian woodland and the taking of birds by falconers.

LISTING: Blue-Listed from 1972 to 1981, accorded **Special Concern** in 1982 and **Local Concern** in 1986. By 1982, Harris' Hawk was stable in the Southwest and Southern Great Plains regions. Because we lack sufficient knowledge of the species' status across the border, variations in local populations should be followed closely.

OSPREY
Pandion haliaetus

NESTING: Usually requires snags or living trees (deciduous trees or conifers) adjacent to or over water. The Osprey builds a platform of sticks, sod, cow dung, seaweed, or rubbish that is used and expanded year after year, becoming very large. It also will nest on poles or cliffs.

FOOD: Mostly fish—dead or alive—but also rodents, birds, other small vertebrates, and crustaceans. The Osprey usually hunts by diving into the water after hovering at heights of 30 to 100 feet. It may also fly low over the water and snatch fish from near the surface. It feeds its young by regurgitation for the first 10 days; a brood of three consumes 6 pounds of fish daily.

RANGE: Almost worldwide. **WINTERS** (North American populations): South to Chile and northern Argentina, with perhaps more than half remaining in Latin America and the West Indies. **IN PERIL:** Possibly in areas such as Chesapeake Bay where fish populations are declining. Estimates of the size of the Alaskan and Canadian populations are not yet complete.

NOTES: The Osprey is the only raptor that turns one of its front talons backward—an adaptation that facilitates the capture of its slippery prey. Fish delivered to nests in Chesapeake Bay in 1985 were smaller than those delivered in 1975, possibly leading to increased sibling aggression, brood reduction, and smaller young.

JEOPARDIZED: By contamination from DDT, degradation and loss of breeding habitat, and shooting. From the 1950's through the 1970's, populations crashed, particularly in the East. Coastal populations recovered, especially after the ban on DDT and the introduction of conservation programs that provided artificial nesting platforms.

LISTING: Blue-Listed 1972–81, **Special Concern** in 1982, and **Local Concern** only in 1986. By 1982 the Osprey was transferred to the Special Concern category in anticipation of specific evidence of increases. One report from the Middle Pacific Coast Region indicated that the number of young per occupied nest increased consistently from 1968 to 1981, and in 1981 the rates were particularly high when compared with records in the literature. But, while the effects of DDT (and its breakdown products, DDE and DDD) were steadily lessening, the effects of acid rain on food availability required watching in the Niagara–Champlain Region. By 1986 the Osprey was accorded only Local Concern, and there were no recommendations for listing at the regional level. As of 1991, disturbing reports of renewed eggshell thinning had been documented in Delaware Bay and at other scattered locations across the U.S.

NORTHERN BOBWHITE

Colinus virginianus

LEWIS' WOODPECKER

Melanerpes lewis

NESTING: In tall grasslands, open woodland, or brushy or cultivated fields. The Bobwhite conceals its nest in a shallow depression by weaving an arch of vegetation overhead.

FOOD: Mostly greens, including leaves, fruits, buds, tubers, and seeds. Also insects, snails, spiders, and smaller vertebrates. While foraging, the Bobwhite usually picks items from the substrate. Over the year, its diet consists of about 85 percent vegetable matter and 15 percent animal matter, although most of the latter is taken in the summer.

RANGE: Breeds from Sonora (formerly Arizona), southeastern Wyoming, and New England south to Guatemala. **WINTER:** Resident. **IN PERIL:** Throughout its U.S. range.

NOTES: Covey formation begins when the young reach an age of 3 weeks. Except when nesting, the Bobwhite feeds and roosts in these coveys, which consist of two or more family groups and up to 30 individuals.

JEOPARDIZED: Reasons are unclear, but a severe toll was exacted by the extreme winter weather during 1979–80. See also the Masked Bobwhite (p. 52), a subspecies of the Northern Bobwhite.

LISTING: Blue-Listed in 1980 and 1981, **Special Concern** in 1982. By 1982 the Bobwhite's recovery from the severe winter of 1979–80 appeared almost complete, and by 1986 the species was only of **Local Concern.**

NESTING: In a cavity in a lifeless stub of a living tree, a snag, or a pole, in open woodlands or forests, including oak, conifer (often ponderosa pine), riparian woodlands, or at orchard edges. Logged or burned coniferous forest is a favored habitat, at elevations up to 9,000 feet. Cavities are often used year after year.

FOOD: Mostly insects; also nuts, including acorns and commercial nuts, pine seeds, and fruit, including berries. While foraging to capture flying insects, Lewis' Woodpecker usually sallies acrobatically from a perch on short flights. It also picks items from the ground or gleans them from tree trunks or branches. To cache acorns and nuts (for use in the nonbreeding season only), it does not drill holes, but rather breaks the nuts, tailoring them to fit natural crevices.

RANGE: Breeds from southern British Columbia south and east to central California, southern New Mexico, and northwestern Nebraska. **WINTERS:** Over most of its breeding range and south irregularly to northwestern Mexico. **IN PERIL:** See under Listing.

NOTES: Territory defense does not extend beyond the immediate nest site and cache. Lewis' is the only woodpecker that perches on wires.

JEOPARDIZED: Populations now appear stable, except for those associated with riparian habitats in arid regions, where drought and overgrazing pose continued threats.

LISTING: Blue-Listed 1975–81, **Special Concern** in 1982, and only **Local Concern** in 1986. Widespread reports and the Breeding Bird Survey suggested long-term losses, but these have not been corroborated consistently.

LEAST FLYCATCHER

Empidonax minimus

NESTING: This flycatcher places its nest, a tight cup of bark, weed stems, and grass, on a horizontal branch of a tree, usually deciduous, sometimes a conifer, or a shrub, in open deciduous or deciduous–coniferous woodlands or wooded suburbs.

FOOD: Mostly insects; also berries and some seeds. While foraging, the Least Flycatcher usually either hovers to glean vegetation or sallies from a perch on short flights to capture flying insects.

RANGE: Breeds from southern Yukon south and east to Montana, Missouri, northern Georgia, and Nova Scotia. **WINTERS:** From northern Mexico south to Panama. **IN PERIL:** Possibly over much of its range.

NOTES: The Least Flycatcher vigorously excludes the ecologically similar American Redstart (see pp. vii and 3) from its nesting territory. It is territorial even in winter.

JEOPARDIZED: Possibly by deforestation in its tropical wintering areas.

LISTING: Blue-Listed in 1980, **Special Concern** in 1981 and 1982, and **Local Concern** in 1986. By 1982 the Least Flycatcher was reported as declining in the Hudson–Delaware, Northeastern Maritime, and Western Great Lakes regions. By 1986 the species was regarded as of only Local Concern because of reports of declines in parts of the Niagara–Champlain, Prairie Provinces, and Southern Great Plains regions, and serious declines in the Western Great Lakes Region (where it still remains in need of systematic surveys). In other areas, however, it was stable or increasing.

CLIFF SWALLOW
Hirundo pyrrhonota

NESTING: Originally on cliffs or other vertical surfaces in open country or savanna, particularly near water; now in much of its range more usually on the underside of bridges or culverts or on walls beneath eaves. On these surfaces the Cliff Swallow cements mud pellets to form its gourdlike nest. Construction takes 5 to 14 days; old nests are frequently repaired and reused.

FOOD: Almost exclusively insects, which the Cliff Swallow usually hunts while in prolonged, continuous flight. It also sometimes takes berries.

RANGE: Breeds from Alaska and northern Canada south to southern Mexico. **WINTERS:** In South America from Paraguay and central and southeastern Brazil to central Argentina. **IN PERIL:** At least in the northeastern U.S.

NOTES: The Cliff Swallow's nesting colonies, sometimes consisting of more than 1,000 pairs, serve as centers for conveying information on foraging: unsuccessful foragers watch successful ones feed their nestlings and follow them when they depart the colony. Buildup of insect nest parasites often leads to the alternation of colony sites from one year to the next.

JEOPARDIZED: The House Sparrow, a species not native to North America, appropriates the Cliff Swallow's nests and may be a factor in its regional decline.

LISTING: Blue-Listed in 1976–77 and in 1981, **Special Concern** in 1982, and **Local Concern** in 1986. In 1982 there were reports of declines in the Southwest, Appalachian, Northeastern Maritime, Niagara–Champlain, and Middlewestern Prairie regions, but the Breeding Bird Survey indicated that populations were stable or increasing in all areas except a few northeastern states. By 1986, declines were reported only in parts of the Northeastern Maritime Region; all other reports were of stable or increasing populations.

GOLDEN-CROWNED KINGLET

Regulus satrapa

NESTING: In trees in open conifer forests, where the birds suspend their open, oblong nest of dead leaves, moss, lichen, spider webs, and plant down.

FOOD: Mostly insects and spiders; also tree sap, some fruit, and seeds. While foraging, the Golden-crowned Kinglet usually gleans foliage, branches, and bark, sometimes while hovering; also will sally from a perch on short flights to capture flying insects. It feeds its young only insects—they will not accept spiders.

RANGE: Breeds from southern Alaska across Canada and south, in mountains, to southern California, Guatemala, and North Carolina. **WINTER:** Retreats from northern Canada and spreads into lowlands in the U.S. The Golden-crowned Kinglet does its best to adhere to conifers even in the winter; it does not migrate to the tropics. San Diego is the southern limit of the species' winter range on the Pacific coast, and the winter range has extended this far south in only the past 30–35 years (presumably with widespread planting of conifers in lowlands). **IN PERIL:** See under Listing.

NOTES: Often forms mixed winter flocks with chickadees, Brown Creepers, and small woodpeckers.

JEOPARDIZED: Populations in most portions of the range seem to have recovered from the losses they sustained in the early 1980's.

LISTING: **Blue-Listed** in 1980 and 1981, **Special Concern** in 1982, and **Local Concern** in 1986. In 1982 the Golden-crowned Kinglet was transferred to the Special Concern category, since it had not entirely rebounded in the Niagara–Champlain, Northern Great Plains, or Central Southern regions, and there were indications of a possible decline in the Mountain West Region. By 1986 the decline of the early 1980's appeared to have reversed completely.

CALIFORNIA GNATCATCHER

Polioptila californica

NESTING: Restricted to lowland, arid scrub. The nest is a compact cup of plant material attached to several twigs of a shrub.

FOOD: Insects and spiders gleaned from foliage and twigs, but no detailed studies have been conducted.

RANGE: Baja California, north on the Gulf side about to Bahía San Luís Gonzaga, and on the Pacific side across the international border to the Palos Verdes Peninsula and Riverside, formerly as far as Ventura County and San Bernardino, California.

WINTER: Resident. **IN PERIL:** In California and in Baja California between Tijuana and Ensenada. A 1980 estimate of 1,135 pairs in the U.S. was revised with better data to 2,000 in 1991, though even this figure is only a rough approximation. Most important is the amount and distribution of protected habitat, which at present is insufficient to preserve the California Gnatcatcher in this country.

NOTES: The California Gnatcatcher was from 1927 to 1988 usually considered conspecific with the Black-tailed Gnatcatcher, *P. melanura,* but in 1988 an extensive area was discovered where the two kinds of gnatcatchers occur together without interbreeding.

JEOPARDIZED: By habitat fragmentation and loss to expanding urban sprawl. Most of the California Gnatcatcher's U.S. range has already been developed, and most of the remaining birds live on private land proposed for housing tracts and golf courses. The areas of native scrub remaining in open-space easements and under public ownership may be too small to support viable populations. Once the birds are eliminated from an isolated patch of habitat, they will likely fail to recolonize because they seldom cross even narrow barriers of unsuitable habitat.

LISTING: In 1982, when the California Gnatcatcher was still considered a subspecies of the Black-tailed Gnatcatcher, the National Audubon Society warranted it of **Special Concern** because of habitat constraints in San Diego County, California. By 1986 it was still accorded **Local Concern.** By mid-September 1991, the U.S. Fish and Wildlife Service was to have responded to petitions requesting that the northern subspecies of the California Gnatcatcher, *P. californica californica* (ranging south to El Rosario), be designated as **Endangered.** (A USFWS working group was established in late 1990 to promote conservation efforts for the coastal scrub population.) Because the demand for land in coastal southern California is so intense, the petitions have sparked heated debate, vigorous opposition from developers, and difficult negotiations among government agencies.

NOT OFFICIALLY LISTED IN THE U.S.: Local Concern

WESTERN BLUEBIRD

Sialia mexicana

NESTING: The Western Bluebird favors open, riparian, burned, or logged woodlands and savanna. It builds its nest, a flimsy cup of grass, weed stems, pine needles, twigs, and, sometimes, hair and feathers in natural cavities or the abandoned excavations of woodpeckers.

FOOD: Mostly insects, earthworms, snails, and other terrestrial invertebrates. While foraging for flying insects, the Western Bluebird usually sallies from a low perch on short flights near the ground. It also gleans fruit, particularly berries, from foliage.

RANGE: Breeds from southern British Columbia and Montana south, mostly in mountains, to northern Baja California and southern Mexico. **WINTER:** Some birds spread into lowland and desert habitats where the species does not breed. **IN PERIL:** At least in northern California.

NOTES: The Western Bluebird will use nest boxes.

JEOPARDIZED: By the clearing of dead trees and the pruning of dead branches, which often eliminate nest holes and heighten competition with other cavity-nesting species—particularly the House Sparrow and European Starling. These introduced species may well be factors in the Western Bluebird's decline.

LISTING: **Blue-Listed** in 1972 and from 1978 to 1981, warranted of **Special Concern** in 1982, but accorded only **Local Concern** in 1986. Efficient nest-box programs might be effective in increasing the Western Bluebird's numbers, especially in areas reporting low numbers over a long term. By 1986 there were reports of decline from the Middle Pacific Coast Region. See the Eastern Bluebird (p. 166).

CONTINENTAL BIRDS
EXTINCT SINCE 1776

Four species native to the continental U.S. and Canada—two seabirds, a pigeon, and a parrot—have become extinct in historic times. What is known of their demises is often told, but we repeat it here as a reminder of what has already been lost.

John James Audubon and Alexander Wilson, the fathers of American ornithology, knew the Labrador Duck as the Pied Duck; others knew this species, which was often found on sandbars, as the Sandshoal Duck. None of them, apparently, anticipated its loss. The biology of this sea duck, whose closest living relatives seem to be the eiders, is virtually unknown, as are the reasons behind its rapid extinction.

The "penguin" that once bred on our shores, the flightless Great Auk, or Garefowl, was a fish-hunting diver that stood some 30 inches high. Widely distributed in the North Atlantic, it was a superlative swimmer, but once on land, it was little more than walking dinner. Its breeding colonies on offshore islands served as stockyards for sailors: the birds could be herded right across gangplanks. The Great Auk was valued for feathers, meat, and eggs, and even its chicks were used—for fish bait. As human numbers increased, those of the Great Auk decreased. Now only the name "penguin" lives on, long since transferred to the ecologically similar but unrelated birds of the Antarctic and southern oceans.

Many think the Passenger Pigeon was once the most abundant bird on the planet, accounting for perhaps one-fourth of all North American landbirds. Wilson estimated that one flock consisted of two *billion* birds. Audubon watched a flock pass overhead *for three days* and estimated that at times more than 300 million pigeons flew by him *each hour*. The Passenger Pigeon was unsurpassed as an easily harvested resource. Collecting fat squabs that had fallen or been knocked from their nests took only a minute, and market hunters had a heyday. Overharvesting led to the bird's demise.

The Carolina Parakeet (or, as it was sometimes called by Europeans, the Illinois Parrot) declined and disappeared from the eastern American forests on about the same schedule as the Passenger Pigeon. Besides the Thick-billed Parrot (assuming that it nested here), the Carolina Parakeet was the only member of the parrot family native to the United States. It was a beautiful, abundant agricultural pest and a common target in the orchards of American farmers.

At least five North American subspecies —a prairie chicken, a wren, and three sparrows—have also been lost, one hunted to oblivion throughout its range and reduced to a single island population on Martha's Vineyard, Massachusetts, where it finally died out, and the other four because their very limited natural range was degraded by habitat destruction or overrun by human development.

In a region as vast as North America, the extinction of just four species and five subspecies of birds may not seem cause for alarm, but as many as ten more species and fifteen more subspecies may be driven to extinction within the next few years. And three of these, the Ivory-billed Woodpecker, the Eskimo Curlew, and Bachman's Warbler, may already be gone.

LABRADOR DUCK
Camptorhynchus labradorius

NESTING: According to Audubon, the Labrador Duck built a nest of large fir twigs. Its nesting habits are thought to have generally resembled those of eiders, but details are unknown.
FOOD: Mostly marine invertebrates; also seaweed. While foraging, the Labrador Duck usually dove from a floating position, seeking food underwater.
RANGE: Bred apparently at least in Labrador, where the only known eggs were supposedly collected. **WINTERED:** Along the Atlantic coast from Nova Scotia to New Jersey.
NOTES: The birds were no longer marketed after 1860, and the last known specimens were collected in the 1870's. Until recently, it had been assumed that there were 31 specimens in North American collections, but another one recently turned up at a garage sale!

JEOPARDIZED: By its very limited breeding range. The Labrador Duck's extinction was likely the result of habitat loss, overhunting of both adults and eggs, and, possibly, the decline in mussels and other shellfish that accompanied the sudden rise in the human population within its range.
EXTINCT: Concern for the conservation of this species did not arise until after it had already disappeared, around 1878.

GREAT AUK
Pinguinus impennis

NESTING: On offshore rocky islands, where the birds laid their eggs on bare or guano-covered rock.
FOOD: Mostly fish, which the Great Auk probably hunted near the sea floor, at depths down to 250 feet or more.
RANGE: Bred on islands around the North Atlantic from the Gulf of St. Lawrence to Britain; probably more widely in prehistoric times. **WINTERED:** At sea, south to South Carolina and Spain.
NOTES: The Great Auk bred in large colonies from New England to Iceland, but data on breeding and diet are largely extrapolated from those for other alcids, the auk's relatives. In contrast, archaeological evidence shows that the Great Auk was an important part of the diet of prehistoric maritime tribes at least as far back as 7,000 B.C.

JEOPARDIZED: By overhunting. The birds were slaughtered as food and bait, or for their fat, their feathers, or, finally (by collectors), their skins. About 80 skins have been preserved.
EXTINCT: The species became extinct so quickly that at one point it was considered a myth. The "original penguin," it was the North Atlantic's largest alcid and the only nonfossil flightless alcid, and was last seen alive on June 3, 1844, in Iceland.

PASSENGER PIGEON

Ectopistes migratorius

NESTING: In trees, usually in beech woods, where colony members crowded their frail platforms onto branching tree forks. The Passenger Pigeon bred in colonies that could be 40 miles long and several miles wide. The largest nesting colony on record was in Wisconsin. It contained at least 135 million adults and extended over 850 square miles.

FOOD: Primarily such items as beechnuts, acorns, chestnuts, and other forest nuts; also fruits, berries, grain, and grass seeds, supplemented with insects, earthworms, and other invertebrates. While foraging, the Passenger Pigeon usually picked items from the substrate or vegetation.

RANGE: Bred within forests, especially the great deciduous forests from Montana, southern Ontario, and Nova Scotia south to Oklahoma, Mississippi, and Georgia.

WINTERED: Mostly from southeastern Missouri, Tennessee, and North Carolina south to the Gulf of Mexico.

NOTES: Native Americans usually avoided killing nesting adults in excess of anticipated need; American market hunters observed no such constraints.

JEOPARDIZED: By the taste of its flesh and the ease of its capture; market hunting led precipitately to the Passenger Pigeon's extinction, but the birds went into their final decline after commercial hunting ceased. Apparently, once their numbers were reduced to the point where huge breeding colonies could no longer be formed, predators or other factors finished the job.

EXTINCT: Concern for conservation came too late for this species, which is thought to have been one of the most abundant on the planet. The last one, a female named "Martha," died in 1914, in the Cincinnati Zoo.

CAROLINA PARAKEET

Conuropsis carolinensis

NESTING: The Carolina Parakeet frequented riverine forest, cypress swamps, and deciduous woodlands. Ornithologists never examined nests in the wild. Reportedly, the nests were placed in abandoned chip-lined or unlined tree cavities, including those excavated by woodpeckers. Up to 50 nests were crowded into one tree.

FOOD: A wide variety of fruit, such as apples and peaches; also mulberries, pecans, grapes, dogwood, and grain. Before the advent of agriculture, the Carolina Parakeet fed on the seeds of grasses, maples, elms, pines, and other trees. Afterward, it still took items from native vegetation but preferred open habitats, especially areas under cultivation and gardens.

RANGE: Eastern Nebraska, southeastern Wisconsin, and New York south to Oklahoma, Louisiana, and Florida. **WINTER:** Was apparently resident.

NOTES: At night the Carolina Parakeet roosted communally in tree hollows, with as many as 30 individuals seeking shelter per tree; individuals crowded out of the hollow would hang on the outside.

JEOPARDIZED: By shooting. Before 1900 the Carolina Parakeet was considered an agricultural pest. Highly gregarious, this species formed apparently cohesive social flocks. It was coveted as a cage bird and for its plumage, and it was hunted for "sport," although, as challenges go, this bird with its habit of flocking around individuals as they were shot was a virtual sitting duck.

EXTINCT: Concern for its conservation was insufficient to prevent this, the only parrot native to the eastern U.S., from going extinct. The last individual died in 1914 in the Cincinnati Zoo, where a breeding program had kept the species going for twenty years.

HEATH HEN

Tympanuchus cupido cupido

NESTING: Presumably in grassland interspersed with brushy areas, where the bird would make a shallow depression.

FOOD: The Heath Hen's diet was probably similar to that of other prairie chickens: seeds, acorns, insects, greens, and fruit. While foraging, it probably picked items from the surface of soil, turf, or sand.

RANGE: The eastern seaboard from Massachusetts to Virginia. **WINTER:** Was resident.

NOTES: The Heath Hen was the eastern subspecies of the Greater Prairie-chicken. The darker subspecies, Attwater's Greater Prairie-chicken (*T. cupido attwateri*), is holding on in southwestern Louisiana and eastern Texas, although it has been listed as Endangered since 1967 (see p. 51).

JEOPARDIZED: By overhunting, habitat loss, predation (especially by cats), and diseases introduced by pheasants and domestic chickens. In 1900, fewer than 100 birds remained on the island of Martha's Vineyard, Massachusetts, the only area where the Heath Hen survived into the twentieth century. By 1916 the population recovered to some 2,000 birds. Then catastrophic fire and heavy raptor predation reduced the numbers to from 100 to 150. Numbers rose to 200 by 1920 and then dropped again—this time for good.

EXTINCT: Concern for its conservation came too late for this resident of fire-maintained grasslands and blueberry barrens. The last individual was seen in 1932.

SAN CLEMENTE BEWICK'S WREN

Thryomanes bewickii leucophrys

NESTING: In dense thickets of thorny shrubs and patches of cactus, where it could find a natural cavity in which to place its twig and grass nest.

FOOD: Presumably insects and spiders.

RANGE: San Clemente Island, California. **WINTER:** Was resident.

NOTES: Another subspecies of the Bewick's Wren was extirpated from Guadalupe Island, off northern Baja California, by the same cause (see below). It was last seen on Guadalupe in 1897. Bewick's Wrens still survive commonly on some of California's other Channel Islands (Santa Rosa, Santa Cruz, Anacapa, and Santa Catalina), where habitat degradation has been less complete than that on San Clemente and Guadalupe.

JEOPARDIZED: Primarily by the introduced goats and sheep that devoured the island's original cover of trees and shrubs, leading to its replacement by weedy foreign grasses, a habitat unsuitable for the wrens or for most of the island's other native birds. Feral sheep and goats foraging on fruit and seeds on the island have prevented the reproduction of woody plants. Goats were introduced in the 1800's. By 1883, there were 10,000 sheep, and in 1897, cattle were also present. The Bald Eagle, Peregrine Falcon, Osprey, Rufous-sided Towhee, and Song Sparrow all formerly bred on San Clemente, and the San Clemente Loggerhead Shrike and San Clemente Sage Sparrow are both Endangered.

LISTING: This subspecies is a Category 3A bird on the federal list, removed from active listing because there is persuasive evidence that it has become extinct.

EXTINCT: The last certain record was in 1941.

TEXAS HENSLOW'S SPARROW

Ammodramus henslowii houstonensis

NESTING: Usually in weedy fields, pastures, prairies, or meadows with a patch of concealing grass (typically providing the nest with a partial roof) or vertical stems (on which the sparrow could attach and elevate its nest, reducing the need for a roof). The Texas Henslow's Sparrow preferred moist areas supporting grass, other herbaceous plants, and scattered shrubs for its cup of coarse grass and forbs.

FOOD: Mostly insects and other terrestrial invertebrates, including some spiders and snails; also some seeds of grass, other herbaceous plants, and sedges. While foraging, the Texas Henslow's Sparrow usually picked items from the substrate. It fed its young insects exclusively.

RANGE: At the time of its description in 1983, the Texas Henslow's Sparrow was known from only one 105-acre field in Houston, Harris County, Texas. **WINTER:** Its historic range is unknown.

NOTES: A census of the population on August 12, 1973, revealed 62 adults and nine immatures. The Texas Henslow's Sparrow was separated by 750 miles from the southernmost known breeding population (Missouri) of other Henslow's Sparrows. Whether or not the Texas Henslow's Sparrow should have been designated a subspecies is somewhat controversial. There is some question about the validity of the differences in the distinguishing characters.

JEOPARDIZED: Presumably by urban growth and industrial development.

EXTINCT: Concern for conservation came too late for this east Texas subspecies, which was removed from the active federal Endangered Species List in the late 1980's and assigned to Category 3A. Category 3A listings are considered to be extinct on the basis of available evidence.

DUSKY SEASIDE SPARROW

Ammodramus maritimus nigrescens

NESTING: Amid grasses, rushes, sedges, and occasional salt-marsh shrubs. The cup and canopy of dried grass and sedges was interwoven into the surrounding grass.

FOOD: Mostly insects and other terrestrial invertebrates, including spiders; also amphipods and the seeds of various marsh plants. While foraging, the Dusky Seaside Sparrow usually picked items from the substrate or gleaned food from foliage.

RANGE: The salt marshes of Orange and Brevard counties on Florida's east-central coast. **WINTERED:** Was resident.

NOTES: Last-ditch efforts to save the subspecies included a captive breeding program in which the Dusky was mated with Scott's Seaside Sparrow (*A. m. peninsulae*), yielding fertile hybrids (see pp. 35–36). As of 1991, two other subspecies, the Wakulla Seaside Sparrow and the Smyrna Seaside Sparrow, continue to be recognized as Category 2 candidates; thus the U.S. Fish and Wildlife Service has information indicating the possible appropriateness of listing, but needs further information.

JEOPARDIZED: By its tiny range (a 10-mile radius) and the destruction of salt marshes, which severely decreased its breeding habitat. DDT, draining of wetlands, development, flooding for mosquito control, and fires also contributed to its extinction and to the virtual extinction of another subspecies, the Cape Sable (*A. m. mirabilis*), listed as Endangered since 1967. The impounding of saltwater also led to a rise in pig frogs and Boat-tailed Grackles, which preyed on nestlings. In 1968, 894 Dusky males were counted; by 1972, counts dropped to 110; by 1973, to 54.

EXTINCT: Conservation efforts began too late. The last pure-bred Dusky died at the age of 13 in 1987.

SANTA BARBARA SONG SPARROW

Melospiza melodia graminea

NESTING: Probably wherever bushes provided cover. The bird placed its cup nest in bushes or beneath them.

FOOD: Probably insects, grass and forb seeds, and some berries.

RANGE: Was limited to Santa Barbara Island, California. **WINTER:** Was resident.

NOTES: Described as "abundant" by the ornithologist C. H. Townsend, who named it in 1890. This sparrow maintained fair numbers as recently as 1958, even after a plague of European hares had severely reduced vegetation over much of the island. Hare-control programs came too late.

JEOPARDIZED: By the near-total destruction of ground cover and other vegetation by the introduced hares. A fire that swept 60 percent of the remaining vegetation in 1967 may have dealt the final blow; there has been no confirmed sighting since.

EXTINCT: Concern came too late for this island subspecies, which was removed from the federal Endangered Species List in 1983 and placed in Category 3A (species considered on the basis of convincing evidence to be extinct). As of 1991, four other subspecies, the Amak Song Sparrow, Suisun Song Sparrow, San Pablo Song Sparrow, and Alameda (South Bay) Song Sparrow, continue to be recognized as Category 2 candidates; thus the U.S. Fish and Wildlife Service has information indicating the possible appropriateness of listing, but further information is still needed.

HAWAIIAN BIRDS
EXTINCT SINCE 1776

The Hawaiian Islands are young, transient (they will eventually be worn away), and more geographically isolated than any other islands on Earth. Although the entire archipelago is spread thinly across almost 1,500 miles, its main islands, all at the southeast of the chain, span less than 400 miles. Its first human settlers, the Polynesians, arrived about 400 A.D., bringing with them bananas, coconuts, yams, and taro. They also introduced junglefowl, dogs, and pigs, and unintentionally carried along Polynesian rats, a few snails, and some weed seeds. It took about 1,250 years for the Polynesian population to peak. By 1650, it was 200,000 strong; all the islands except Oahu were more heavily peopled than they are today. Many believe the human population had begun to decline in the face of dwindling resources even before it was devastated by European diseases and exploitation. The Polynesians destroyed much of the dry forest and exterminated many species of forest birds. Archaeological excavations reveal that at least 50 percent of the original bird species were lost, including two flightless ibises and at least seven flightless geese, which were hunted to extinction.

In 1778 Captain Cook sailed into the area, and the islands had their first contact with Western culture. That culture eventually introduced cattle, sheep, goats, pigs, rats, mongooses, cats, mosquitoes, other insects, and birds—all critically dangerous to the native birds, either directly or indirectly. More bird species have been successfully introduced to Hawaii than to any other area of equivalent size; some of these brought avian diseases that may have been the final blow for much of the native avifauna, already pressured by the shrinkage and degradation of the native habitat.

Western culture also brought more than 4,600 plant species (three times the number of native species); of these, about 460 became naturalized and almost 100 have become pests. By dramatically altering the character and composition of the islands' vegetation in many areas, the introduced plants have affected the native birds as powerfully as have the introduced animals.

Species extinctions were often the result of multiple pressures. Habitat degradation, fragmentation, and conversion, introduced predators, competitors, disease-transmitting insects, and, in some cases, poaching and hunting all contributed to the overall loss. How many of the 30 Hawaiian birds now federally listed as Threatened or Endangered will be added to the list of extinctions is difficult to judge, but few ornithologists are optimistic. Many interested in the conservation of birds have devoted great effort to minimizing the toll, but if they are to succeed in stabilizing the dwindling populations, many more will need to join their ranks.

The 23 birds that follow (17 species and 6 subspecies) have been lost in just the 220 years since Captain Cook's first visit, and as many as 15 other Hawaiian birds may be extinct within decades, despite the best efforts of government, science, and concerned citizens. Two of these are probably already gone, and four more may also be extinct. It should be remembered, however, that although the *rate* of extinctions accelerated with the arrival of Western culture, the *number* of extinctions in the prior centuries had been considerable. The fossil remains of more than 40 bird species extirpated during the tenure of the Polynesians have so far been discovered. In part, this catastrophic drop reflects the nature of island biotas: worldwide in the last 300 years or so, island species have accounted for more than 80 percent of avian extinctions.

REFERENCES: Berger, 1981; Freed et al., 1987; Pratt et al., 1989; Scott et al., 1986.

HAWAIIAN RAIL, or MOHO

Porzana sandwichensis

NESTING: Apparently, the Hawaiian Rail inhabited open scrub and grass-covered hills adjoining forest clearings or forests, but its nest was never described.

FOOD: Never described.

RANGE: The Hawaiian Rail was probably restricted to the main Hawaiian islands, and in historic times was found on Hawaii and perhaps Molokai. **WINTER:** Was resident.

NOTES: The first specimen known to Western science was collected on Captain Cook's final voyage, in 1780. This small flightless bird (less than 6 inches in length) was presumably well known to native Hawaiians, and Hawaiian chiefs apparently hunted it for sport. At least eight flightless rail species formerly inhabited the Hawaiian Islands. The Hawaiian Rail is also referred to as the Sandwich Rail.

JEOPARDIZED: Probably by dogs, cats, rats, and, perhaps, the mongoose, which was introduced in Hawaii in 1883, when the bird was already almost gone.

EXTINCT: The last individual recorded was seen in 1884.

LAYSAN RAIL

Porzana palmeri

NESTING: Apparently in thickets or grass tussocks, which would conceal the side entrance of the domed, ball-shaped nest of grass.

FOOD: Presumably mostly insects (including flies and their larvae, moths, caterpillars, beetles, and earwigs) and spiders; also the eggs of petrels and small terns, the flesh of decaying seabird carcasses, some seeds, and green plant material.

RANGE: Originally restricted to Laysan Island (northwestern Hawaiian Islands), the species was later introduced on Midway. **WINTER:** Was resident.

NOTES: Also known as the Laysan Crake, this flightless bird was discovered in 1828. It was active, quick-moving, and reputedly curious and fearless of people.

JEOPARDIZED: On Laysan, by starvation first, as a result of the destruction of vegetation by introduced rabbits and, with it, the rail's food supply; then by roof rats and flooding, which presumably decimated the population.

EXTINCT: By 1912 an estimated 2,000 rails remained on Laysan, but within 20 years they were essentially gone. The population introduced on Midway was exterminated by black rats, the last rail seen having been recorded there in 1944.

'AMAUI
Myadestes oahuensis

NESTING: Apparently lived along the forest edge, according to the record in Bloxam's diary (see below).
FOOD: Unknown.
RANGE: Oahu. **WINTER:** Was resident.
NOTES: All specimens collected in historical times have been lost, but fossil remains have been discovered on Oahu. Descriptions date back to Andrew Bloxam, naturalist on the *H.M.S. Blonde,* who sailed to Honolulu from London with Lord Byron when he returned the bodies of King Liholiho and Queen Kamamalu. Bloxam recorded in his diary (May 1825) that this thrush inhabited the forest fringe of east Oahu. This bird has been listed under various names, including *Phaeornis obscura oahuensis* and the Oahu Thrush.

JEOPARDIZED: The conditions leading to the 'Amaui's extinction are unknown.
EXTINCT: Not reported since the 1820's.

KAUAI 'O'O, or 'O'O'A'A
Moho braccatus

NESTING: The Kauai 'O'o was lately restricted to dense, wet forests, in which it nested in tree cavities. It apparently preferred canyons at higher elevations. The first nest (located in a cavity) was discovered in 1971.
FOOD: Mostly invertebrates (spiders, moths, crickets, and other insects); also the nectar of the lobelia and ohia, and olapa fruit.
RANGE: Kauai. **WINTER:** Was resident.
NOTES: This little-studied, acrobatic honeycreeper was Hawaii's smallest 'O'o. Its distinctive call made censusing its very rugged remaining habitat in the Alakai Swamp somewhat easier during breeding. Most biologists doubt that the 'O'o could still survive, because there were so few birds left that even a captive breeding program could not be established.
JEOPARDIZED: By deforestation (conversion for agriculture), habitat degradation (rooting, browsing, and trampling by feral pigs and goats, which encouraged the invasion of introduced plants), predation by introduced black rats, and the transmission of avian diseases by introduced insects.
EXTINCT: Listed as **Endangered** in March 1967. The last sightings were of two birds in 1981, one in 1983, and one or possibly two in 1984, but researchers concur that the Kauai 'O'o is almost certainly extinct.

OAHU 'O'O
Moho apicalis

NESTING: Never described, but the other species of 'O'o on the other islands apparently nested in the cavities of large ohia trees.

FOOD: Undescribed, but other 'O'os ate insects, spiders, nectar, and berries.

RANGE: Known only from Oahu.

WINTER: Was resident.

NOTES: No information on behavior relevant to the species' extinction is available.

JEOPARDIZED: As were all species of 'o'o, by native plume hunters, changes in the environment, and nest predation by rats, but little information on the Oahu species is available. In total, only five specimens were ever taken, and none remain in Hawaii (two went to Germany, three others to Great Britain).

EXTINCT: The last individual was recorded in 1837.

HAWAII 'O'O
Moho nobilis

NESTING: Apparently, the Hawaii 'O'o inhabited forest canopy in ohia and koa–ohia forests, but its nests were never described.

FOOD: Mostly nectar, especially that of ohia and lobelia flowers, but also bracts of the ieie vine, insects (especially caterpillars), and fruit, taken in tall trees. The Hawaii 'O'o may have moved on a daily basis into mamane forest to forage on rich nectar resources.

RANGE: Was restricted to the island of Hawaii, and was commonly sighted 100 years ago at elevations of from 1,300 to 3,800 feet. **WINTER:** Was resident.

NOTES: The Hawaii 'O'o was first collected on Captain Cook's third voyage, when it was common in the lower and middle forests, especially in trees growing near lava. An aggressive bird, it dominated the other nectarivores, including the Hawaii Mamo, Apapane, and Iiwi.

JEOPARDIZED: By hunters (even by the turn of the century more than 1,000 birds were taken for plumes for feather wreaths, by hunters who apparently discovered a previously overlooked population), destruction of the forest (especially by cattle), and (according to George Munro) avian diseases carried by fowl brought in by coffee farmers.

EXTINCT: Presumably so, since the last sure record dates to 1898, and the last call was reported in 1934. An attempt in 1892 to introduce the species to Kauai failed. There is still a very remote possibility that the species continues to survive on Hawaii.

KIOEA

Chaetoptila angustipluma

NESTING: Apparently in forest canopy, but the nest was never described in the literature. It has been suggested from the fossil record and from anecdotal notes that the Kioea primarily inhabited dry woodland or scrubland below 600 feet elevation.

FOOD: Presumably nectar and some insects, including caterpillars, taken from the canopy.

RANGE: In historic times the Kioea was restricted to the island of Hawaii, although fossil remains have been discovered on other Hawaiian islands. **WINTER:** Was resident.

NOTES: Very little is known about the biology of this rather large (13-inch) forest bird. The few collectors who saw it reported merely that it was graceful and active. Its name, Kioea, means to stand tall, as on long legs.

JEOPARDIZED: By factors unknown. The Kioea was apparently rare in pre-human times; no explanations for its loss have been offered, and it was neither prized by nor even familiar to the native people.

EXTINCT: By about 1859, when the last few specimens were taken (only four were ever obtained).

LANAI HOOKBILL

Dysmorodrepanis munroi

NESTING: Unknown.

FOOD: Uncertain, but clearly included the fruit of the akoko. The bill of this species was unique. The mandibles were curved toward each other, leaving an opening so that only the tip of the lower mandible touched the upper, in an exaggerated version of the bill of the Nukupu'u, but more finchlike (serving perhaps as pincers).

RANGE: Lanai, where it was known only from the Kaiholena Valley and at Waiakeakau on the southwestern forest edge, at about 2,000 feet. **WINTER:** Was resident.

NOTES: Discovered in February 1913 by George Munro, who shot it, mistaking it for an 'O'u. It was also known as the Hook-bill Lanai Finch. Munro saw two more individuals, one in 1916 and another in 1918. The only museum specimen known to exist had been considered an aberrant female 'O'u until 1986, when its

skull was extracted, replaced with a cast, analyzed, and determined to be a unique honeycreeper.

JEOPARDIZED: The conditions leading to the Lanai Hookbill's extinction are unknown. Munro assumed that the bird was associated with the large akoko forest of the Lanai plains, which was later converted into fields of pineapple; recent ornithologists agree. Presumably, the destruction of this forest led to the final demise of the bird.

EXTINCT: Sometime after 1918, but the exact date is unknown.

LESSER KOA-FINCH

Rhodacanthis flaviceps

NESTING: Never described in the literature.

FOOD: Apparently similar to that of the Greater Koa-finch (although the two species' bills differed), including koa pods taken in the tops of trees.

RANGE: By the nineteenth century, evidently, the Lesser Koa-finch was restricted to the upland koa forests of the leeward slopes of Mauna Loa, on the island of Hawaii. Fossils indicate that it was once widespread in the lowlands and also found on Oahu. **WINTER:** Was resident.

NOTES: The Lesser Koa-finch was also known as the Yellow-headed Koa-finch. Only a few specimens were collected; the species was so rare that it was at first thought to be a hybrid. The Lesser Koa-finch formed mixed flocks with Greater Koa-finches.

JEOPARDIZED: By factors unknown; apparently the Lesser Koa-finch was already on the verge of extinction when it was discovered.

EXTINCT: The last specimen was taken in 1891.

GREATER KOA-FINCH, or HOPUE

Rhodacanthis palmeri

NESTING: Apparently in the high branches of large koa trees; the species was most common in koa forests between 2,800 and 3,800 feet elevation.

FOOD: Primarily seeds from the pods of koa trees, often taken in the upper branches; also other seeds and insects (including caterpillars), sometimes gleaned from smaller trees.

RANGE: The Greater Koa-finch was restricted to the island of Hawaii, where it was seen among koa and other acacia trees.

WINTER: Was resident.

NOTES: This species was also called the Orange Koa-finch, and some early references assigned it the name "Hopue," but that apparently was not the native Hawaiian name. The first specimen was taken in 1891 at an elevation above 5,000 feet. The Greater Koa-finch was the largest member of the Hawaiian honeycreeper family that has been known in historic time. It sometimes formed mixed flocks with the Lesser Koa-finch.

JEOPARDIZED: By factors unknown.

EXTINCT: The last specimens were taken in 1896.

KONA GROSBEAK

Chloridops kona

NESTING: Apparently limited to a very small area of recent lava flows at elevations between 3,500 and 5,000 feet where there were medium-sized trees and little undergrowth. No descriptions of nests were ever published.

FOOD: Mostly kernels of the hard, dry naio fruits; also some green leaves and caterpillars.

RANGE: Was restricted to one district on the island of Hawaii. **WINTER:** Was resident.

NOTES: The Kona Grosbeak was a slow-moving bird, often located by the sounds of its cracking of naio kernels during foraging. It was also known as the Kona Finch, the Grosbeak Finch, and, erroneously, the Palila; the native Hawaiians apparently did not give it a name. By the time it was discovered by Scott Wilson in 1887, the Kona Grosbeak was already very rare. It is one of at least nine finchlike honeycreepers that formerly inhabited the Hawaiian Islands.

JEOPARDIZED: By factors unknown.

EXTINCT: Last recorded about 1894–96.

GREATER 'AMAKIHI, or GREEN SOLITAIRE

Hemignathus sagittirostris

NESTING: Apparently in areas of dense lowland ohia rain forest.

FOOD: Mostly insects, including crickets, caterpillars, and beetles, but also spiders, all gleaned from leaves, vines, and the loose bark of ohia trees. The Greater 'Amakihi also apparently took some nectar. It had a fairly straight bill and probably did not forage by creeping.

RANGE: Was restricted to the island of Hawaii on slopes between 500 and 4,000 feet elevation along the Wailuku River.

WINTER: Was resident.

NOTES: Easily overlooked, the Greater 'Amakihi was first recorded in 1892. Three years later it was the subject of a two-week study by a second researcher apparently unaware that the species had already been discovered. It was known to native Hawaiians, but not well, and they gave it no name. Its green plumage was apparently not prized enough by the Hawaiians to interest them in collecting the bird.

JEOPARDIZED: By factors unknown, but virtually all of the Greater 'Amakihi's native habitat has been replaced by introduced plant species.

EXTINCT: The last individual was recorded in the early 1900's, and the last specimen was taken in 1901. In the very unlikely event that the species has survived, however, it could reside only in the forests along Hawaii's Hamakua coast.

KAUAI 'AKIALOA

Hemignathus procerus

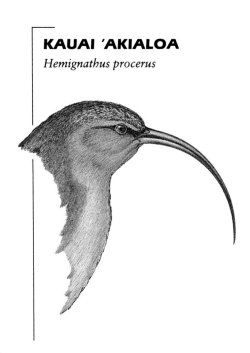

NESTING: Was restricted to dense, wet ohia forests.

FOOD: Insects and spiders gleaned from leaves and bark, from under lichens, and from within the bases of ieie leaves; also nectar from the flowers of ohia and lobelia trees.

RANGE: Kauai. The species was considered abundant in the 1890's, but declines were evident by the early 1900's, and the Kauai 'Akialoa was restricted ultimately to undisturbed portions of the Alakai Swamp.

WINTER: Was resident.

NOTES: This sickle-billed honeycreeper was scarcely studied. The Kauai 'Akialoa and Hawaii 'Akialoa differed in size. Until 1950, 'akialoas from all islands were considered one species, and their names remain in dispute.

JEOPARDIZED: Probably by deforestation (conversion for agriculture and pasture), habitat degradation (including the invasion of introduced plants), insect-borne diseases, competition from introduced birds, and predators. The bird's habit of moving to the forest edge and lower elevations apparently subjected it to introduced insect-borne disease, to which it was very susceptible.

EXTINCT: Although the Kauai 'Akialoa remains on the federal Endangered Species List, to which it was added in March 1967, it is generally thought to be already extinct, for no birds have been recorded since 1965, when only two individuals were seen. 'Akialoas formerly occupied all of the larger Hawaiian Islands except Maui, but are now generally considered to be extinct on all, most recently on Kauai (see also Hawaii 'Akialoa).

HAWAII 'AKIALOA

Hemignathus obscurus

NESTING: Was restricted to dense, wet ohia forests.

FOOD: Insects and spiders gleaned from leaves and bark, from under lichens, and from within the bases of ieie leaves; also nectar from the flowers of ohia and lobelia trees.

RANGE: Formerly occupied Lanai, Oahu, and the island of Hawaii; fossils have been found on Molokai. **WINTER:** Was resident.

NOTES: This sickle-billed honeycreeper was scarcely studied. Locating this species was made somewhat easier by the bird's conspicuous tapping and calls. Until 1950, 'akialoas from all islands were considered one species, and their names remain in dispute.

JEOPARDIZED: By deforestation (conversion for agriculture and pasture) and habitat degradation (including the invasion of introduced plants, insects, competitive birds, and predators).

EXTINCT: The species remains on the federal Endangered Species list, to which it was added in March 1967, despite the lack of sightings (outside of a possible observation in 1940) during this century. Various 'akialoas formerly occupied the larger Hawaiian Islands (except Maui), but all are now considered by most to be extinct.

ULA-'AI-HAWANE

Ciridops anna

NESTING: Unknown.

FOOD: Apparently the blossoms and unripe fruit of the hawane (loulu) palm, but possibly also insects taken from foliage. The Ula-'ai-hawane's bill was short and straight.

RANGE: In historic times the Ula-'ai-hawane was restricted to the island of Hawaii, occurring in the Kohala, Kona, and Hilo districts. Fossils have been found on Kauai, Molokai, and Oahu. **WINTER:** Was resident.

NOTES: Virtually nothing of the species' biology is known; only five specimens were collected, the first in 1859. Apparently the bird was shy. Its name means "the red bird that feeds on the hawane palm."

JEOPARDIZED: By factors unknown, but perhaps by the scarcity of the hawane palm.

EXTINCT: Even with rewards offered, only one specimen (an immature) was obtained after the early 1890's.

HAWAII MAMO

Drepanis pacifica

NESTING: Presumably in forest canopy.

FOOD: Presumably, the nectar of flowers that fit its sickle-shaped bill (lobelia, loulu palm, mamane, and ohia), and it also took insects high in ohia trees and berries of the Hawaiian mistletoe, but records are contradictory. Its lower mandible was much shorter than the upper.

RANGE: Restricted to the island of Hawaii. **WINTER:** Was resident.

NOTES: The Hawaii Mamo was also referred to as the Hoohoo, by the naturalists on the Cook expedition, who had probably mistaken it for the 'o'o, another black-and-yellow bird. Several specimens date to 1859. After the lava flow of 1880, many were shot, and the species was extremely rare by the 1890's. King Kamehameha I possessed a full-length cloak consisting solely of Hawaii Mamo feathers (about 500,000, requiring 80,000 to 90,000 birds, each of which provided only six to eight plucked feathers). Later cloaks were made of the feathers of the 'o'o and other birds. The Hawaii Mamo was an aggressive bird, often displacing other nectarivores from favored feeding sites.

JEOPARDIZED: By plume hunters who prized the yellow feathers. Hunters easily grasped the bill of the Hawaii Mamo by squeezing a flower as the bird probed for nectar. Some say the birds, once plucked of their yellow feathers, were released; others say they were kept as meat. Either way, the arrival of avian diseases and of guns probably led to their ultimate demise.

EXTINCT: The last sighting was in 1899.

BLACK MAMO
Drepanis funerea

NESTING: Apparently (at least by the time it was discovered in 1893) in the underbrush of higher wet forest (elevations above 5,000 feet) where the ground was boggy and soft.

FOOD: Presumably, nectar taken from the flowers of lobelias and the ohia-lehua.

RANGE: Restricted to Molokai.

WINTER: Was resident.

NOTES: The Black Mamo was bold and curious, not frightened by the close approach of people. Its head was often covered with pollen. Like the Hawaii Mamo, the Black Mamo was aggressive and dominated all other nectarivores except the 'O'o. It was also known as Perkins' Mamo, after the ornithologist who discovered it in 1893, or by its Hawaiian names Hoa and 'O'o-nuku-umu.

JEOPARDIZED: By habitat degradation: introduced cattle and deer trampled the vegetation, thinning it and drying out the area. Rare even when Perkins discovered it, the Black Mamo was finally depleted by collectors.

EXTINCT: The last individual was sighted in 1907.

LAYSAN MILLERBIRD
Acrocephalus familiaris familiaris

NESTING: Presumably restricted to areas supporting dense shrubs or bunch grass—habitat originally common on Laysan.

FOOD: Probably insects, mostly moths, flies, and small beetles, gleaned from leaves, bushes, grass, and the soil surface or hawked in flight.

RANGE: Restricted to Laysan Island (northwestern Hawaiian Islands), but see also the Nihoa Millerbird (p. 71). *Acrocephalus* is an Old World genus, represented also on many other Polynesian islands. **WINTER:** Was resident.

NOTES: The Laysan Millerbird was an active, abundant ground bird. It apparently was not shy of people, entering windows in search of moths, and landing on people if they remained quiet. Its name derives from its habit of feeding on noctuid ("miller") moths. The Laysan and Nihoa Millerbirds are considered separate species (rather than different subspecies) by some. The first specimen of the Laysan was collected in 1891.

JEOPARDIZED: By starvation in its limited range when introduced rabbits began stripping the island of vegetation. The rabbits were introduced in 1903 and 1904 by an agent of the North Pacific Phosphate and Fertilizer Company, who reportedly hoped to establish a canning business.

EXTINCT: Even though the species was still rather common in 1913, the last individual was reported in 1923.

LANAI THRUSH, or OLOMA'O

Myadestes lanaiensis lanaiensis

NESTING: Apparently in low forest trees and thick underbrush, probably in areas supporting the ieie vine or staghorn fern. The Lanai forest covered no more than 5,000 acres and rose to an elevation of only 3,400 feet.

FOOD: Primarily fruit, especially berries, and insects.

RANGE: The island of Lanai. **WINTER:** Was resident.

NOTES: The Lanai Thrush was collected and described in 1891 by Scott Wilson, together with the related Molokai Thrush; in 1908 the Molokai Thrush was described as a distinct species. Apparently the differences between the two thrushes included their songs; only those on Molokai were melodious. George Munro considered the Lanai Thrush common until 1923.

JEOPARDIZED: By the growth of Lanai City, which encroached upon the forest, and by disease-bearing poultry brought into the city (mosquitoes carried the diseases to the forest birds). The herd of sheep introduced to Lanai in the 1920's proved disastrous for the habitat, and the planting of pineapple fields was also probably a factor; there is virtually no native forest left on Lanai.

EXTINCT: The last individual was seen in 1933.

OAHU NUKUPU'U

Hemignathus lucidus lucidus

NESTING: Apparently restricted to the lower forest on Oahu where koa trees were available.

FOOD: Recorded as taking nectar from banana flowers rather than the insects and larvae that are gleaned from tree trunks and branches by other subspecies of the Nukupu'u.

RANGE: Oahu. **WINTER:** Was resident.

NOTES: This little-studied honeycreeper had a distinctive bill; its sickle-shaped upper mandible was double the length of the lower. One specimen was taken in 1837; few others remain in collections.

JEOPARDIZED: By its limited range, even though it was said to be fairly numerous on Oahu in the 1860's. The Oahu Nukupu'u's forest habitat was eventually trampled by feral cattle.

EXTINCT: By the 1890's, no individuals could be found.

LANAI CREEPER, or 'ALAUAHIO

Paroreomyza montana montana

NESTING: Apparently in forest from 2,000 feet elevation to the heights of the island, which were covered in dense brush and thick mist. The bird may have constructed a tight nest of grass and decayed leaves, but this was never confirmed.

FOOD: Presumably insects found on the bark of trees and branches, sometimes pursued after short flights.

RANGE: The island of Lanai. **WINTER:** Was resident.

NOTES: Specimens were first collected in 1894. Some do not consider this bird a true honeycreeper, since it lacked the characteristic odor, tongue morphology, song, tendency to mob predators, and other behaviors typical of Hawaiian honeycreepers.

JEOPARDIZED: By deforestation, habitat degradation, avian diseases, and introduced insects that eliminated native insects that had been eaten by these creepers.

EXTINCT: Common 100 years ago in the Lanai forest, the Lanai Creeper declined along with other birds on the island, becoming very scarce by the 1930's. The last pair was seen in 1937.

OAHU 'AKEPA, or 'AKOPEU'IE

Loxops coccineus rufus

NESTING: Probably in a cavity in a large tree, as are the nests of other 'akepas, but specifics about nesting were not reported for the Oahu subspecies.

FOOD: Insects (especially caterpillars) and spiders, and occasional nectar from ohia and other flowers visited within the forest canopy. Like the other 'akepas, this bird's specialized jaw musculature and asymmetrical bill allowed it to capture insects by twisting apart buds, galls, small green seed pods, and leaf clusters.

RANGE: Oahu. **WINTER:** Was resident.

NOTES: This small, finchlike honeycreeper was often found in small flocks. The generic name *Loxops* means "twisted face" and refers to the 'akepa's unequal mandibles (a condition evident only at close range). Specimens were collected in 1825 and 1893.

JEOPARDIZED: By factors unknown, but probably those affecting other forest birds on Oahu.

EXTINCT: Considered rare and only locally distributed 100 years ago, the Oahu 'Akepa is now feared lost. Assumed extinct since 1981 by Andrew Berger, it has not been sighted since 1976, and even that record is in some doubt.

LAYSAN HONEYCREEPER

Himatione sanguinea freethii

NESTING: Apparently in the interior of the island near the lagoon, where tall grass and low bushes were available.

FOOD: Presumably insects, including cryptically colored caterpillars and noctuid "miller" moths, and probably some nectar.

RANGE: Laysan Island (northwestern Hawaiian Islands). **WINTER:** Was resident.

NOTES: The Laysan Honeycreeper was a subspecies of the Apapane, the most abundant Hawaiian honeycreeper. It was first collected in 1891 and named (originally misspelled) after the manager of the North Pacific Phosphate and Fertilizer Company, which was mining the island.

JEOPARDIZED: By starvation in its limited habitat, when introduced rabbits began stripping the island of vegetation. The rabbits were introduced in 1903 and 1904 by an agent of the fertilizer company, who reportedly hoped to establish a canning business.

EXTINCT: By 1906, the Laysan Honeycreeper was the rarest of Laysan birds. The last three individuals were lost in a three-day sandstorm in 1923.

BIRDS OF PUERTO RICO EXTINCT SINCE 1776

The fossil and subfossil remains of a few bird species now extinct have been discovered in Puerto Rico. The losses apparently predate the arrival of the Europeans, and some may not be the result of human activities at all. The Puerto Rican Woodcock (*Scolopax anthonyi*) and the Puerto Rican Quail-dove (*Geotrygon larva*), for example, were gone before the arrival of Columbus. The Puerto Rican Barn-owl (*Tyto cavatica*) may have lasted into the colonial period, but the records for the period are doubtful. DeBooy's Rail (*Neso-trochis debooyi*) probably did disappear early in the colonial period.

The Culebran Puerto Rican Parrot (treated here) and the Puerto Rican Parakeet (*Aratinga maugei*) are the only birds endemic to the island known to have gone extinct since 1776. (No specimens of the Puerto Rican Parakeet, however, were collected. This bird apparently dropped from sight in the late 1890's, a victim, perhaps, of hunting or of the disastrous hurricane of 1899. Records of its existence are limited to some fossil bones and hearsay, and with so much speculation surrounding the bird, we have not provided it with a separate treatment.)

The Puerto Rican populations of a number of birds that continue to survive elsewhere have been extirpated. The White-necked Crow (*Corvus leucognaphalus*), last sighted in Puerto Rico in 1963, remains on Hispaniola. The Cuban Crow (*Corvus nasicus*) persists on Cuba's main island and on the Isle of Pines, and in the Bahamas. Populations of the Greater Flamingo (*Phoenicopterus ruber*) exist throughout the Caribbean. The Black Rail (*Laterallus jamaicensis*) and the Black-bellied Whistling Duck (*Dendrocygna autumnalis*) occur widely through North and South America, but now appear in Puerto Rico only as rare visitors or vagrants. (Because populations of these birds persist elsewhere, they are not treated here.)

Worldwide in the last 300 years or so, as we have noted previously, island species have accounted for more than 80 percent of avian extinctions. Thus Puerto Rico, like Hawaii, is a case study of the impact of humanity on island avifaunas.

REFERENCES: Raffaele, 1989; Wiley, 1985.

CULEBRAN PUERTO RICAN PARROT

Amazona vittata gracilipes

NESTING: Apparently required deep cavities in large, old trees in forests or woodlands.

FOOD: Fruit, seeds, and leaves.

RANGE: The subspecies was restricted to Culebra Island. **WINTER:** Was resident.

NOTES: Common as late as 1899, this parrot was considered an agricultural pest.

JEOPARDIZED: By 1912, nearly all of Puerto Rico had been cleared for agriculture (see p. 94). The Puerto Rican Parrot, in general, was threatened by the loss of its forest habitat, hunting, and capture of chicks for pets.

EXTINCT: The last individual was seen around 1912.

CONSERVING
BIOLOGICAL DIVERSITY

Conserving biological diversity, long a priority among biologists, is becoming a priority among policymakers as well. Keeping it high on political agendas in North America is imperative for restoring and maintaining our natural heritage. Success requires a comprehensive approach founded on biological research, accurate species inventories, agreement on research priorities, continuity of leadership, coordination within cooperative networks of conservation biologists and conservation organizations, and easy public access to information.

The best way to proceed, many in the U.S. believe, is to establish a central base of operations with an independent scientific advisory committee that has authority over appropriations, the means to coordinate activities among agencies, the personnel to train new leadership, and the opportunity to set "the right kind" of worldwide example. The Hawaiian case is instructive: the rescue efforts extended to Hawaii's many severely Endangered forest species (17 of its 30 federally listed Endangered birds) could encourage comparable preservation efforts for jeopardized tropical forest species elsewhere.

The Endangered Species Act, law now for nearly 20 years, was written to protect individual species from extinction and to preserve their habitats. The next stage of legislation calls for the protection of biological diversity in general. At this writing, however, the Bush administration, like the Reagan administration before it, remains opposed to the National Biological Diversity Conservation and Environmental Research Act, which was introduced in March 1988.

In the interim, the need for accurate data on the changing status of species under threat is growing more urgent. In recent years especially, birders have turned their energies and their expertise to the censusing of avian populations, and have set an extraordinary example of coordinated voluntary participation (see pp. 223, 225). The National Audubon Society's Christmas Bird Counts and the U.S. Fish and Wildlife Service's Breeding Bird Survey—just to name two—set the standard for public effort in establishing and interpreting species inventories. Of course, one cannot equate data collected by an army of volunteers devoting one day per year to the censusing of local birds with the data gleaned by ornithologists devoting perhaps years of professional attention to the assembling of precise demographic information on a limited number of populations. Both efforts are important to avian conservation, but despite these contributions it remains difficult to stay abreast of the changing status of our vulnerable species. Eventually, as various sources of data are better integrated, more information will come into the hands of the public. Until then, to some degree, inconsistency and contradiction are likely to be partners in our efforts to maintain current knowledge on the status of our birds.

REFERENCES: Blockstein, 1988; Lowe, Matthews, and Moseley, 1990.

The equivalent, roughly, of 30 pages, altogether, from the authors' *The Binder's Handbook* (Simon & Schuster, 1988) has been incorporated into the next several pages, and used by permission.

HABITAT LOSS, DISEASE, COWBIRDS, AND CHEMICALS

All manner of forces put populations of birds at risk, some of them natural, others—such as habitat loss and degradation and the introduction of predators—directly imposed by people. But even such natural events as the felling of Red-cockaded Woodpecker nest trees by Hurricane Hugo are exacerbated by the preexisting and ongoing human alteration of the environment. What follows are some examples of that array of forces.

Habitat Loss

Habitat loss and degradation pose the greatest threat to North American birds. From forests to wetlands, avian habitats are everywhere endangered. Riparian areas (corridors of water-loving vegetation along streams and rivers) are especially vulnerable and of critical importance.

We began this book with a discussion of the effects of habitat loss on the North American avifauna. As we mentioned in the Introduction, large tracts of forest are better able than are woodlots or small parks to maintain forest bird populations, because unbroken forest is less likely to harbor the nest predators—in particular, cats, jays, crows, and cowbirds—that thrive on forest edges. Much of North America's forest is long since lost. For example, longleaf pine woodland previously covered 60–70 million acres and extended from Virginia to Texas. Today, it covers less than 10 million acres, is primarily second growth, and continues to be degraded by land use and fire-

prevention policies. Outmoded silvicultural practices still replace mixed-forest ecosystems with single-species plantations able to support fewer birds and other animals. Development projects typically convert forest into areas that can support few, if any, of their former avian inhabitants. Though the effects of forest loss on bird populations may be starkly apparent, the effects of forest degradation may be quite insidious, yielding long-term reconfigurations of breeding-bird communities by favoring some species over others.

Wetlands include a broad array of habitats, from mangrove swamps, marshes, seeps, springs, ponds, vernal pools, and prairie potholes to bottomland hardwood forests. Wetlands improve water quality, increase the recharge rate for groundwater, and reduce erosion and downstream flooding. They also support a great diversity of organisms, some depending on them for their entire lives, and others, including millions of migratory birds, requiring wetland shelter and food only as they move between their wintering and breeding grounds. According to U.S. Fish and Wildlife Service estimates, by the mid-1970's the U.S. had lost more than half of its original wetland acreage. Today, under 100 million acres remain, and losses continue at up to 450,000 acres yearly. Where is it all going? Almost 90 percent of recent wetland losses are the result of agricultural practices (some 60 percent of the U.S. land base is used for crops and pastureland). Some areas, of

course, have been hit harder than others: less than 10 percent of California's natural historical wetlands remain. Similarly, some wetland-dependent species have been affected more than others. An estimated one-third of the Threatened or Endangered plants in the U.S. depend upon wetlands, and more than one in five Endangered species would benefit from wetland restoration.

In eastern North America, riparian ecosystems often encompass wide areas, such as floodplains or bottomlands. In the West, they are essentially confined to narrow belts of vegetation along streams and rivers, and cover less than 1 percent of the land area. In the Southwest and in the Great Basin, riparian habitat supports more than half of the region's avian species. This rare habitat is especially endangered: riparian belts have been converted for agriculture, grazed, channelized, developed for recreational uses, logged, and invaded by exotic plants, such as salt cedar, that have crowded out the native plant species upon which native animals depend. Land-use policies are struggling to keep up with these threats, and losses of riparian bird populations continue.

The challenge of long-term habitat management is compounded by the prospect of global warming and the difficulty of protecting corridors and buffer zones between critical habitats. Global warming threatens to lead to changes in regional temperature, precipitation, rate of evaporation, sea level, and even soil and water chemistry. And its effects will threaten some species more than others. For those birds already in jeopardy, warming may reduce their range and increase the extent of protected habitat (often already marginal) on which they are dependent. Moreover, the ability of already reduced populations to adapt to rapidly changing environmental conditions may be limited. Foraging specialists, such as the Everglade Snail Kite, will be at extreme risk if their prey (for that kite, a single species of snail) fails to adapt to changing conditions. Tundra-nesting migratory shorebirds and other high-latitude breeders (where the effects of warming are predicted to be greater) may find less habitat that is able to support them. Coastal wintering habitat, such as the Texas site used by the Whooping Crane, would be reduced by any significant rise in sea level.

In light of continued habitat loss and degradation and the potential effects of global warming, our deliberations over which species to save can only become much more agonizing, and the measures we adopt drastically less effective. Today, the listing process emphasizes identifying those species most likely to go extinct unless helped, while managers target those most likely to recover. Increasingly, however, biologists must persuade policy-makers that it is far more promising to preserve entire ecosystems or habitats than it is to continue to focus on individual species.

Diseases and Parasites

Birds may be host to disease-causing microorganisms, such as protozoans, bacteria, fungi, viruses, or rickettsiae (tiny bacteria-like organisms). They may also be host to other parasites—larger organisms that are small enough to live on or in birds indefinitely, and may or may not make them sick.

There is a great variety of avian diseases, from malaria (caused by close relatives of the protozoans that cause human malaria) or aspergillosis (a fungal infection) to tuberculosis (not the same pathogen that causes human tuberculosis). Newcastle disease, fowl plague, avian pox, and avian influenza are among hundreds of kinds of infections that can sicken or kill a bird. Indeed, disease may wipe out entire populations or even species. The mosquito species *Culex pipiens,* accidentally introduced into the Hawaiian Islands in 1826, transmits avian pox virus, malarial protozoans, and other pathogens. Many lowland Hawaiian honeycreepers proved extremely susceptible to the pathogens (see pp. 63–64).

Botulism is a global problem that kills millions of waterfowl. Death is brought on by a toxin produced by a bacterium, *Clostridium botulinum,* which thrives in the oxygen-poor environments created by decaying plant and animal matter (the bacterium is unable to survive in an oxygen-rich environment—it is anaerobic). Birds are exposed when feeding on rotting plants or flesh. The toxin affects their nervous system and may lead to paralysis, preventing flight. Infected birds may hold their head to the side, and may find walking difficult or impossible. Death comes from drowning, starvation, or respiratory failure.

Although aquatic birds are most often subject to botulism, sometimes in great numbers (an estimated 250,000 ducks succumbed on Great Salt Lake in 1932), the toxin has been found in more than 20 avian families. Most epidemics take place in the summer when hot weather and low water levels decrease the level of oxygen and increase the alkalinity of lakes and marshes, creating ideal conditions for *Clostridium* to thrive in and produce higher levels of the toxin. Warmer climates and declining hab-

itats may eventually make botulism an important agent of extinction for waterfowl.

A great variety of parasites take their nourishment from birds. Some are external, such as the chewing bird-lice (Mallophaga) that invade plumage and live on accumulated "dandruff" or on fluids, including blood. Blood-suckers include louse flies (Hippoboscidae), fleas, small bugs (Hemiptera, relatives of bedbugs), ticks, and mites. Internally, birds host tapeworms, flukes, roundworms, and others, which live either in the digestive tract or in the blood vessels. The impact of parasites on natural populations of birds remains unclear, but there are indications that it can be considerable, especially in populations of colonially nesting species.

One survey of parasitic infestation, carried out by biologists Charles and Mary Brown of Princeton University, showed that more "swallow bugs" (bedbuglike parasites) could be expected in the nests of Cliff Swallows nesting in large colonies than in those of swallows nesting in small colonies. Apparently, the smaller colonies may switch sites in alternate years, or return to the same sites even less frequently, leaving their parasites to starve in empty nests. Clearly, then, habitat loss and degradation limit the options available to colonial breeders, and, as seen here, could limit the ability of populations to switch sites to reduce their parasite loads.

Though the presence of diseases and parasites is normal, populations of imperiled birds are small and often restricted to limited habitat on reserves, where the spread of pathogens may be rapid.

Cowbirds as Killers

A brood parasite is a bird that lays some or all of its eggs in the nests of "host" birds. The Brown-headed Cowbird is an obligate brood parasite that always lays all of its eggs in the nests of other species. It is a supreme generalist, having been recorded as parasitizing 220 species, 144 of them successfully. Formerly limited largely to the Great Plains, this cowbird has expanded its range greatly in historic time, so that it now occupies most of our continent below the Arctic. It followed human populations as they converted forest lands into farms and pastures, and rapidly invaded to the north and west, especially between 1900 and 1930. By 1925 it was common in Los Angeles, by 1960 it had reached the Oregon border, and today it poses a major threat to the continued survival of a number of the species and subspecies that it now regularly parasitizes. And it is not alone: the Shiny Cowbird was first recorded in continental North America in 1985, having moved up from South America through the Caribbean, reaching Puerto Rico by the 1940's and Cuba by 1982, crossing the 100 miles to Florida in 1985, reaching Georgia, Louisiana, and the Carolinas in 1989, and Texas and Oklahoma in 1990. In the process it devastated Puerto Rico's Yellow-shouldered Blackbirds (see p. 96).

As a defense, many parasitized species reject cowbird eggs (by either destroying the egg, rebuilding the nest to cover the egg, or abandoning the nest); others fail as foster parents, never rearing the cowbird chick. But if they do rear the young cowbird, their own young invariably suffer. Cowbird eggs usually hatch one day ahead of the host's eggs, and the cowbird young develop very rapidly, usually outpacing the host young and garnering far more than an equal share of the food brought to the nest. The hosts may abandon their nest, but then may fail to breed at all that season. Clearly, the cost to the host species is high.

Despite the Brown-headed Cowbird's population explosion, only an estimated 3 percent of its eggs survive to adulthood. Females have a long reproductive period and only a short break between clutches, and their reproductive organs do not regress following clutch completion (a phenomenon unique among passerines yet studied). The laying cycle takes advantage of a continuous, two-month supply of host nests. In her lifetime a typical female lays about 80 eggs (40 per year for two years). With about 3 percent of those 80 eggs surviving, each female produces an average of 2.4 adults. Each pair of cowbirds, on average, therefore replaces itself with an average of 1.2 pairs—which doubles the cowbird population every eight years. And, of course, each of those 80 eggs presents an obstacle—sometimes insurmountable—to the breeding efforts of a host pair.

There is circumstantial evidence that at least some female Brown-headed Cowbirds specialize in host species that are particularly vulnerable. Some of the most heavily affected have been subjected to parasitism only recently, as the range of the cowbird has expanded. This appears to be true for both the Kirtland's Warbler (see p. 34) and the California subspecies of Bell's Vireo, the Least Bell's Vireo (see p. 56). Other passerines such as the Willow Flycatcher (see p. 162), the Blue-gray Gnatcatcher, and the Yellow Warbler (see p. 168) have also been declining in lowland California with the invasion of cowbirds.

Without proper management, it is quite possible that this exceedingly successful bird could drive a host species to extinction. For 20 years now, managers have removed thousands of cowbirds from Kirtland Warbler habitat and cleared Kirtland nests of parasitic eggs. But under current conditions, such activities will remain critical to the warbler's survival.

The recent spread of the Shiny Cowbird into North America surely warrants great concern. It parasitizes more than 180 host species and seems to be as efficient as the Brown-headed in its role of generalist, obligate brood parasite.

If cowbird parasitism in general is to be effectively managed, we must restrict the conversion of forest into habitat that favors cowbirds. Although cowbirds favor areas under cultivation, recent findings indicate that the effects of parasitism are most significant along forest edges. Large, unbroken blocks of forest minimize the relative extent of forest-edge habitat, and should be sustained wherever possible.

Birds Versus Powerlines

Many owls and raptors are killed at the crossbars of high-voltage power poles. Owls apparently prefer to perch there, where they are less conspicuous than when perched in the middle of an open line. Unfortunately, both ground and hot wires are attached close together, and it is easy for the birds to touch both during landing and take-off. Golden Eagles, particularly younger, less experienced birds, also have been susceptible to electrocution on power poles. In 1981, in a single survey, some 350 Golden Eagles were found dead beneath 24 sections of powerlines in a six-state area (Idaho, Oregon, Nevada, Utah, New Mexico, and Wyoming). Modification of power pole design has been promising, but many miles of powerlines require updating before this hazard is removed.

Birds and Oil

When oil tankers clean their tanks or generate accidental spills, marine birds such as loons, grebes, cormorants, murres, puffins, razorbills, auklets, gulls, and sea ducks are placed in jeopardy. Some birds may smell fresh oil and flee the area of a spill, but many others cannot. Birds subject to newly released oil may swallow or inhale toxins while preening and later suffer pneumonia, liver and kidney damage, or other problems. It apparently takes very little oil to stress birds, interfere with foraging, slow the growth of young, and even kill the eggs during the first half of incubation.

Hazards remain after the toxins have dissolved or evaporated, for although the oil is then relatively inert, it mats plumage, limiting insulation and buoyancy. In their vain attempt to remain warm and afloat, many soiled birds die.

About 3.5 million tons of oil (about one-tenth of one percent of the total pumped from the ground each year) are spilled into the oceans annually. This percentage, we hope, is decreasing, barring aberrations like the huge, deliberate spillage during the Persian Gulf War. Seagoing nations have been legislating increasingly strict measures to contain the problem at its source: stringent sanctions have been imposed against deliberate injection into the oceans, and methods to contain or neutralize accidental spills appear to be improving, although their efficacy in the *Exxon Valdez* disaster in Alaska was not heartening, and in the Persian Gulf, even in peacetime, million-gallon spills have occurred regularly, without cleanup.

Seabirds may help to monitor the problem of coastal spills. Petroleum residues have been detected in the stomach oil of storm-petrels. These birds and other, related ocean birds feed at the surface (where pollutants are concentrated), forage intermittently over vast areas, digest oils slowly, and regurgitate readily. Storm-petrels thus might be used as part of an oceanic pollution monitoring system, as suggested by the studies carried out on them by Dee Boersma at the University of Washington.

Oil contamination of fresh water poses its own set of threats. Our waterways will continue to suffer leaks and spillage as long as they serve as distribution networks for petroleum shipments. And many more birds die each year in the oil-collection ponds of oil facilities than perish in major oil spills—in spite of the enormous toll taken by the latter.

For example, the playa lakes region, which covers parts of Kansas, Oklahoma, Texas, and New Mexico, is riddled with open pits (and ponds) that appear hospitable from the air but contain oil and industrial wastes. Hundreds of thousands of birds, especially waterfowl and shorebirds, mistake the oil pits and their reflective surfaces for bodies of fresh water. The U.S. Fish and Wildlife Service requires that screens cover the pits (or that fines of up to $5,000 per bird be paid), but the problem remains. Only New Mexico has screened most of its pits; Texas and Oklahoma are only at the stage of proposing the requisite screens. Elsewhere, Louisiana, for example, where exemptions for oil companies from waste-disposal laws continue, losses include not just wetland birds but the wetlands themselves, which revert to open water once stabilizing vegetation is poisoned and dies.

Metallic Poisons: From Lead to Mercury

Shotguns kill millions of ducks and geese annually. But many of these deaths are accidental and caused indirectly. Lead pellets that fail to reach their targets drop into ponds, lakes, and marshes where many are later swallowed by aquatic birds. An estimated 1,400 pellets (about half a pound) are left behind by hunters for every bird carried away. It takes only one pellet, swallowed with food or taken as grit and ground in the gizzard, to contaminate the bloodstream with enough lead to kill a duck. Poisoning from swallowed lead pellets has been occurring for a long time over a large area. In 1948 more than 100,000 Mallards died in Illinois; in 1974 more than 500 Tundra Swans were killed in a North Carolina refuge. Canvasbacks and Canada Geese seem to suffer the heaviest mortality among wildfowl, either because they eat hard seeds and grains that resemble lead shot, or because they use their bills to dig for aquatic tubers and seeds in areas where the pellets are lodged.

Poisoned waterfowl characteristically hold their wings in a "roof-shaped" or drooped position, walk with a staggering gait, are reluctant to fly, seek isolation, or fail to join others in migration. In all, some 1.5 to 3 million waterfowl die yearly in North America from lead poisoning. In the last decade more than 60 Bald Eagles ingested enough lead from the waterfowl they preyed upon to die as well.

A phased ban on lead shot was announced by the U.S. Fish and Wildlife Service beginning in the 1987–88 season, making its use illegal in the United States by 1991. From the point of view of ballistics and shotgun barrel wear, the steel substitutes are not ideal, and although the ban is today generally accepted by the hunting public, some hunters are not content. Other sources of lead, including weights used by anglers, also cause lead poisoning of waterfowl, but their impact, although significant, is probably minimal compared to that of shot.

A second, although less threatening, metallic toxin reducing North American bird populations is mercury. Mercury may be eaten in contaminated fish or swallowed along with seeds that have been treated with mercury-loaded pesticides. Organic mercury pesticides used on rice fields extirpated White Storks from Japan, and mercury pollution of lakes and streams is not insignificant on our continent, especially where gold is mined and separated from gravel by the addition of mercury (a threat that increases with the price of gold). Where mercury occurs it can further stress bird populations jeopardized by other human activities.

Pesticides

As noted in the Introduction, birds have played a primary role in alerting us to the problems created by pollution. In the fable that began her 1962 classic *Silent Spring,* Rachel Carson wrote, "It was a spring without voices. On the mornings that had once throbbed with the dawn chorus of robins, catbirds, doves, jays, wrens, and scores of other bird voices there was now no sound; only silence lay over the fields and woods and marsh." The pesticide industry attacked *Silent Spring,* as did narrowly trained entomologists, but there is no dispute in North America today: misuse of pesticides is now widely recognized to threaten not only birds but also people and ecosystems in general.

Carson's book alerted the public to the potentially lethal impact of DDT on birds and led eventually to changes in the gigantic "broadcast spray" programs that had been part of North American insect control. These changes, however, did not come in time to prevent substantial damage. DDT, its breakdown products, and the other chlorinated hydrocarbon pesticides (and nonpesticide chlorinated hydrocarbons such as PCBs) are persistent and tend to concentrate as they move through the feeding sequences in communities that ecologists call "food chains."

Unlike botulism or lead poisoning, large concentrations of chlorinated hydrocarbons do not usually kill the bird outright. Instead, DDT and its relatives disrupt calcium metabolism in birds and lead to eggshell thinning. Incubating Brown Pelicans and Bald Eagles heavily contaminated with DDT simply cracked their eggs when they sat on them. This process led to the decimation of the Brown Pelican populations in much of North America and to the extermination of the Peregrine Falcon from the eastern United States and southeastern Canada. Until DDT was banned in 1972, shell-thinning also caused declines in populations of Golden and Bald Eagles, Ospreys, and White Pelicans, among others.

The population declines, fortunately, were reversible, and soon after the ban, recoveries were apparent in Ospreys and even American Robins, which in most cases returned to their pre-DDT levels of breeding success within a decade or less. Unfortunately, the banning of DDT led to other pesticide problems. The newer organophosphate pesticides that in part replaced the organochlorines, such as parathion and TEPP (tetraethyl pyrophosphate), are less persistent and therefore do not accumulate in food chains, but they are nonetheless highly toxic. Parathion applied to winter wheat, for instance, killed some 1,600 waterfowl, mostly Canada Geese, in the Texas panhandle in 1951. Recent findings show that concentrations of DDT in the tissues of starlings in Arizona and New Mexico, however, have been rising. DDT has been shown to be present as a contaminant in the widely used toxin dicofol (a key ingredient in, among others, the pesticide Kelthane). Dicofol is a chemical formed by adding single oxygen atoms to DDT molecules. Unfortunately, not all the DDT gets oxygenated, so that dicofol may be contaminated with as much as 15 percent DDT.

More than 2.5 million pounds of dicofol, containing about 250 thousand pounds of DDT, are used annually in pesticides. Understanding of the breakdown products of dicofol is limited, but we know that these products include DDE, a breakdown product of DDT and a substance identified as the major cause of reproductive failure in several bird species. With DDT still in use illegally in some areas of the United States, and with migratory birds possibly picking it up in their tropical wintering grounds (where DDT application is still permitted, as is that of other pesticides now banned in the United States but exported legally to developing nations), the threat of DDT to bird populations continues.

Unhappily, knowledge of the ways that pesticides and related industrial chemicals affect both bird and human populations remains very incomplete. Much scientific effort has been directed at determining whether or not various compounds cause cancer; much less has been focused on their possible disruption of development, depression of immune system function, and toxicity to the nervous system. Dioxin, a byproduct of the defoliant Agent Orange, is such a potent concoction that only five parts per trillion can cause tumors in rats. Peregrine Falcon embryos tested in California had absorbed five to ten times the amount of dioxin capable of killing a chicken embryo. But reactions in birds are highly variable: turkey embryos can tolerate 20 times more dioxin than chicken embryos can. That these findings should be of great concern is indicated by such phenomena as distorted sex ratios in California Gulls and the decline of Bald Eagles, Common Terns, and Black Terns in the Great Lakes region—all apparently traceable to exposure to these chemicals.

In 1988, roughly one in five of the federally listed Endangered species were threatened in part by pesticides. Pesticide control is of particular importance to birds such as the Northern Aplomado Falcon, whose range includes extensive agricultural areas, and the Everglade Snail Kite, which feeds on pesticide-sensitive prey.

REFERENCES: Beaver, 1980; Bonney, 1986; Boersma, 1986; Brown and Brown, 1986; Carson, 1962; Darley, 1982; Dunstan, 1990; Ehrlich et al., 1977, 1988; Friedmann and Kiff, 1985; Goldwasser et al., 1980; Henny et al., 1984; Knopf et al., 1988; Moss and Camin, 1970; Myers and Colborn, 1991; Nettleship and Birkhead, 1985; Norton, 1988; Noss, 1988; Peters, 1988; Rollfinke et al., 1990; Sanderson and Bellrose, 1986; Scott and Ankney, 1983; Spitzer et al., 1978; Teather and Robertson, 1986; Terres, 1981; White et al., 1982; Wilcove, 1988; Woodard, 1983.

KEEPING TRACK OF BIRD POPULATIONS— AND WHAT IMPERILS THEM

Birders and ornithologists participate in cooperative research programs of the National Audubon Society, the U.S. Fish and Wildlife Service, the Laboratory of Ornithology at Cornell University, and various bird observatories. Such "cooperative research" programs coordinate the observations of a large number of people collecting similar kinds of information in many different locations and make them available to the birding community and to scientists, as well.

The Christmas Bird Count, sponsored by the National Audubon Society, is one of the oldest cooperative research projects in North America. Organized in 1900, this data-gathering effort now involves nearly 40,000 people in North America, Central America, Hawaii, and parts of the Caribbean and collects millions of records annually. These records consist of the number of birds of each species seen within standardized 177-square-mile-diameter circles on a single day within two weeks of Christmas. The data are used to analyze early-winter population trends of individual species, and to monitor changes in the relative abundance of species over large geographic areas.

The Breeding Bird Census, begun in 1937 and also sponsored by the National Audubon Society, records the numbers of breeding pairs seen on particular study sites that vary in size from about 10 to more than 400 acres. Each census includes at least eight visits to the same site during a single breeding season. Some 2,000 volunteers, who know local birds by both sight and sound, participate annually. The goal is to make repeated censuses on the sites over successive years in order to gain an understanding of local and regional population trends and to collect information on the habitat requirements of breeding species.

The U.S. Fish and Wildlife Service's Breeding Bird Survey is another highly regarded cooperative census. This survey was initiated in 1965 as concern over the effects of pesticides on bird populations grew and a continent-wide monitoring program was deemed imperative. Indeed, many ornithologists consider the Breeding Bird Survey the best method for censusing birds and their population sizes, because it is statistically solid for all but the more cryptic species. In addition, its findings can be controlled to account for changes in habitat. Since 1949, the Winter Bird Populations Study has conducted similar censuses during the winter, often at the same sites, with the goal of understanding wintering populations. These programs are administered through the Cornell Laboratory of Ornithology, and their results are published in the *Journal of Field Ornithology*.

The Nest Record Card Program sponsored by the Cornell Laboratory of Ornithology was started in 1965 and now includes more than 300,000 records of individual bird nests. Each record may include a description of the nesting habitat, clutch size, length of incubation and nesting periods, fledging success, and a variety of other pertinent pieces of information. Besides adding to our knowledge of breeding biology, these records can be extremely useful for understanding reproductive success. The Laboratory also sponsors the Colonial Bird Register, which contains more than 37,000 records collected over the past 20 years. Each record contains the number of breeding pairs in a colony or mixed colony of birds, and the records cover more than 60 species of colonially breeding waterbirds, including pelicans, cormorants, herons, egrets, ibises, gulls, terns, and alcids.

Finally, the Laboratory also runs Project Feeder Watch, in which participants record birds visiting their feeders periodically during the winter and then submit forms tallying the results.

Data from all of these research programs are now stored at the Laboratory of Ornithology. You can obtain further information on them as well as standard forms for submitting your data by writing to Bird Population Studies, Cornell Laboratory of Ornithology, Sapsucker Woods Road, Cornell University, Ithaca, NY 14850.

Other important cooperative research projects in North America include the Western Hemisphere Shorebird Reserve Network, a multi-organization venture based at the Manomet Bird Observatory; the Hawk Migration Association of North America's Hawk Migration Surveys; and the compilation of breeding bird atlases sponsored by various state and provincial agencies. Information on these projects is available through the Audubon Society. Write to the National Audubon Society, 950 Third Avenue, New York, NY 10022.

Further information on the federal (U.S.) monitoring, research, and management strategies for nongame birds is available in the U.S. Fish and Wildlife's *Strategies for Conservation of Avian Diversity in North America* (USFWS, Office of Migratory Bird Management, Mail Stop 634, ARLSQ, Washington, D.C. 20240).

Determining the vulnerability of birds also relies on work carried out in the laboratory. Important data from experimental avian research have been gathered for more than a century and provide us with the understanding of the biology of birds that is the first step toward conserving them. In 1985 alone, more than 9,300 articles on birds were indexed in the Zoological Record. Finding out about what the birds are doing in the field and what others have learned in their studies of them in the laboratory has never been easier—or more important.

REFERENCE: Konishi et al., 1989.

HELPING TO CONSERVE BIRDS

Fortunately we, as individuals, can do a great deal to help fend off the silent spring that will surely be upon us if the degradation of North American habitats and the tropical wintering grounds of so many of our birds continues. In fact, each of us can make substantial contributions to the conservation of birds, not only at local and national levels but at the international level as well.

At the Local Level

Working at the local level is personally rewarding, and results tend to be quick and relatively easy to observe. Whether planting trees, shrubs, or native ground cover and providing a source of fresh water to create a haven for birds in your back yard, or urging limits on the use of pesticides among your neighbors (which can benefit them as well), you can lend birds a hand. Your local Audubon Society chapter can provide important information about birds in your area. For another source of details on the plants and foods used by the birds around you, refer to Stephen Kress's excellent *Audubon Society Guide to Attracting Birds*.

The focus of local political action is the preservation of high-quality bird habitats. Loss of natural vegetation usually leads to declines in local bird populations, but this need not generate resistance to all development. The challenge is to encourage conservationally sound development, and especially to endorse development in areas that

have already been seriously disturbed. Relatively undisturbed habitat should be left alone. Greenbelts and riparian strips along streams and waterways that run through cities and towns (freeing them from concrete encasement where flood control is not a genuine concern) encourage birdlife. The edges of roads and freeways can be planted to provide perches and cover native to the area. Hedgerows and old railroad rights-of-way can be viewed as valued resources that provide protection to a diversity of birds and other animals. City park vegetation can be planned to host a maximum of species (indeed, it may be the only bird habitat that some urban birders can frequent). Even though they are located in the middle of the busiest cities of North America, the larger urban parks are visited by hundreds of bird species annually.

As described elsewhere in this volume, participation in censusing and other data-collecting programs (see p. 223) can be one of the most pleasing and satisfying forms of local participation. Census information is central to informed planning, and the proper use of birds as indicators of changes in environmental quality is critical to arresting deteriorating conditions before damage control is either too costly or too late. Whether you are noting if Common Terns are competing with imperiled Roseate Terns for preferred positions in their foraging area, or keeping watch for tell-tale cat and dog tracks at the edge of Clapper Rail habitat, your participation adds to the

long-range goal of developing integrated programs that help to make the most out of every dollar earmarked for conservation.

At the National Level

Participation at this level usually involves group political activities. Membership in the Audubon Society, which disseminates information on bird conservation through its magazines *Audubon* and *American Birds* and the newsletters of local chapters, or other conservation-oriented organizations such as the Sierra Club, Wilderness Society, and the World Wildlife Fund, makes it easier to keep informed about issues affecting bird conservation. Whether you support the Nature Conservancy, which raises money to purchase habitats that are important for conserving various species, or become an associate of the Laboratory of Ornithology at Cornell University (see p. 223), which is a major center for keeping track of the conservation status of North American birds, your help will be valued.

In the United States, individual contributions such as purchase of the annual $7.50 duck stamp (available through most U.S. post offices) are another approach. Although the stamp is required of waterfowl hunters over the age of 15, the popularity of the stamps is increasing as nonhunters begin to collect them. More than 4 million acres of wetland have been purchased with the more than $300 million in revenue generated by stamp sales. Many states, as well, now issue their own duck stamps. Thus, the harvesting of a living resource finances the preservation of habitat for future generations.

A number of conservation organizations offer coordinated national political action by informing their members of the appropriate times for letter writing and lobbying, and by providing reports to U.S. Congressmen, members of the Canadian Parliament, and other members of the leadership, detailing what is at stake on important votes that affect the preservation of the biological riches of the continent. Political action includes not only encouraging legislation and international treaties protecting birds but pressing for more general environmental legislation as well (see p. 228). It is important, for example, to support legal abatement of acid precipitation, which is damaging freshwater and forest habitats and apparently threatening the populations of many aquatic birds, such as loons, that depend on freshwater fishes.

Reminding North American decision-makers of the degree to which humans compete with birds (and most other animals) for both habitat and food resources, and pressing for steps to limit (and then gradually reduce) the scale of human activities on our continent, are perhaps the most basic actions we can take to ensure a future for our nonhuman residents.

At the Global Level

Membership in many of the conservation organizations helps to protect species and habitat both within and outside of North America. Heading the list is the International Council for Bird Preservation (ICBP), which is the oldest worldwide conservation organization. The ICBP, a federation devoted solely to the protection of birds and their habitats, has a membership totaling over 10 million, with 330 member organizations in 100 countries. The Worldwide Fund for Nature (formerly the World Wildlife Fund) is important here, and the Nature Conservancy, although active mostly within the United States, is increasing its involvement in other countries. North Americans can also work to protect birds elsewhere by influencing the international marketplace. For example, the meat import policies of both the United States and Canada affect the Central and South American forests that are the winter homes of a great many of our birds. Significant portions of those forests have already been cleared to provide pastures for cattle destined for consumption here, as we should continue to remind our representatives.

Assisting our own nation and other nations with programs to protect their human populations by keeping their numbers at safe levels is obviously important from the viewpoint of conserving both birds and human beings. Political battles over whether the U.S. should control its own population size, or whether foreign aid should be provided to further such purposes elsewhere, will continue, but means for limiting the growth of the human population, and then gradually (and humanely) reducing it, are essential if bird populations are to thrive. A decade ago, *Homo sapiens* was already using, destroying, or diverting almost 40 percent of the food resources of Earth's land surface. If the human population continues to expand, the healthy variety of our avifauna will gradually give way, and "weedy" species that thrive in human-altered environments will take over. We can avoid declining into a world of hungry, discontented people whose avian companions are largely cowbirds, House Sparrows, European Starlings, Rock Doves, Common Crows, and Herring Gulls. Supporting conservation organizations financially, volunteering your time, keeping politically informed, and voting appropriately can only help.

It is unlikely that victory in the war against environmental destruction will occur during your lifetime, but the lines of defense must hold if Earth's avifauna is to survive to consume insects, pollinate plants, disperse seeds, recycle phosphorus from the sea, and carry out all of the other roles birds play in keeping our planet's ecosystems functioning—while giving future generations of people the kinds of pleasure they have given to us. There are an estimated 300 thousand to 1.8 million active or committed birders in North America, and this arsenal of bird conservationists represents a powerful and growing lobby, one that increasingly helps the securing of those pleasures. A decade ago, according to the U.S. Fish and Wildlife Service, U.S. birders were already spending more than $20 billion each year on bird-related activities and materials. A survey of just the 43,000 participants in the 1988 Christmas Bird Counts indicated that they spent nearly $80 million on activities related to birding, and, on average, subscribed to more than one birding magazine, had joined three conservation organizations, and bought more than four books about birds or nature.

Today some $500 million (roughly $2 for every American) is given to conservation organizations each year, a total that exceeds the 1989 federal expenditures for U.S. Threatened and Endangered species by more than $450 million! (See p. 14.)

Major Broad-Based Memberships

International Council for Bird Preservation (ICBP)
219c Huntingdon Road
Cambridge, CB3 0DL
United Kingdom

National Audubon Society
(*Audubon, American Birds*)
950 Third Avenue
New York, NY 10022

National and International Wildlife Federations
1412 Sixteenth Street, NW
Washington, DC 20036

Sierra Club
730 Polk Street
San Francisco, CA 94109

Friends of the Earth
218 D Street SE
Washington, DC 20003

Zero Population Growth
1346 Connecticut Avenue, NW
Washington, DC 20036

Californians for Population Stabilization
1025 Ninth St., No. 217
Sacramento, CA 95814

Wildlife and Habitat Conservation

Defenders of Wildlife
1244 Nineteenth Street, NW
Washington, DC 20036

Nature Conservancy
1800 N. Kent Street
Arlington, VA 22209

Wilderness Society
1400 I Street, NW
Washington, DC 20005

World Wildlife Fund (USA)
1255 Twenty-third Street, NW
Washington, DC 20037

The Legal Front

Environmental Defense Fund
257 Park Avenue
New York, NY 10010

Natural Resources Defense Council
1725 I Street, NW, Suite 600
Washington, DC 20006

Sierra Club Legal Defense
2044 Fillmore Street
San Francisco, CA 94115

University Outreach Programs

Center for Conservation Biology
Department of Biological Sciences
Stanford University
Stanford, CA 94305

Laboratory of Ornithology
Cornell University
(*Living Bird Quarterly*)
159 Sapsucker Woods Road
Ithaca, NY 14850

For Information on Canadian Wildlife

Committee on the Status of Endangered Wildlife in Canada (COSEWIC)
Secretariat
Canadian Wildlife Service
Ottawa, ONT K1A 0H3

World Wildlife Fund Canada
90 Eglinton Avenue East
Toronto, ONT M45 2Z7

REFERENCES: Canadian Wildlife Service, 1988, 1989, 1991; Ehrlich and Ehrlich, 1981, 1987; Kress, 1985; Safina, 1990; Soulé, 1986; Soulé and Wilcox, 1980; Vitousek et al., 1986.

LAWS TO PROTECT BIRDS

Most people interested in birds know that millions of Passenger Pigeons were killed and shipped to markets, but few realize that an enormous variety of other native birds and their eggs once found their way to shops and onto dining-room tables. John James Audubon had firsthand experience with more than a few of these birds. Numerous accounts in his classic *Birds of America*, published in the early 1840's, describe hunting and eating the eggs and adults of not only game birds such as ducks, geese, and prairie-chickens, but also shorebirds including the Dunlin, Eskimo Curlew, and Golden Plover, and even such species as the Belted Kingfisher, American Robin, and Dark-eyed Junco.

In Audubon's time, attitudes on wildlife were much like those that prevailed in the days of the Roman Empire. Free-ranging birds were the property of no one; once shot or trapped, they became the property of the shooter or trapper. The exceptions were those birds found on private land, which could be taken only by the owner. Early on in Europe, wildlife became the property of royalty. Later, ownership was assigned to the state, but that doctrine was slow to emerge on the frontier continent of North America. (In fact, it was not until the turn of this century that the U.S. federal government got into the business of protecting birds.)

In Europe, concern over hunted species had been expressed off and on for centuries. Interestingly, even after cities grew to the point that market hunters threatened overharvesting, the first international law to protect European birds focused on species of value to farmers.

In North America, by contrast, the early state and provincial laws protected hunted birds. Largely in response to the fate of the Passenger Pigeon and the notorious excesses of the plume hunters, the Lacey Act was passed in 1900, making illegal the interstate transport of birds killed in violation of state laws. The turning point in bird conservation, however, came in 1918 when legislation was enacted to implement the landmark Migratory Bird Treaty, which had been signed in 1916 by the United States and Great Britain (on behalf of Canada). The treaty designated three groups of migratory birds: game birds, insectivorous birds, and other nongame birds, and provided a season in which the birds of each group could not be taken "except for scientific or propagating purposes under permits." With minor exceptions for hunting by Native Americans, the closed season on the second and third categories was year-round. For migratory game birds, hunting seasons were not to exceed three and a half months. The taking of nests or eggs of any migratory birds was prohibited, except for scientific purposes. Thus ended the hobby of oology (egg collecting). Penalties for breaking the law were six months in prison and $500 in fines, or both. Similar treaties were signed with Mexico in 1936, Japan in 1972, and the Soviet Union in 1976. In the

Mexican treaty, additional avian groups were specified, more or less completing the basic legal protection of North American birds.

In the U.S., the protection of nonmigratory species has included passage of the Bald Eagle Protection Act in 1940 (see p. 107) and passage of the Endangered Species Act in 1966 (see p. 12), which extended protection to species in peril. As of 1991, 38 continental North American birds and another 32 (plus two birds still listed but considered already extinct by researchers) from Hawaii and Puerto Rico are federally listed as Threatened or Endangered and 51 are candidates for federal listing.

Under special permits, protected (but not Endangered) nongame native species may be killed if they become serious *local* pests. This provision has been used primarily with regard to species of blackbirds, crows, and cowbirds (see p. 219), particularly when their gigantic fall and winter roosting flocks become nuisances, although control programs have not been without controversy. House Sparrows and European Starlings, both non-native species, are not protected. No other birds, except those for which there are designated hunting seasons, can be legally killed, trapped, harassed, or possessed (including birds found dead). Even the "adoption" of young birds that appear to have been deserted by their parents is illegal without a permit. If found, these apparently unattended young should be left alone since, more often than not, the adults are not far away. In Canada or the United States, anyone witnessing the molestation of protected birds in any way should report it to the state or provincial department of fish and game or the U.S. Fish and Wildlife Service.

Since the 1970's, four major international treaties that pertain to birds (but are not restricted to them) have been written, and, when taken together, affect the conservation of many avian species and an enormous number of the planet's other plants and animals. Ramsar (named after the Iranian town where the treaty was signed in 1971) addresses the problem of wetland preservation (it is formally but infrequently known as The Convention on Wetlands of International Importance Especially as Waterfowl Habitat). The World Heritage Convention, signed in 1972, protects some 50 areas of outstanding natural (rather than cultural) value. CITES (see p. 12), signed in 1973, forbids international trade in Endangered species. And the Bonn Convention, signed in 1979, protects migratory species throughout their ranges. Collectively, these treaties close the gaps in and between preceding agreements and, in theory, ease international cooperation. Nonetheless, about 900 of the world's 9,000-plus bird species are threatened with global extinction during our lifetimes.

The breakthrough in protective legislation in the 1970's coincided with public concern that the value of wildlife in general and birds in particular extends beyond utilitarian roles. Previously seen as sources of food, opportunities for sport, and aids to agriculture (especially to control insect pests), birds are increasingly recognized for their aesthetic, recreational, and scientific value, as well as their importance to the natural environment and their right to coexist. International wildlife treaties cover most continents, but a worldwide treaty to protect the habitats of imperiled species or imperiled ecosystems has yet to be drafted. Meanwhile, as the public grows increasingly alarmed about overhunting and deliberate damage to habitats, we can hope that more stringent regulations with greater penalties for noncompliance will be legislated.

REFERENCES: Bean, 1983; Council on Environmental Quality, 1977; Ehrlich, Dobkin, and Wheye, 1988; Lyster, 1985; Versteeg, 1984.

REGIONAL QUICK CHECK OF
BIRDS IN JEOPARDY

Listing birds in groups according to their regional vulnerability is an inexact exercise, in part because their demographic and ecological conditions, our understanding of them, and the response of various agencies and conservation organizations to them shifts with time. Similarly, vulnerability may differ in different portions of a single region. Endangered Light-footed Clapper Rail populations, for example, may be increasing in one set of marshes but declining precipitously in other nearby marshes. Furthermore, a species like the Clapper Rail (with its many subspecies and their varying vulnerabilities) presents a very complex picture, and may appear to be less (or more) imperiled than it is. Three Clapper Rail subspecies in California (California Clapper, Light-footed Clapper, and Yuma Clapper) are Endangered, and a fourth (the Mangrove Clapper, found in Florida) remains a candidate for federal listing, but several other Clapper subspecies in the southeastern U.S. are not currently at risk in the eyes of the National Audubon Society or the U.S. Fish and Wildlife Service, even though data on their populations are not easily had. And finally, although the federal listing system will qualify species, subspecies, or even populations for listing, the Blue List and its auxiliary lists of birds of Special or Local Concern include only species. As a result, some birds, such as the Loggerhead Shrike, are on more than one list: the San Clemente Island subspecies is Endangered, the Migrant Loggerhead subspecies is a candidate for federal listing,

and the species as a whole is Blue-Listed.

Given these constraints, what is this Quick Check useful for? It will tell you which birds in your region have been identified by the U.S. Fish and Wildlife Service or the National Audubon Society as undergoing significant regional declines. The Quick Check will list a bird found in your region *only* if data clearly show the species to be declining *there*. Hence, it will provide you with only *the minimal subset of imperiled or declining species in each region*. It will omit species that may in fact be imperiled or declining if indications of these conditions have escaped the data on which the National Audubon Society lists are based. We believe that many such cases exist, but they will not be documented adequately until more refined survey techniques and more extensive geographic coverage are in place. With environmental conditions changing rapidly in many species' breeding and wintering grounds, a timely update of the Blue List is urgently needed. For further information, check the "Listing" portion of the individual species accounts.

Note, however, that although the following birds are listed as Vulnerable in Canada (see p. 13), they are not given individual accounts in this book: Ross's Gull, Ivory Gull, Caspian Tern, Flammulated Owl, Great Gray Owl, Prairie and Prothonotary warblers, Louisiana Waterthrush, and Ipswich Sparrow (a subspecies of the Savannah Sparrow).

Note, too, that for seven species warranting Special Concern by the National Au-

dubon Society in 1986 (Western Grebe, Clark's Grebe, Reddish Egret, Swainson's Hawk, Ferruginous Hawk, Crested Caracara, and Sharp-tailed Grouse) and six species warranting Local Concern in 1986 (American White Pelican, Double-crested Cormorant, Harris' Hawk, Osprey, Lewis' Woodpecker, and Golden-crowned Kinglet), reports in *American Birds* did not specify the bird's area or region of concern. Finally, Hawaii and Puerto Rico were not included on the lists compiled by the National Audubon Society.

In each of the groupings below, the birds are listed in taxonomic order.

The Quick Check combines the 1991 federal listings of Threatened and Endangered birds, the 1990 candidates for federal listings (primarily breeding ranges), the 1986 National Audubon Society's listings (Blue-Listed birds and birds of Special Concern or Local Concern), and the 1991 Canadian listings of Endangered, Threatened, or Vulnerable birds. The regions delineated, including those for Canada, are essentially those used by the National Audubon Society.

The birds discussed in Birds Reflecting the Spectrum of Protection (p. 234) are not included here; and birds that occur in particular regions only as brief visitors are not listed under those regions.

Note that the Blue List and its auxiliary lists are compiled for species only, not for subspecies or populations.

Legend for Regional Map for Quick Check

U.S. REGIONS

1 Northeast Region

(including southeastern Canada)

Includes:

Atlantic Provinces Region (New Brunswick, Nova Scotia, Prince Edward Island, Newfoundland)

Northeastern Maritime Region (Maine, New Hampshire, Massachusetts, Rhode Island, Connecticut)

Niagara-Champlain Region (most of New York, Vermont)

Hudson-Delaware Region (southeastern New York, New Jersey, eastern Pennsylvania, Delaware)

2 Middle Atlantic Coast Region

eastern Maryland, District of Columbia, eastern Virginia

3 Southern Atlantic Coast Region

most of North and South Carolina, most of Georgia

4 Florida Region

all but western Florida

5 Appalachian Region

western Pennsylvania, West Virginia, southeastern Ohio, eastern Kentucky, eastern Tennessee, western Virginia, western North Carolina, northwestern South Carolina, northern Georgia, northeastern Alabama

6 Western Great Lakes Region

Michigan, Wisconsin, Minnesota

7 Middlewestern Prairie Region

most of Ohio, western Kentucky, Indiana, Illinois, Missouri, Iowa

8 Central Southern Region

western Florida, most of Alabama, western Tennessee, Mississippi, Louisiana, Arkansas

9 Northern Great Plains Region

North and South Dakota, eastern Montana

10 Southern Great Plains and Texas Region

Includes:

Southern Great Plains Region (Nebraska, Kansas, Oklahoma, northern Texas)

South Texas Region (southern Texas)

11 Northern Rocky Mountain-Intermountain Region

western Montana, Idaho, eastern Washington, eastern Oregon

12 Mountain West Region

Wyoming, Colorado, Utah, Nevada

13 Southwest Region

New Mexico, Arizona

14 Northern Pacific Coast Region

western Oregon, western Washington, coastal British Columbia

15 Middle Pacific Coast Region

northern California

16 Southern Pacific Coast Region

southern California

17 Alaska Region

Alaska, including Aleutian Islands

18 Hawaiian Islands Region

Hawaii, including Laysan and other far-northwestern islands

19 Puerto Rico Region

CANADIAN REGIONS

1 Atlantic Provinces Region

New Brunswick, Nova Scotia, Prince Edward Island, Newfoundland (but see Northeast Region, under U.S. above)

2 Quebec Region

3 Ontario Region

4 Prairie Provinces Region

Manitoba, Saskatchewan, Alberta

5 Northwestern Canada Region

most of British Columbia (see also Northern Pacific Coast Region, under U.S. above), Yukon Territory, Northwest Territories

UNITED STATES

1 Northeast Region

(Combining Four "Regions"; including southeastern Canada; see map)

Federally Listed as Threatened or Endangered

Piping Plover; Roseate Tern; Bald Eagle; Peregrine Falcon

Candidates for Federal Listing

Migrant Loggerhead Shrike

National Audubon Society's Blue List

Horned Grebe; Least and American Bitterns; Cooper's, Sharp-shinned, and Red-shouldered Hawks; Northern Harrier; Upland Sandpiper; Black Tern; Short-eared Owl; Whip-poor-will; Common Nighthawk; Ruby-throated Hummingbird; Loggerhead Shrike; Grasshopper Sparrow

National Audubon Society's Birds of Special Concern

American Black Duck; Merlin; Common Barn-owl; Eastern Screech-owl; Hairy Woodpecker; Eastern Phoebe; Purple Martin; Sedge Wren; Eastern Bluebird; Golden-winged Warbler; Eastern Meadowlark; Orchard Oriole; Henslow's Sparrow

National Audubon Society's Birds of Local Concern

Common Loon; Black-crowned Night Heron; Great Blue Heron; Northern Bobwhite; Cliff Swallow; Least Flycatcher

2 Middle Atlantic Coast Region

Federally Listed as Threatened or Endangered

Piping Plover; Bald Eagle; Peregrine Falcon

Candidates for Federal Listing

Migrant Loggerhead Shrike; Appalachian Bewick's Wren; Bachman's Sparrow

National Audubon Society's Blue List

Horned Grebe; Least and American Bitterns; Loggerhead Shrike

National Audubon Society's Birds of Special Concern

Common Barn-owl; Eastern Meadowlark

3 Southern Atlantic Coast Region

Federally Listed as Threatened or Endangered

Wood Stork; Piping Plover; Bald Eagle; Peregrine Falcon; Red-cockaded Woodpecker; Bachman's Warbler

Candidates for Federal Listing

Southeastern American Kestrel; Migrant Loggerhead Shrike; Appalachian Bewick's Wren; Bachman's Sparrow

National Audubon Society's Blue List

Horned Grebe; Least and American Bitterns; Cooper's and Red-shouldered Hawks; Black Tern; Whip-poor-will; Common Nighthawk; Ruby-throated Hummingbird; Bewick's Wren; Loggerhead Shrike; Bachman's Sparrow

National Audubon Society's Birds of Special Concern

Fulvous Whistling-duck; Common Barn-owl; Eastern Screech-owl; Red-headed and Hairy Woodpeckers; Eastern Phoebe; Eastern Bluebird; Henslow's Sparrow

National Audubon Society's Birds of Local Concern

Red-necked Grebe; Black Vulture

4 Florida Region

Federally Listed as Threatened or Endangered

Wood Stork; Piping Plover; Roseate Tern; Everglade Snail Kite; Bald Eagle; Peregrine Falcon; Audubon's Crested Caracara; Red-cockaded Woodpecker; Florida Scrub Jay; Cape Sable Seaside and Florida Grasshopper Sparrows

Candidates for Federal Listing

Reddish Egret; Southeastern American Kestrel; Mangrove Clapper Rail; Southeastern Snowy Plover; White-crowned Pigeon; Stoddard's Yellow-throated Warbler; Bachman's, Wakulla Seaside, and Smyrna Seaside Sparrows

National Audubon Society's Blue List

Loggerhead Shrike; Grasshopper Sparrow

National Audubon Society's Birds of Special Concern

Reddish Egret; Snowy Plover; Common Barn-owl; Burrowing Owl; Red-headed Woodpecker; Eastern Bluebird

National Audubon Society's Birds of Local Concern

Common Loon; Black-crowned Night Heron; Black Vulture

5 Appalachian Region

Federally Listed as Threatened or Endangered

Bald Eagle; Peregrine Falcon; Red-cockaded Woodpecker; Bachman's Warbler

Candidates for Federal Listing

Migrant Loggerhead Shrike; Appalachian Bewick's Wren; Bachman's Sparrow

National Audubon Society's Blue List

Least Bittern; Sharp-shinned, Cooper's, and Red-shouldered Hawks; Northern Harrier; Upland Sandpiper; Yellow-billed Cuckoo; Whip-poor-will; Ruby-throated Hummingbird; Bewick's Wren; Loggerhead Shrike; Grasshopper Sparrow

National Audubon Society's Birds of Special Concern

Common Barn-owl; Eastern Screech-owl; Red-headed and Hairy Woodpeckers; Eastern Phoebe; Purple Martin; Golden-winged and Yellow Warblers; Eastern Meadowlark; Orchard Oriole; Henslow's Sparrow

National Audubon Society's Birds of Local Concern

Northern Bobwhite

6 Western Great Lakes Region

Federally Listed as Threatened or Endangered

Piping Plover; Bald Eagle; Peregrine Falcon; Kirtland's Warbler

Candidates for Federal Listing

Migrant Loggerhead Shrike

National Audubon Society's Blue List

Least and American Bitterns; Sharp-shinned and Cooper's Hawks; Upland Sandpiper; Black Tern; Whip-poor-will; Common Nighthawk

National Audubon Society's Birds of Special Concern

Merlin; Common Barn-owl; Eastern Phoebe; Purple Martin; Eastern Bluebird; Yellow Warbler

National Audubon Society's Birds of Local Concern

Great Blue Heron; Common Tern; Northern Bobwhite; Least Flycatcher

7 Middlewestern Prairie Region

Federally Listed as Threatened or Endangered

Least Tern; Bald Eagle; Peregrine Falcon

Candidates for Federal Listing

Migrant Loggerhead Shrike; Bachman's Sparrow

National Audubon Society's Blue List

American Bittern; Sharp-shinned, Cooper's, and Red-shouldered Hawks; Northern Harrier; Upland Sandpiper; Black Tern; Yellow-billed Cuckoo; Short-eared Owl; Common Nighthawk; Ruby-throated Hummingbird; Bewick's Wren; Loggerhead Shrike; Grasshopper and Bachman's Sparrows

National Audubon Society's Birds of Special Concern

American Black Duck; Common Barn-owl; Eastern Screech-owl; Red-headed and Hairy Woodpeckers; Eastern Phoebe; Purple Martin; Sedge and Carolina Wrens; Golden-winged Warbler; Orchard Oriole; Dickcissel

National Audubon Society's Birds of Local Concern

Common Loon; Black-crowned Night Heron; Great Blue Heron; Northern Bobwhite

8 Central Southern Region

Federally Listed as Threatened or Endangered

Brown Pelican; Wood Stork; Mississippi Sandhill Crane; Piping Plover; Least Tern; Bald Eagle; Peregrine Falcon; Red-cockaded Woodpecker; Bachman's Warbler

Candidates for Federal Listing

Southeastern American Kestrel; Southeastern Snowy Plover; Migrant Loggerhead Shrike; Appalachian Bewick's Wren; Stoddard's Yellow-throated Warbler; Bachman's Sparrow

National Audubon Society's Blue List

Least Bittern; Northern Harrier; Upland Sandpiper; Short-eared Owl; Whip-poor-will; Bewick's Wren; Loggerhead Shrike; Grasshopper Sparrow

National Audubon Society's Birds of Special Concern

Reddish Egret; Common Barn-owl; Red-headed and Hairy Woodpeckers; Eastern Phoebe; Yellow Warbler; Orchard Oriole; Henslow's Sparrow; Dickcissel

National Audubon Society's Birds of Local Concern

Black-crowned Night Heron; Turkey and Black Vultures

9 Northern Great Plains Region

Federally Listed as Threatened or Endangered

Piping Plover; Least Tern; Bald Eagle; Peregrine Falcon

Candidates for Federal Listing

Mountain Plover; Long-billed Curlew; Ferruginous Hawk; Columbian Sharp-tailed Grouse

National Audubon Society's Blue List

American Bittern; Upland Sandpiper; Loggerhead Shrike

National Audubon Society's Birds of Special Concern

Willow Flycatcher; Orchard Oriole

National Audubon Society's Birds of Local Concern

Common Loon; Northern Bobwhite

10 Southern Great Plains and Texas Region

Federally Listed as Threatened or Endangered

Whooping Crane; Brown Pelican; Piping Plover; Eskimo Curlew; Least Tern; Bald Eagle; Peregrine and Northern Aplomado Falcons; Attwater's Greater Prairie-chicken; Red-cockaded Woodpecker; Black-capped Vireo; Golden-cheeked Warbler

Candidates for Federal Listing

Reddish Egret; White-faced Ibis; Western Snowy and Mountain Plovers; Long-billed Curlew; Ferruginous and Northern Gray Hawks; Spotted Owl; Cactus Ferruginous Pygmy-owl; Migrant Loggerhead Shrike; Tropical Parula (Olive-backed) Warbler; Brownsville Common Yellowthroat; Texas (Sennett's) Olive, Bachman's, and Texas Botteri's Sparrows; Audubon's Oriole;

Mexican Hooded and Sennett's Hooded Orioles

National Audubon Society's Blue List

Least Bittern; Northern Harrier; Black Tern; Yellow-billed Cuckoo; Short-eared Owl; Common Nighthawk; Ruby-throated Hummingbird; Bewick's Wren; Loggerhead Shrike; Grasshopper Sparrow

National Audubon Society's Birds of Special Concern

Reddish Egret; Snowy Plover; Long-billed Curlew; Common Barn-owl; Hairy Woodpecker; Carolina Wren; Bell's Vireo; Yellow Warbler; Orchard Oriole; Dickcissel

National Audubon Society's Birds of Local Concern

Turkey and Black Vultures; Least Flycatcher

11 Northern Rocky Mountain-Intermountain Region

Federally Listed as Threatened or Endangered

Whooping Crane; Piping Plover; Least Tern; Bald Eagle; Peregrine Falcon; Northern Spotted Owl

Candidates for Federal Listing

Western Sage Grouse; Western Snowy Plover; Long-billed Curlew; Ferruginous Hawk; Columbian Sharp-tailed Grouse; Tricolored Blackbird

National Audubon Society's Birds of Special Concern

Sage Grouse; Common Barn-owl

National Audubon Society's Birds of Local Concern

Trumpeter Swan

12 Mountain West Region

Federally Listed as Threatened or Endangered

Whooping Crane; Least Tern; Bald Eagle; Peregrine Falcon

Candidates for Federal Listing

White-faced Ibis; Columbian Sharp-tailed Grouse; Western Snowy and Mountain Plovers; Long-billed Curlew; Ferruginous Hawk; Spotted Owl; Southwestern Willow Flycatcher

National Audubon Society's Blue List

Cooper's Hawk; Common Nighthawk

National Audubon Society's Birds of Special Concern

Common Barn-owl

National Audubon Society's Birds of Local Concern

Black-crowned Night Heron; Great Blue Heron; Trumpeter Swan

13 Southwest Region

Federally Listed as Threatened or Endangered

Whooping Crane; Yuma Clapper Rail; Least Tern; Bald Eagle; Peregrine and Northern Aplomado Falcons; Masked Bobwhite; Thick-billed Parrot

Candidates for Federal Listing

White-faced Ibis; Fulvous Whistling-duck; California Black Rail; Ferruginous and Northern Gray Hawks; Apache Northern Goshawk; Western Snowy and Mountain Plovers; Long-billed Curlew; Spotted Owl; Cactus Ferruginous Pygmy-owl; Southwestern Willow Flycatcher

National Audubon Society's Blue List

Cooper's Hawk

National Audubon Society's Birds of Special Concern

Fulvous Whistling-duck; Common Barn-owl

14 Northern Pacific Coast Region

Federally Listed as Threatened or Endangered

Aleutian Canada Goose; Piping Plover; California Least Tern; Bald Eagle; Peregrine Falcon; Northern Spotted Owl

Candidates for Federal Listing

White-faced Ibis; Western Snowy Plover; Long-billed Curlew; Marbled Murrelet; Tricolored Blackbird

National Audubon Society's Blue List

Common Nighthawk

National Audubon Society's Birds of Special Concern

Sage Grouse; Common Barn-owl; Hairy Woodpecker

National Audubon Society's Birds of Local Concern

Trumpeter Swan

15 Middle Pacific Coast Region

Federally Listed as Threatened or Endangered

Aleutian Canada Goose; Brown Pelican; California Clapper Rail; California Least Tern; Bald Eagle; Peregrine Falcon; Northern Spotted Owl

Candidates for Federal Listing

White-faced Ibis; Fulvous Whistling-duck; Western Snowy Plover; Long-billed Curlew; California Black Rail; Marbled Murrelet; Spotted Owl; Tricolored Blackbird; San Pablo, Suisun, and Alameda (South Bay) Song Sparrows

National Audubon Society's Blue List

Yellow-billed Cuckoo; Short-eared Owl

National Audubon Society's Birds of Special Concern

Common Barn-owl; Burrowing Owl; Willow Flycatcher

National Audubon Society's Birds of Local Concern

Black-crowned Night Heron; Western Bluebird

16 Southern Pacific Coast Region

Federally Listed as Threatened or Endangered

Brown Pelican; California, Light-footed, and Yuma Clapper Rails; California Least Tern; California Condor; Bald Eagle; Peregrine Falcon; San Clemente Loggerhead Shrike; Inyo California Towhee; Least Bell's Vireo; San Clemente Sage Sparrow

Candidates for Federal Listing

White-faced Ibis; Fulvous Whistling-duck; Western Snowy Plover; California Black Rail; Elegant Tern; Spotted Owl; California Gnatcatcher; Saltmarsh Common Yellowthroat; Belding's Savannah Sparrow; Tricolored Blackbird

National Audubon Society's Blue List

Northern Harrier; Yellow-billed Cuckoo

National Audubon Society's Birds of Special Concern

Fulvous Whistling-duck; Reddish Egret; Snowy Plover; Common Barn-owl; Burrowing Owl; Purple Martin; Willow Flycatcher

National Audubon Society's Birds of Local Concern

California Gnatcatcher

17 Alaska Region

Federally Listed as Threatened or Endangered

Aleutian Canada Goose; Bald Eagle; Peregrine Falcon; Eskimo Curlew

Candidates for Federal Listing

Bristle-thighed Curlew; Marbled Murrelet; Amak Song Sparrow

18 Hawaiian Islands Region

Federally Listed as Threatened or Endangered

Newell's Shearwater; Dark-rumped Petrel; Nene or Hawaiian Goose; Koloa or Hawaiian Duck; Laysan Duck; Hawaiian Gallinule or Moorhen; Hawaiian Coot; Hawaiian Stilt; 'Io or Hawaiian Hawk; 'Alala or Hawaiian Crow; Nihoa Millerbird; Kama'o or Large Kauai Thrush; Oloma'o or Molokai Thrush; Puaiohi or Small Kauai Thrush; Kauai 'O'o; Laysan Finch; Nihoa Finch; 'O'u; Palila; Maui Parrotbill; Nukupu'u; 'Akiapola'au; Kauai 'Akialoa; Hawaii Creeper; Oahu Creeper; Molokai Creeper; Maui 'Akepa; Hawaii 'Akepa; 'Akohekohe or Crested Honeycreeper; Po'ouli (The Kauai 'O'o and Kauai 'Akialoa, though listed, are thought to be extinct.)

Candidates for Federal Listing

Bristle-thighed Curlew (winter only); Bishop's 'O'o

19 Puerto Rico Region

Federally Listed as Threatened or Endangered

Piping Plover; Roseate Tern; Puerto Rican Parrot; Puerto Rican Plain Pigeon; Puerto Rican Nightjar; Yellow-shouldered Blackbird

Candidates for Federal Listing

Southeastern Snowy Plover; Caribbean Coot; Puerto Rican Broad-winged Hawk; Virgin Islands Screech-owl; Lesser White-cheeked Pintail; West Indian Ruddy Duck; West Indian Whistling-duck; Elfin Woods Warbler

National Audubon Society's Birds of Local Concern

Reddish Egret

CANADA

The 1991 report of the Committee on the Status of Endangered Wildlife in Canada (COSEWIC), to which we referred in compiling this portion of the Regional Quick Check, does not provide range information. For our purposes here, we list Canadian birds regionally according to their breeding range as described by the American Ornithological Union, although in some cases the birds may be especially protected wherever they are spotted on Canadian soil.

C-1 Atlantic Provinces Region

(see Northeast Region, under U.S., above)

Listed by Canada as Threatened or Endangered

Harlequin Duck (eastern populations); Piping Plover; Roseate Tern; Arctic Peregrine Falcon

Listed by Canada as Vulnerable

Least Bittern; Caspian Tern; Cooper's and Red-shouldered Hawks; Ipswich Sparrow; Eastern Bluebird

C-2 Quebec Region

Listed by Canada as Threatened or Endangered

Harlequin Duck (eastern populations); Piping Plover; Arctic Peregrine Falcon; Loggerhead Shrike

Listed by Canada as Vulnerable

Least Bittern; Caspian Tern; Cooper's and Red-shouldered Hawks; Eastern Bluebird

C-3 Ontario Region

Listed by Canada as Threatened or Endangered

Piping Plover; Loggerhead Shrike; Kirtland's Warbler; Henslow's Sparrow

Listed by Canada as Vulnerable

Least Bittern; King Rail; Caspian Tern; Cooper's and Red-shouldered Hawks; Common Barn-owl; Great Gray Owl; Prairie and Prothonotary Warblers; Louisiana Waterthrush; Eastern Bluebird

Candidate for Federal Listing in the U.S.

Appalachian Bewick's Wren

National Audubon Society's Blue List

Least and American Bitterns; Red-shouldered Hawk; Northern Harrier; Upland Sandpiper; Black Tern; Short-eared Owl; Loggerhead Shrike; Grasshopper Sparrow

National Audubon Society's Birds of Special Concern

American Black Duck; Snowy Plover; Common Barn-owl; Red-headed Woodpecker; Eastern Phoebe; Sedge and Carolina Wrens; Eastern Bluebird; Golden-winged and Yellow Warblers; Eastern Meadowlark

National Audubon Society's Birds of Local Concern

Black-crowned Night Heron

C-4 Prairie Provinces Region

Listed by Canada as Threatened or Endangered

Whooping Crane; Piping and Mountain Plovers; Ferruginous Hawk; American Peregrine Falcon; Burrowing Owl; Loggerhead Shrike; Baird's Sparrow

Listed by Canada as Vulnerable

Least Bittern; Ross's Gull; Caspian Tern; Trumpeter Swan; Cooper's Hawk; Great Gray Owl; Eastern Bluebird

Candidates for Federal Listing in the U.S.

Long-billed Curlew; Ferruginous Hawk; Western Sage Grouse; Columbian Sharp-tailed Grouse; Migrant Loggerhead Shrike

National Audubon Society's Blue List

American Bittern; Northern Harrier; Short-eared Owl; Loggerhead Shrike

National Audubon Society's Birds of Local Concern

Merlin; Least Flycatcher

C-5 Northwestern Canada Region

Listed by Canada as Threatened or Endangered

Whooping Crane; Eskimo Curlew; Marbled Murrelet; American and Arctic Peregrine Falcons; Northern Spotted and Burrowing Owls

Listed by Canada as Vulnerable

Trumpeter Swan; Ross's and Ivory Gulls; Caspian Tern; Cooper's Hawk; Peale's Peregrine Falcon; Common Barn-owl; Flammulated and Great Gray Owls

SOURCES

The arrangement of the species accounts within each text section follows the essentially taxonomic order used in the National Geographic Society's *Field Guide to the Birds of North America* (1987), which formed the basis of the sequence used in *The Birder's Handbook* (Ehrlich et al., 1988). Accounts of the birds of Hawaii and Puerto Rico follow the sequences established in the Hawaii Audubon Society's *Hawaii's Birds* and Herbert A. Raffaele's *A Guide to the Birds of Puerto Rico and the Virgin Islands*. We drew much information on the general requirements for nesting and feeding (including major habitats, nesting materials, foraging techniques, and so forth) and most of the material in the Commentaries from *The Birder's Handbook*. A variety of other sources, particularly those published since *The Birder's Handbook* and sources covering individual subspecies and Hawaiian and Puerto Rican birds, were also consulted, and are listed in the Bibliography.

North American wintering-range information was gleaned from a variety of sources, including *The Birder's Handbook* and the *A.O.U. Checklist of North American Birds*. Other range information came from, among others, Richard Howard and Alick Moore's *A Complete Checklist of the Birds of the World*, Michael Walters' *Complete Birds of the World*, W. Earl Godfrey's *Birds of Canada*, H. Douglas Pratt, Phillip L. Bruner, and Delwyn G. Berrett's *The Birds of Hawaii and the Tropical Pacific*,

and Raffaele's *A Guide to the Birds of Puerto Rico and the Virgin Islands*.

For information on worldwide endangerment, we consulted the U.S. Fish and Wildlife Service's "Systematic List of the World's Threatened Bird Species," compiled by Nigel Collar and Paul Andrew for the 1988 International Union for the Conservation of Nature and Natural Resources' "List of Threatened Animals," which can be found in Guy Mountfort's *Rare Birds of the World*. An older work (1981), Endangered Birds of the World: The ICBP Bird Red Data Book, compiled by Warren B. King, was also a valuable guide.

Considerable information is available on the imperilment, status, and plans for recovery of populations of birds formally listed as Threatened or Endangered. In addition to the lists prepared by the U.S. Fish and Wildlife Service (see the Bibliography), the World Wildlife Fund's two-volume *Official Guide to Endangered Species of North America*, the *Audubon Wildlife Reports* (1985–90), and the *Forest Bird Communities of the Hawaiian Islands*, by Scott, Mountainspring, Ramsey, and Kepler, were consulted frequently during the preparation of this book.

For information on the threats to and status of the remaining birds in jeopardy treated in this volume, we relied on a wide variety of journals, personal contacts, and the reports of the National Audubon Society's field journal, *American Birds*. For 15 years *American Birds* has published the

Blue List, to provide an overview of species that are not listed as Threatened or Endangered by the U.S. Fish and Wildlife Service but are still at risk in all or parts of their ranges. The Blue List is based on data taken by an army of dedicated birders and professional ornithologists and has drawn its summaries from the three main field counts organized by the National Audubon Society: the Christmas Bird Counts, which have been carried out annually for the last 91 years, the Breeding Bird Census, which has surveyed breeding birds for the last 54 years, and the Winter Bird Populations Study, which has been conducted for 42 years (see p. 223).

FURTHER READING

Of the many valuable books and research papers published on the conservation of birds, only a few will be easy reading for most readers. The following are some of the easily located sources that expand on the information and themes of *Birds in Jeopardy*.

On Birds, Worldwide:

Anthony W. Diamond, Rudolf L. Schreiber, Walter Cronkite, and Roger Tory Peterson. 1989. *Save the Birds*. Houghton Mifflin, Boston. A richly illustrated treatment of bird conservation with global coverage. Part of each purchase price goes to the International Council for Bird Preservation (ICBP).

Warren B. King. 1981. *Endangered Birds of the World: The ICBP Bird Red Data Book*. Smithsonian Institution Press/International Council for Bird Preservation, Washington, D.C. One- to two-page species accounts of the world's most vulnerable birds. Available in paperback.

N. J. Collar and P. Andrew. 1988. *Birds to Watch: The ICBP World Checklist of Threatened Birds*. ICBP Technical Publication No. 8. Cambridge, England. An interim volume providing paragraph-long species treatments that summarize the latest data on threatened birds for readers wishing to keep up to date while awaiting publication of the next Red Data volume.

G. Mountfort. 1988. *Rare Birds of the World: A Collins/ICBP Handbook*. Stephen Greene Press, Lexington, Mass. Offers fine global coverage of avian species at risk.

On North American Birds:

Paul R. Ehrlich, David S. Dobkin, and Darryl Wheye. 1988. *The Birder's Handbook: A Field Guide to the Natural History of North American Birds*. Simon and Schuster, New York. Information on the ecology, behavior, and conservation of all North American bird species, accompanied by 250 essays providing a comprehensive overview of their biology. Some of the information found in *Birds in Jeopardy* was developed as a result of preparing the 800-page *Handbook*. Available in paperback.

John Terborgh. 1989. *Where Have All the Birds Gone?* Princeton University Press, Princeton, N.J. An excellent extended essay on the decline of North American birds. Highly recommended.

National Audubon Society. *American Birds*. A fine periodical for those interested in North American bird biology, with frequent coverage of environmental issues. (950 Third Avenue, New York, N.Y. 10022)

Cornell Laboratory of Ornithology. *The Living Bird Quarterly*. This journal often covers conservation issues. (159 Sapsucker Woods Road, Ithaca, N.Y. 14850)

On Canadian Birds:

W. Earl Godfrey. 1986. *The Birds of Canada* (Revised Edition). National Museums of Canada, Ottawa, Ont. The standard work for treatments on Canada's avifauna.

On Hawaiian Birds:

H. Douglas Pratt, Phillip L. Bruner, and Delwyn G. Berrett. 1987. *The Birds of Hawaii and the Tropical Pacific*. Princeton University Press, Princeton, N.J. An indispensable guide for those interested in the birds of the Pacific. Available in paperback.

Andrew J. Berger. 1981. *Hawaiian Birdlife* (Second Edition). University Press of Hawaii, Honolulu. The most detailed treatment of the birds of the Hawaiian Islands.

On Puerto Rican Birds:

Herbert A. Raffaele. 1989. *A Guide to the Birds of Puerto Rico and the Virgin Islands* (Revised Edition). Princeton University Press, Princeton, N.J. Another indispensable source, the definitive field guide for the avifauna of Puerto Rico. Available in paperback.

On the Root Causes of Bird Imperilment:

Paul R. Ehrlich and Anne H. Ehrlich. 1981. *Extinction: The Causes and Consequences of the Disappearance of Species*. Random House, New York. Comprehensive treatment of the extinction crisis. Available in paperback.

Paul R. Ehrlich and Anne H. Ehrlich. 1990. *The Population Explosion*. Simon and Schuster, New York. The basics of the demographic situation, showing how human numbers contribute to the deterioration of the human environment—and explaining

BIBLIOGRAPHY

why the most serious population problems occur in rich nations. Available in paperback.

Paul R. Ehrlich and Anne H. Ehrlich. 1991. *Healing the Planet.* Addison Wesley, New York. An overview of the most basic environmental problems—global warming, ozone depletion, acid rain, desertification, and so forth—and how to solve them.

Stephen H. Schneider. 1989. *Global Warming.* Sierra Club Books, San Francisco. The best overview of the environmental threat potentially most deadly for both birds and people. Available in paperback.

Alvo, R. 1987. The acid test. *Living Bird Quarterly,* Spring: 25–30.

Anon. 1987. Seized parrots could restore a lost species. *Audubon,* July: 22.

Anon. 1988. Eyes on the Eskimo Curlew. *Natural History,* April: 6.

Anon. 1988. Fatal shock. *Living Bird Quarterly,* Winter: 33.

Anon. 1990. Spotted Owl committee conservation plan calls for protection of larger habitat areas. *Center for Conservation Biology Update* 4: 7.

Arbib, R. 1971. Announcing—The Blue List: An "early warning system" for birds. *American Birds* 25: 948–49.

Arnold, K. A. 1983. A new subspecies of Henslow's Sparrow (*Ammodramus henslowii*). *Auk* 100: 504–5.

Atwood, J. L., and B. W. Massey. 1988. Site fidelity of Least Terns in California. *Condor* 90: 389–94.

Atwood, J. L., and D. E. Minsky. 1983. Least Tern foraging ecology at three major California breeding colonies. *Western Birds* 14: 57–72.

Audubon, J. J. 1842. *Birds of America,* vols. 1–9. (Published by the author.)

Avise, J. C., and W. S. Nelson. 1989. Molecular genetic relationships of the extinct Dusky Seaside Sparrow. *Science* 243: 646–48.

Bailey, E. P., and J. L. Trapp. 1984. A second wild breeding population of the Aleutian Canada Goose. *American Birds* 38: 284–86.

Bancroft, G. T. 1989. Status and conservation of wading birds in the Everglades. *American Birds* 43: 1258–65.

Banks, R. C. 1988. Geographic variation in the Yellow-billed Cuckoo. *Condor* 90: 473–77.

Barzen, J. A., and J. R. Serie. 1990. Nutrient reserve dynamics of breeding Canvasbacks. *Auk* 107: 75–85.

Bean, M. J. 1983. *The Evolution of National Wildlife Law.* Praeger, New York.

Beaver, D. L. 1980. Recovery of an American Robin population after early DDT use. *Journal of Field Ornithology* 51: 220–28.

Bednarz, J. C. 1988. A comparative study of the breeding ecology of Harris' and Swainson's Hawks in southeastern New Mexico. *Condor* 90: 311–23.

———. 1990. The hunters of Los Medanos. *Natural History,* October: 56–62.

Beissinger, S. R. 1990. Alternative foods of a diet specialist, the Snail Kite. *Auk* 107: 327–33.

Beissinger, S. R., A. Sprunt, IV, and R. Chandler. 1983. Notes on the Snail (Everglade) Kite in Cuba. *American Birds* 37: 262–65.

Bengtson, S. A. 1984. Breeding ecology and extinction of the Great Auk (*Pinguinus impennis*): Anecdotal evidence and conjectures. *Auk* 101: 1–12.

Benson, R. H., and K. L. P. Benson. 1991. Reply to Scott and Garton. *Condor* 93: 470–72.

Berger, A. J. 1981. Hawaiian Birdlife (second edition). University Press of Hawaii, Honolulu.

Bixby, K. 1987. CITES: Old problems and

new challenges. *Endangered Species Technical Bulletin Reprint* 4(7): 1–3.

Blankinship, D. R., and K. A. King. 1984. A probable sighting of 23 Eskimo Curlews in Texas. *American Birds* 38: 1066–67.

Blockstein, D. E. 1988. U.S. legislative progress toward conserving biological diversity. *Conservation Biology* 2: 311–13.

Blockstein, D. E., and H. B. Tordoff. 1985. Gone forever: A contemporary look at the extinction of the Passenger Pigeon. *American Birds* 39: 845–51.

Boersma, P. D. 1986. Ingestion of petroleum by seabirds can serve as a monitor of water quality. *Science* 231: 373–76.

Bonney, R. E. 1986. Dicofol stays on the market. *Audubon,* January: 124–25.

Botkin, D., D. Woodby, and R. Nisbet. 1991. Kirtland's Warbler habitats: A possible early indicator of climatic warming. *Biological Conservation,* in press.

Brigham, R. M. 1989. Roost and nest sites of Common Nighthawks: Are gravel roofs important? *Condor* 91: 722–24.

Brisbin, I. L. 1968. The Passenger Pigeon, a study in the ecology of extinction. *Modern Game Breeding* 4: 13–20.

Brooks, B. L., and S. A. Temple. 1990. Dynamics of a Loggerhead Shrike population in Minnesota. *Wilson Bulletin* 102: 441–50.

Brown, C. R., and M. B. Brown. 1986. Ectoparasitism as a cost of coloniality in Cliff Swallows (*Hirundo pyrrhonota*). *Ecology* 67: 1206–18.

Browning, M. R. 1990. Taxa of North American birds described from 1957 to 1987. *Proceedings of the Biological Society of Washington* 103: 432–51.

Buchanan, J. B. 1988. North American Merlin populations: An analysis using Christmas Bird Count data. *American Birds* 42: 1178–80.

Burger, J. 1988. Social attraction in nesting Least Terns: Effects of numbers, spacing, and pair bonds. *Condor* 90: 575–82.

Burger, J., and M. Gochfeld. 1988. Nest-site selection by Roseate Terns in two tropical colonies on Culebra, Puerto Rico. *Condor* 90: 843–51.

Canadian Wildlife Service. 1988. Transactions 1988, Fifty-Second Federal-Provincial/Territorial Wildlife Conference. Victoria, B.C., June 14–17. Environment Canada.

Canadian Wildlife Service. 1989. Transactions 1989, Fifty-Third Federal-Provincial/Territorial Wildlife Conference. St. John's, Nfld., June 20–23. Environment Canada.

Canadian Wildlife Service. 1991. Annual Report to Canadian Wildlife Directory Meeting for COSEWIC. June 18–20.

Carothers, J. H., S. R. Sabo, and R. B. Hansen. 1983. Ecological observations on an endangered species: The Maui Parrotbill, *Pseudonestor xanthrophrys.* *American Birds* 37: 820–21.

Carson, R. 1962. *Silent Spring.* Houghton Mifflin, Boston.

Chandler, W. J. (ed.). 1988. *Audubon Wildlife Report 1988/1989.* Academic Press, San Diego.

Clark, C. F. 1988. Observations on the nesting success of Bell's Vireos in southern Arizona. *Western Birds* 19: 177–20.

Collar, N. J., and P. Andrew. 1988. *Birds to Watch: The ICBP World Check-list of Threatened Birds.* Technical Bulletin No. 8. International Council for Bird Preservation, Cambridge, England.

Conant, S., and M. S. Kjargaard. 1984. Annotated checklist of birds of Haleakala National Park, Maui, Hawaii. *Western Birds* 15: 97–110.

Council on Environmental Quality. 1977. *The Evolution of National Wildlife Law.* U.S. Government Printing Office, Washington, D.C.

Craig, T. H., J. W. Connelly, E. H. Craig, and T. L. Parker. 1990. Lead concentrations in Golden and Bald Eagles. *Wilson Bulletin* 102: 130–33.

Cruz, F., and J. B. Cruz. 1990. Breeding, morphology, and growth of the endangered Dark-rumped Petrel. *Auk* 107: 317–26.

Culbert, R., and R. Blair. 1989. Recovery planning and endangered species. *Endangered Species Update* 6(10): 2–8.

Darley, J. A. 1982. Territoriality and mating behavior of the male Brown-headed Cowbird. *Condor* 84: 15–21.

Delannoy, C. A., and A. Cruz. 1988. Breeding biology of the Puerto Rican Sharp-shinned Hawk (*Accipiter striatus venator*). *Auk* 105: 649–62.

Diamond, J. M. 1985. Salvaging single-sex populations. *Nature* 316: 104.

———. 1988. Red books or green lists? *Nature* 332: 304–5.

———. 1990. Bob Dylan and moas' ghosts. *Natural History,* October: 26–31.

Dijak, W. D., B. Tannenbaum, and M. A. Parker. 1990. Nest-site characteristics affecting success and reuse of Red-shouldered Hawk nests. *Wilson Bulletin* 102: 480–86.

Di Silvestro, R. L. (ed.). 1987. *Audubon Wildlife Report 1987.* Academic Press, Orlando.

Dobson, A., and D. Miller. 1989. Infectious diseases and endangered species management. *Endangered Species Update* 6(9): 1–5.

Dunstan, T. C. 1989. The Golden Eagle. *In* Chandler, W. J. (ed.). *Audubon Wildlife Report 1989/1990.* Academic Press, San Diego, pp. 499–511.

Duvall, F. P., and S. Conant. 1986. Current status of the Hawaiian Crow. *Endangered Species Technical Bulletin* 3(11): 1–2.

Eddleman, W. R., F. L. Knopf, B. Meanley, F. A. Reid, and R. Zembal. 1988. Conservation of North American rallids. *Wilson Bulletin* 100: 458–75.

Ehrlich, A. H., and P. R. Ehrlich. 1987. *Earth.* Methuen, London.

Ehrlich, P. R. 1990. Birding for fun: People vs. birds. *American Birds* 44: 193–96.

Ehrlich, P. R., Dobkin, D. S., and D. Wheye. 1988. *The Birder's Handbook: A Field*

Guide to the Natural History of North American Birds. Simon and Schuster, New York.

Ehrlich, P. R., and A. H. Ehrlich. 1981. *Extinction: The Causes and Consequences of the Disappearance of Species*. Random House, New York.

Ehrlich, P. R., A. H. Ehrlich, and J. P. Holdren. 1977. *Ecoscience: Population, Resources, Environment*. Freeman, San Francisco.

Fields, R. H. 1985. The Snail Kite, an endangered species. *Endangered Species Technical Bulletin* 10(12): 3–4.

Findholt, S. L. 1986. New American White Pelican nesting colony in Wyoming. *Western Birds* 17: 136–38.

Forbes, L. S. 1991. Intraspecific piracy in Ospreys. *Wilson Bulletin* 103: 111–12.

Freed, L. A., S. Conant, and R. C. Fleischer. 1987. Evolutionary ecology and radiation of Hawaiian passerine birds. *Trends in Ecology and Evolution* 2: 196–203.

Friedmann, H., and L. F. Kiff. 1985. The parasitic cowbirds and their hosts. *Proceedings of the Western Foundation for Vertebrate Zoology* 2: 226–304.

Gabel, R. R., and S. J. Dobrott. 1988. Saving the Masked Bobwhite. *Endangered Species Technical Bulletin* 13(5): 6–7.

Garrison, B. A., J. M. Humphrey, and S. A. Laymon. 1987. Bank Swallow distribution and nesting ecology on the Sacramento River, California. *Western Birds* 18: 71–76.

Gawlik, D. E., and K. L. Bildstein. 1990. Reproductive success and nesting habitat of Loggerhead Shrikes in north-central South Carolina. *Wilson Bulletin* 102: 37–48.

Godfrey, W. E. 1986. The Birds of Canada (revised edition). National Museums of Canada, Ottawa.

Goldwasser, S., D. Gaines, and S. R. Wilbur. 1980. The Least Bell's Vireo in California: A de facto endangered race. *American Birds* 34: 742–45.

Gollop, J. B. 1988. The Eskimo Curlew. *In*

W. J. Chandler (ed.). *Audubon Wildlife Report 1988/89*. Academic Press, San Diego, pp. 583–95.

Gowaty, P. A. 1988. Daughters dearest. *Natural History*, April: 80–81.

Gradwohl, J., and R. Greenberg. 1989. The Golden Eagle. *In* Chandler, W. J. (ed.). *Audubon Wildlife Report 1989/1990*. Academic Press, San Diego, pp. 297–328.

Graham, F., Jr. 1990. Kite vs. stork. *Audubon*, May: 104–10.

Haggerty, T. M. 1988. Aspects of the breeding biology and productivity of Bachman's Sparrow in central Arkansas. *Wilson Bulletin* 10: 247–55.

Halliday, T. 1978. *Vanishing Birds: Their Natural History and Conservation*. Holt, Rinehart and Winston, New York.

Handel, C. M., and C. P. Dau. 1988. Seasonal occurrence of migrant Whimbrels and Bristle-thighed Curlews on the Yukon–Kuskokwim Delta, Alaska. *Condor* 90: 782–90.

Haney, J. C. 1990. Winter habitat of Common Loons on the continental shelf of the southeastern United States. *Wilson Bulletin* 102: 253–63.

Harwood, M. 1983. A clannish problem. *Audubon*, July, 30–32.

Hector, D. P. 1987. The decline of the Aplomado Falcon in the United States. *American Birds* 41: 381–89.

Henny, C. J., L. J. Blus, A. J. Krynitsky, and C. M. Bunck. 1984. Current impact of DDE on Black-crowned Night Herons in the intermountain west. *Journal of Wildlife Management* 48: 1–13.

Hindman, L. J. 1985. The Trumpeter Swan blasts back. *American Birds* 39: 260.

Houston, C. S. 1990. Saskatchewan Swainson's Hawks. *American Birds* 44: 215–20.

Howard, R., and A. Moore. 1980. *A Complete Checklist of the Birds of the World*. Oxford University Press, Oxford, England.

Hunt, C. E. 1989. Creating an Endangered

Ecosystems Act. *Endangered Species Update* 6(3–4): 1–5.

Hutcheson, W. H., and W. Post. 1990. Shiny Cowbird collected in South Carolina: First North American specimen. *Wilson Bulletin* 102: 561.

Ingold, D. J. 1991. Nest-site fidelity in Red-headed and Red-bellied Woodpeckers. *Wilson Bulletin* 103: 118–22.

Jackson, J. A. 1986. Biopolitics and management of federal lands and the conservation of the Red-cockaded Woodpecker. *American Birds* 40: 1162–68.

James, F. C. 1991. Signs of trouble in the largest remaining population of Red-cockaded Woodpeckers. *Auk* 108: 419–23.

James, H. F., R. L. Zusi, and S. L. Olson. 1989. *Dysmorodrepanis munroi* (Fringillidae: Drepanidini), a valid genus and species of Hawaiian finch. *Wilson Bulletin* 101: 159–79.

Johnsgard, P. A. 1990. *Hawks, Eagles, and Falcons of North America*. Smithsonian Institution Press, Washington, D.C.

Johnson, K. W., J. E. Johnson, R. O. Albert, and T. R. Albert. 1988. Sightings of Golden-cheeked Warblers (*Dendroica chrysoparia*) in northeastern Mexico. *Wilson Bulletin* 100: 130–31.

Johnson, R. R., and L. T. Haight. 1987. Endangered habitats versus endangered species: A management challenge. *Western Birds* 18: 89–96.

Jones, S. 1989. The implications of Hurricane Hugo on the recovery of the Red-cockaded Woodpecker. *Endangered Species Update* 7(1–2): 6.

Jorgensen, P. D., and H. L. Ferguson. 1984. The birds of San Clemente Island. *Western Birds* 15: 111–30.

Kale, H. W., II, and D. S. Maehr. 1990. *Florida's Birds*. Pineapple Press, Sarasota, Fla.

King, D. B., Jr., M. Baumgartel, J. De Beer, and T. Meyer. 1987. The birds of San Elijo Lagoon, San Diego County, California. *Western Birds* 18: 177–208.

King, W. B. 1981. *Endangered Birds of the World: The ICBP Bird Red Data Book.* Smithsonian Institution Press/International Council for Bird Preservation, Washington, D.C.

———. 1987. The Puerto Rican Parrot: New directions. *American Birds* 41: 28–34.

Knopf, F. L., R. R. Johnson, T. Rich, F. B. Samson, and R. C. Szaro. 1988. Conservation of riparian ecosystems in the United States. *Wilson Bulletin* 100: 272–84.

Kohm, K. A. (ed.). 1991. *Balancing on the Brink of Extinction: The Endangered Species Act and Lessons for the Future.* Island Press, Washington, D.C.

Konishi, M., S. T. Emlen, R. E. Ricklefs, and J. C. Wingfield. 1989. Contributions of bird studies to biology. *Science* 246: 465–72.

Kress, S. W. 1985. *Audubon Society Guide to Attracting Birds.* Charles Scribner's Sons, New York.

Kuhn, L. 1989. Stalk the muddy waters. *Living Bird Quarterly,* Autumn: 31.

Laymon, S. A. 1987. Brown-headed Cowbirds in California: Historical perspectives and management opportunities in riparian habitats. *Western Birds* 18: 63–70.

Lennartz, M. R., and P. W. Stangel. 1989. Few and far between. *Living Bird Quarterly,* Autumn: 15–17, 20.

Lowe, D. W., J. R. Matthews, and C. J. Moseley (eds.). 1990. *The Official World Wildlife Fund Guide to Endangered Species of North America.* Beacham, Washington, D.C.

Lowe, J. D., and G. S. Butcher. 1990. Population dynamics of the Loggerhead Shrike in winter: 1963–1987. *Birdscope Newsletter* 4: 4.

Luoma, J. R. 1987. Black Duck decline: An acid rain link. *Audubon,* May: 19–24.

Lyster, S. 1985. *International Wildlife Law: An Analysis of International Treaties Concerned with the Conservation of Wildlife.* Grotius, Cambridge, England.

Mackenzie, J. P. S. 1977. *Birds in Peril.* Houghton Mifflin, Boston.

MacPherson, S. L. 1987. History and status of the endangered Puerto Rican Parrot. *Endangered Species Technical Bulletin* 12(7): 6–7.

MacWhirter, R. B. 1989. On the rarity of intraspecific brood parasitism. *Condor* 91: 485–92.

Marshall, D. B. 1988. The Marbled Murrelet joins the old-growth forest conflict. *American Birds* 42: 202–11.

———. 1989. The Marbled Murrelet. *In* Chandler, W. J. (ed.). *Audubon Wildlife Report 1989/1990.* Academic Press, San Diego, pp. 435–55.

Marshall, J. T. 1988. Birds lost from a giant sequoia forest during fifty years. *Condor* 90: 359–72.

Mayfield, H. F. 1988. Where were Kirtland's Warblers during the last ice age? *Wilson Bulletin* 100: 659–60.

McHenry, E. N., and J. C. Dyes. 1983. First record of juvenal "white-phase" Great Blue Heron in Texas. *American Birds* 37: 119.

McLean, P. K., and M. A. Byrd. 1991. Feeding ecology of Chesapeake Bay Ospreys and growth and behavior of their young. *Wilson Bulletin* 103: 105–11.

McMillen, J. L., D. H. Ellis, and D. G. Smith. 1987. The role of captive propagation in the recovery of the Mississippi Sandhill Crane. *Endangered Species Technical Bulletin* 12(5–6): 6–8.

Morin, M. P., and S. Conant. 1990. Nest substrate variation between native and introduced populations of Laysan Finches. *Wilson Bulletin* 102: 591–604.

Morton, E. S., L. Forman, and M. Braun. 1990. Extra-pair fertilizations and the evolution of colonial breeding in Purple Martins. *Auk* 107: 275–83.

Moss, W. W., and J. H. Camin. 1970. Nest parasitism, productivity, and clutch size in Purple Martins. *Science* 168: 1000–1003.

Mountainspring, S., T. L. C. Casey, C. B. Kepler, and J. M. Scott. 1990. Ecology, behavior, and conservation of the Po'o-uli (*Melamprosops phaeosoma*). *Wilson Bulletin* 102: 109–22.

Mountfort, G. 1988. *Rare Birds of the World: A Collins/ICBP Handbook.* Stephen Greene, Lexington, Mass.

Munro, G. C. 1944. Birds of Hawaii. Tongg, Honolulu; reprinted 1960 by Charles E. Tuttle, Tokyo.

Myers, J. P., and T. Colburn. 1991. Blundering questions, weak answers lead to poor pesticide policies. *Chemical and Engineering News,* January 7: 40–43, 53–54.

Myers, J. P., R. Morrison, P. Antas, B. Harrington, T. Lovejoy, M. Salaberry, S. Senner, and A. Tarak. 1987. Conservation strategy of migratory species. *American Scientist* 75: 19–26.

Nelson, J. 1989. Agriculture, wetlands, and endangered species: The Food Security Act of 1985. *Endangered Species Technical Bulletin* 14(5): 1, 6–8.

Nettleship, D. N., and T. R. Birkhead (eds.). 1985. *The Atlantic Alcidae: The Evolution, Distribution, and Biology of the Auks Inhabiting the Atlantic Ocean and Adjacent Water Areas.* Academic Press, London.

Nicholls, J. L., and G. A. Baldassarre. 1990. Winter distribution of Piping Plovers along the Atlantic and Gulf coasts of the United States. *Wilson Bulletin* 102: 400–412.

Norton, B. G. 1988. Avoiding the triage question. *Endangered Species Update* 5(8–9): 1–4.

Noss, R. F. 1988. The longleaf pine landscape of the southeast: Almost gone and almost forgotten. *Endangered Species Update* 5(5): 1–5.

Nuechterlein, G. L., and D. P. Buitron. 1989. Diving differences between Western and Clark's Grebes. *Auk* 106: 467–70.

O'Brien, S. J., and E. Mayr. 1991. Bureaucratic mischief: Recognizing endangered species and subspecies. Science 251: 1187–88.

Office of Migratory Bird Management. 1987. *Migratory Nongame Birds of Management Concern in the United States: The 1987 List.* U.S. Fish and Wildlife Service, Washington, D.C.

Ogden, J. C. 1983. The abundant, endangered flinthead. *Audubon*, January: 90–101.

Otis, D. R. 1989. The big loser. *Living Bird Quarterly,* Autumn: 18–19.

Paradiso, J. L. 1986. Audubon's Crested Caracara, one of Florida's most distinctive raptors, proposed for listing. *Endangered Species Technical Bulletin* 11(7): 1–2.

Parker, W. 1985. Creating Wood Stork habitat: An important management strategy. *Endangered Species Technical Bulletin* 10(2): 7.

Pattee, O. H. 1987. The role of lead in condor mortality. *Endangered Species Technical Bulletin* 12(9): 6–7.

Perrigo, G., R. Brundage, R. Barth, N. Damude, C. Benesh, C. Fogg, and J. Gower. 1990. Spring migration corridor of Golden-cheeked Warblers in Tamaulipas, Mexico. *American Birds* 44: 28.

Peters, R. L. 1988. Effects of global warming on species and habitats: An overview. *Endangered Species Update* 5(7): 1–8.

Philp, T. 1990. Bird dooms logging proposal. *San Jose Mercury News,* July 7: 1.

Piatt, J. F., C. J. Lensink, W. Butler, M. Kendziorek, and D. R. Nysewander. 1990. Immediate impact of the 'Exxon Valdez' oil spill on marine birds. *Auk* 107: 387–97.

Pimm, S. L. 1988. Rapid morphological change in an introduced bird. *Trends in Ecology and Evolution* 3: 290–91.

Pratt, H. D., P. L. Bruner, and D. G. Berrett. 1987. *The Birds of Hawaii and the Tropical Pacific.* Princeton University Press, Princeton, N.J.

Pratt, T. K. 1988. New hope for survival of the 'Alala. *Endangered Species Technical Bulletin* 13(11–12): 10.

Prior, K. A. 1990. Turkey Vulture food habits in southern Ontario. *Wilson Bulletin* 102: 706–10.

Pulich, W. M. 1976. *The Golden-cheeked Warbler.* Texas Parks and Wildlife Department, Austin, Tex.

Raffaele, H. A. 1989. *A Guide to the Birds of Puerto Rico and the Virgin Islands* (revised edition). Princeton University Press, Princeton, N.J.

Rappole, J. H., M. A. Ramos, and K. Winker. 1989. Wintering Wood Thrush movements and mortality in southern Veracruz. *Auk* 106: 402–10.

Rauzon, M. J. 1991. Save our shearwaters! *Living Bird,* Spring: 28–32.

Rees, M. D. 1989. Aleutian Canada Goose proposed for reclassification. *Endangered Species Technical Bulletin* 14(11–12): 8–9.

Rodgers, J. A., Jr., S. T. Schwikert, and A. S. Wenner. 1988. Status of the Snail Kite in Florida: 1981–1985. *American Birds* 42: 30–35.

Rollfinke, B. F., R. H. Yahner, and J. S. Wakeley. 1990. Effects of forest irrigation on long-term trends in breeding-bird communities. *Wilson Bulletin* 102: 264–78.

Rowell, G. 1991. Falcon rescue. *National Geographic,* April 106–14.

Rudolph, D. C., H. Kyle, and R. N. Conner. 1990. Red-cockaded Woodpeckers vs rat snakes: The effectiveness of the resin barrier. *Wilson Bulletin* 102: 14–22.

Safina, C. 1990. Foraging habitat partitioning in Roseate and Common Terns. *Auk* 107: 351–58.

Sakai, H. F. 1988. Avian response to mechanical clearing of a native rainforest in Hawaii. *Condor* 90: 339–48.

Sakai, H. F., and T. C. Johanos. 1983. The nest, egg, young, and aspects of the life history of the endangered Hawaii Creeper. *Western Birds* 14: 73–84.

Sanderson, G. C., and F. C. Bellrose. 1986. A review of the problem of lead poisoning in waterfowl. *Illinois Natural History Survey, Special Publication* 4.

Sauer, J. R., and S. Droege. 1990. Recent population trends of the Eastern Bluebird. *Wilson Bulletin* 102: 239–52.

Schorger, A. W. 1955. *The Passenger Pigeon: Its Natural History and Extinction.* University of Oklahoma Press, Norman, Okla.

Schulenberg, J. H., and M. B. Ptacek. 1984. Status of the Interior Least Tern in Kansas. *American Birds* 38: 975–81.

Scott, D. M., and C. D. Ankney. 1983. The laying cycle of Brown-headed Cowbirds: Passerine chickens? *Auk* 100: 583–92.

Scott, J. M., and E. O. Garton. 1991. Population estimates of the Black-capped Vireo. *Condor* 93: 469–70.

Scott, J. M., S. Mountainspring, F. L. Ramsey, and C. B. Kepler. 1986. Forest bird communities of the Hawaiian Islands: Their dynamics, ecology, and conservation. *Studies in Avian Biology* 9.

Senner, S. E. 1988. Saving birds while they are still common: An historical perspective. *Endangered Species Update* 5(6): 1–4.

Shaffer, M. L. 1981. Minimum population sizes for species conservation. *BioScience* 31: 131–34.

Sidle, J. G., J. J. Dinan, M. P. Dryer, J. P. Rumancik, Jr., and J. W. Smith. 1988. Distribution of the Least Tern in interior North America. *American Birds* 42: 195–201.

Sidle, J. G., W. H. Koonz, and K. Roney. 1985. Status of the American White Pelican: An update. *American Birds* 39: 859–64.

Singer, S. W., N. L. Noslund, S. A. Singer, and C. J. Ralph. 1991. Discovery and observations of two tree nests of the Marbled Murrelet. *Condor* 93: 330–39.

Smith, M. 1986. From a strike to a kill. *New Scientist,* May 29: 44–47.

Smith, P. W., and A. Sprunt, IV. 1987. The Shiny Cowbird reaches the United States. *American Birds* 41: 370–71.

Snyder, N. F. R., S. R. Beissinger, and R. E. Chandler. 1989. Reproduction and demography of the Florida Everglade (Snail) Kite. *Condor* 91: 300–316.

Soulé, M. E. (ed.). 1986. *Conservation Biology: The Science of Scarcity and Diversity.* Sinauer Associates, Sunderland, Mass.

Soulé, M. E., and B. A. Wilcox (eds.). 1980. *Conservation Biology: An Evolutionary–Ecological Approach.* Sinauer Associates, Sunderland, Mass.

Sparling, D. W. 1987. The endangered Palila of Hawaii. *Endangered Species Technical Bulletin* 12(9): 6–7.

Spendelow, J. A., and J. D. Nichols. 1989. Annual survival rates of breeding adult Roseate Terns. *Auk* 106: 367–74.

Spitzer, P. R., R. W. Risebrough, W. Walker, R. Hernandez, A. Poole, D. Puleston, and I. C. T. Nisbet. 1978. Productivity of Osprey in Connecticut–Long Island increases as DDE residues decline. *Science* 202: 333–35.

Stine, P. A. 1986. Refuge established for endangered Hawaiian forest birds. *Endangered Species Technical Bulletin* 11(1): 5.

———. 1987. Captive 'Alala moved to new breeding facilities. *Endangered Species Technical Bulletin* 12(1): 5–6.

Stoddard, P. K. 1988. The "bugs" call of the Cliff Swallow: A rare food signal in a colonially nesting bird species. *Condor* 90: 714–15.

Takekawa, J. E., and S. R. Beissinger. 1989. Cyclic drought, dispersal, and the conservation of the Snail Kite in Florida: Lessons in critical habitat. *Conservation Biology* 3: 302–11.

Tate, J., Jr. 1981. The Blue List for 1981: The first decade. *American Birds* 35: 3–10.

———. 1986. The Blue List for 1986. *American Birds* 40: 227–36.

Tate, J., Jr., and D. J. Tate. 1982. The Blue List for 1982: A restructured list redefines and refines the analysis of data from the field. *American Birds* 36: 126–35.

Teather, K. L., and R. J. Robertson. 1986. Pair bonds and factors influencing the diversity of mating systems in Brown-headed Cowbirds. *Condor* 88: 63–69.

Terborgh, J. 1989. *Where Have All the Birds Gone?* Princeton University Press, Princeton, N.J.

Terres, J. K. 1981. Diseases of birds—How and why some birds die. *American Birds* 35: 255–60.

Thomas, L. 1989. Pesticides and endangered species: New approaches to evaluating impact. *Endangered Species Technical Bulletin* 14(1–2): 1, 7–8.

Turner, J. L. 1985. The deadly wild-bird trade. *Defenders* 60: 20–29.

Unitt, P. 1987. *Empidonax traillii extimus:* An endangered subspecies. *Western Birds* 18: 137–62.

U.S. Fish and Wildlife Service. 1989. Endangered and Threatened Wildlife and Plants. Annual Notice of Review. Part 17. January 6.

U.S. Fish and Wildlife Service. 1990. Endangered and Threatened Wildlife and Plants. 50 CFR 17.11 and 17.12. April 15.

U.S. Fish and Wildlife Service. 1990. *Federal and State Endangered Species Expenditures, Fiscal Year 1989.* USFWS, Washington, D.C.

Versteeg, H. 1984. The protection of endangered species: A Canadian perspective. *Ecology Law Quarterly* 11: 267–90.

Vitousek, P. M., P. R. Ehrlich, A. H. Ehrlich, and P. A. Matson. 1986. Human appropriation of the products of photosynthesis. *BioScience* 36: 368–73.

Walker, L. 1989. Endangered species and Florida's pesticide program. *Endangered Species Technical Bulletin* 14(6): 3, 10.

Walters, M. 1981. *The Complete Birds of the World.* David and Charles, New York.

Warkentin, I. G., P. C. James, and L. W. Oliphant. 1990. Body morphometrics, age structure, and partial migration of urban Merlins. *Auk* 107: 25–34.

Warkentin, I. G., and L. W. Oliphant. 1988.

Seasonal predation of large prey by Merlins. *Wilson Bulletin* 100: 137–39.

White, D. H., C. A. Mitchell, L. D. Wynn, E. L. Flickinger, and E. J. Kolbe. 1982. Organophosphate insecticide poisoning of Canada Geese in the Texas panhandle. *Journal of Field Ornithology* 53: 22–27.

White, R. P. 1983. Distribution and habitat preference of the Upland Sandpiper (*Bartramia longicauda*) in Wisconsin. *American Birds* 37: 16–22.

Whitlock, R. 1981. *Birds at Risk.* Moonraker Press, Wiltshire, England.

Wiedner, D., and P. Kerlinger. 1990. Economics of birding: A national survey of active birders. *American Birds* 44: 209–13.

Wilbur, S. R. 1979. The Bell's Vireo in California: A preliminary report. *American Birds* 33: 252.

Wilbur, S. R., P. D. Jorgensen, B. W. Massey, and V. A. Basham. 1979. The Light-footed Clapper Rail: An update. *American Birds* 33: 25.

Wilcove, D. 1988. Changes in the avifauna of the Great Smoky Mountains: 1947–1983. *Wilson Bulletin* 100: 256–71.

———. 1989. Predicting the future for endangered species. *Endangered Species Update* 6(10): 40.

———. 1990. A quiet exit. *Living Bird,* Autumn: 10–11.

Wiley, J. W. 1985. Bird conservation in the United States Caribbean. *In* Temple, S. A. (ed.). *Bird Conservation,* vol. 2. International Council for Bird Preservation, United States Section. University of Wisconsin Press, Madison, pp. 107–60.

———. 1988. Host selection by the Shiny Cowbird. *Condor* 90: 289–303.

Wiley, J. W., and R. Zembal. 1989. Concern grows for Light-footed Clapper Rail. *Endangered Species Technical Bulletin* 14(3): 6–7.

Wilson, A. 1811. American Ornithology, vols. 1–9. Bradford and Inskeep, Philadelphia.

Wilson, S. B. 1974. Aves Hawaiienses: The

Birds of the Sandwich Islands. Arno Press, New York. (Reprint of the 1890–99 edition published by R. H. Porter, London.)

Woodard, P. W. 1983. Behavioral ecology of fledgling Brown-headed Cowbirds and their hosts. *Condor* 85: 151–63.

Zembal, R., and J. M. Fancher. 1988. Foraging behavior and foods of the Light-footed Clapper Rail. *Condor* 90: 959–62.

Zembal, R., K. J. Kramer, R. J. Bransfield, and N. Gilbert. 1988. A survey of Belding's Savannah Sparrows in California. *American Birds* 42: 1233–36.

Zembal, R., and B. W. Massey. 1981. A census of the Light-footed Clapper Rail in California. *Western Birds* 12: 87–99.

———. 1985. Distribution of the Light-footed Clapper Rail in California, 1980–1984. *American Birds* 39: 135–37.

Zimmerman, J. L. 1988. Breeding season habitat selection by the Henslow's Sparrow (*Ammodramus henslowii*) in Kansas. *Wilson Bulletin* 100: 17–24.

Zusi, R. L. 1989. A modified jaw muscle in the Maui Parrotbill (*Pseudonestor:* Drepanididae). *Condor* 91: 716–20.

Zusi, R. L., and G. D. Bentz. 1978. The appendicular morphology of the Labrador Duck (*Camptorhynchus labradorius*). *Condor* 80: 407–18.

Zwank, P. J. 1987. Survival of captive, parent-reared Mississippi Sandhill Cranes released on a refuge. *Conservation Biology* 1: 165–68.

Zwank, P. J., J. P. Geaghan, and D. A. Dewhurst. 1988. Foraging differences between native and released Mississippi Sandhill Cranes: Implications for conservation. *Conservation Biology* 2: 386–90.

Zwank, P. J., P. M. McKenzie, and E. B. Moser. 1988. Fulvous Whistling-duck abundance and habitat use in southwestern Louisiana. *Wilson Bulletin* 100: 488–94.

ABOUT THE CENTER FOR CONSERVATION BIOLOGY

Established at Stanford University in 1984, the Center for Conservation Biology carries out research, policy, and educational activities in conservation biology—the science of preserving biological diversity (biodiversity) by preserving genetic resources, populations, species, habitats, and ecosystems.

The Center's objectives include promoting communication within and between the scientific and conservation communities, applying existing scientific information to conservation efforts, carrying out basic ecological research, and disseminating information to wildlife and resource managers, teachers, politicians, administrators, and others concerned with conservation. We hope that *Birds in Jeopardy*, published with the counsel and assistance of the Center, will become a resource for managers, teachers, others concerned with conservation, and the birding community at large.

The Center also carries out policy research on the global environmental problems responsible for the decline of birds and other elements of biodiversity. These root causes include the interlocking problems of human population growth, wasteful consumption, waste disposal, and the use of technologies and practices that unnecessarily damage the environment. Together they are responsible for the major threats to biodiversity—thus to avian diversity—including deforestation, desertification, acid precipitation, ozone depletion, and global warming, all of them problems which, if not solved, are likely to negate the decades of effort exerted by conservation biologists to safeguard plants and animals.

Under its President, Professor Paul R. Ehrlich, and its Director, Dr. Dennis D. Murphy, the Center is an institute within the Department of Biological Sciences at Stanford University. It is supported by foundation grants, contracts, and donations from corporations and individuals. Subscriptions to *Update*, the Center's biannual newsletter, are available for donations of $15 or more. (See p. 227 for address.)

INDEX

Full text treatments of particular species and subspecies are indicated by page numbers in **boldface** type.